MORBID SYMPTOMS

Stanford Studies In Middle Eastern and Islamic Societies and Cultures

Morbid Symptoms

Relapse in the Arab Uprising

Gilbert Achcar

Stanford University Press
Stanford, California

Stanford University Press
Stanford, California

©2016 by Gilbert Achcar. All rights reserved.

Published by Stanford University Press

Printed in the United States of America on acid-free, archival-quality paper

Library of Congress Cataloging-in-Publication Data

Names: Achcar, Gilbert, author.
Title: Morbid symptoms : relapse in the Arab uprising / Gilbert Achcar.
Description: Stanford, California : Stanford University Press, 2016. |
Includes bibliographical references and index.
Identifiers: LCCN 2016011912 (print) | LCCN 2016012450 (ebook) |
ISBN 9781503600300 (cloth : alk. paper) |
ISBN 9781503600317 (pbk. : alk. paper) | ISBN 9781503600478 (eBook)
Subjects: LCSH: Arab Spring, 2010- | Protest movements--Arab countries. |
Syria--History--Civil War, 2011- | Egypt--History--Protests, 2011- |
Syria--Politics and government--2000- | Egypt--Politics and
government--21st century.
Classification: LCC JQ1850.A91 A335 2016 (print) | LCC JQ1850.A91 (ebook) |
DDC 909/.097492708312--dc23
LC record available at http://lccn.loc.gov/2016011912

Cover design: Christian Fuenfhausen
Cover cartoon: Ali Ferzat

The crisis consists precisely in the fact that the old is dying and the new cannot be born; in this interregnum a great variety of morbid symptoms appear.

Antonio Gramsci, *Prison Notebooks* (1930)

With this system I'll make my fortune quickly; then I will kill everybody and leave.

Alfred Jarry, *King Ubu* (1896)

Contents

Preface

As happens quite often, this book did not start as a full book project. My initial intention was to write an updated chapter for a second edition of *The People Want: A Radical Exploration of the Arab Uprising* (2013). I therefore embarked on drafting an assessment of the developments that had occurred since I finished writing that previous book in October 2012. In order not to exceed the limits of a chapter, I decided to focus my assessment on the tragic developments in two key countries – Syria and Egypt – with a brief survey of the other theatres of the 2011 regional uprising.

Unsurprisingly, the chapter soon turned into much more than could be accommodated as an appendix to a book that is already quite thick. I therefore decided to go for a new book, and thus use all the space I needed for a thorough assessment of the most recent events. *The People Want* will be reprinted as it is: a book dedicated to explaining the economic, social and political roots and causes of the upheaval that engulfed the whole Arab region in 2011, and is not anywhere near ending, as well as examining the determinants and parameters of the revolutionary dynamics that it unleashed, with a balance sheet of its first two years. As such, it can surely be discussed, but it did not become obsolete. Readers will judge whether or not I am right in my contention that none of the diagnoses and prognoses I made in 2012 were contradicted by subsequent events.

This new book is therefore both a sequel to *The People Want* and a book that stands on its own, written on the assumption that the reader may not have read the former. For this reason, I have briefly summarised for each of the cases that I discuss here what my assessment was in the autumn of 2012, taking the analysis from there – or from an earlier stage when needed, in order to make the developments that I am describing fully understandable – and assessing the prospects as they seem after five years of upheaval. I hope that this new book will stand the test of time as the previous one has. But I would be very much happier if ongoing events were to disprove the pessimism of my assessment.

London, 21 December 2015

On Transliteration of Arabic

The transcription of Arabic words and names in the Latin alphabet in this book is a simplified version of the transliteration in use in specialised literature. This is in order to make it easier for non-specialists to read the text, while allowing Arabic-readers to recognise the original. Special characters and diacritical marks have been avoided, except for the inverted apostrophe representing the Arabic letter 'ayn. The common spellings of the names of the best-known individuals and groups have been retained. Finally, Arab authors' and organisations' own transliterations of their names in the Latin alphabet have been respected.

Acknowledgements

I am deeply grateful to Ali Ferzat for having graciously authorised me to adorn the cover of this book with one of his drawings. The recipient of many awards, Ali Ferzat has become one of the world's most famous political cartoonists. Circumventing censorship, his drawings have provided a radical critique of injustice and oppression over decades in Syria, his homeland, and across the Arab world. In 2011, he was assaulted by pro-regime gunmen who beat him up, breaking his hands and fingers.

Special thanks are due to Sarah Cleave at Saqi Books and Kate Wahl at Stanford University Press with whom it was my pleasure to prepare this book. I am also thankful to my good friend Omar El Shafei and the two anonymous reviewers solicited by SUP for their useful remarks on the manuscript.

Introduction

Of Revolutionary Cycles and Seasons

Lo, Winter comes! – the grief of many graves,
The frost of death, the tempest of the sword,
The flood of tyranny, whose sanguine waves
Stagnate like ice at Faith, the enchanter's word,
And bind all human hearts in its repose abhorred.

Percy Bysshe Shelley, *The Revolt of Islam* (1818)

The designation "Arab Spring" was most often used sarcastically during the fifth year since the Arab uprising commenced. Such sarcasms had actually started multiplying ever since the regional revolutionary upheaval began turning sour, in the autumn of 2011. They were facilitated by the fact that "Arab Spring", in the mind of most of its users at the early stage of the uprising, was not meant to designate one phase in an open-ended sequence of revolutionary seasons, where autumn and winter were to follow spring and summer. It was rather meant as a one-time political mutation; to use a word related to the same metaphor, it was seen as the long-overdue "blossoming" of democracy in the Arab region. According to this view, Arab-speaking countries were finally, albeit belatedly, joining what Samuel Huntington had identified as the "third wave of democratization" – a chain of political mutations that started in the 1970s.[1]

"Democratic Transition" and Revolutionary Process

The mood was all the more euphoric in 2011 because the Arab uprising happened at a time when the cautious pessimism of the arch-"realist" Huntington looked more and more vindicated. Countering the blissful optimism and Western triumphalism encapsulated in Francis Fukuyama's 1989 "end of history" delusion,[2] Huntington – in his 1991 *The Third Wave* – had warned of the possibility of what he called a "third *reverse* wave", enumerating its potential causes with much perspicacity.[3] Indeed, on the eve of the Arab upheaval most indicators pointed in that very direction. The 2008 annual report on *Freedom in the World*, produced by the veteran US-based organisation Freedom House, had already asked worriedly: "Freedom in retreat: is the tide turning?"[4] The question soon became a gloomy assertion: in 2010, the same organisation noted that 2009 was the fourth consecutive year during which "global declines in freedom outweighed gains".[5] This, were we told, constituted "the longest continuous period of decline for global freedom in the nearly 40-year history of the report". A fifth consecutive year, 2010, confirmed the sad record.[6]

Hence the deep sigh of relief that the "Arab Spring" occasioned in 2011. The discussion thereafter turned on whether this dramatic sequence of democratic upheavals represented a continuation of the "third wave of democratization", or the beginning of a *fourth* wave, after a short reverse interlude. For not only did "the political uprisings that swept across the Arab world over [that] year represent the most significant challenge to authoritarian rule since the collapse of Soviet communism", as Freedom House's report stated, but they were taking place moreover "in a region that had seemed immune to democratic change".[7] This purported immunity of Arab countries to democracy was widely held by Western pundits to be due to Islam. Huntington himself made that very tendentious observation in his later best-selling book upholding the Bernard Lewis-inspired "clash of civilizations" thesis, where he asserted that "Islamic culture explains in large part the failure of democracy to emerge in much of the Muslim world."[8]

In 1991, however, the same Huntington could still conjecture that "the wave of democratization that had swept about the world from region to region in the 1970s and 1980s could become a dominant feature of Middle Eastern and North African politics in the 1990s."[9] This is because *The Third Wave*'s author was still heedful in his appraisal of Islam, asserting that the Islamic doctrine "contains elements that may be both congenial and uncongenial to democracy".[10] By contrast, Fukuyama, his former student turned challenger, did not bother with nuances: in the 1992 book in which he developed his "end of history" thesis, one finds statements on "Islam" of a staggeringly crude "Orientalist", i.e. essentialist, character. Islam, without qualification, is said to constitute "a systematic and coherent ideology, just like liberalism and communism" (*sic*) that "has indeed defeated liberal democracy in many parts of the Islamic world, posing a grave threat to liberal practices even in countries where it has not achieved political power directly."[11] The author sought consolation, however, in the fact that Islam has "virtually no appeal outside those areas that were culturally Islamic to begin with" and that "the Islamic world would seem more vulnerable to liberal ideas in the long run than the reverse."[12]

In the immediate wake of the attacks of 11 September 2001, Fukuyama went yet further. He observed candidly: "There does seem to be something about Islam, or at least the fundamentalist versions of Islam that have been dominant in recent years, that makes Muslim societies particularly resistant to modernity."[13] More candid yet in its reproduction of Islamophobic clichés was his dismissal of the "politically correct" view that only a tiny minority of Muslims supported "terrorism":

> The answer that politicians East and West have been putting out since Sept. 11 is that those sympathetic with the terrorists are a "tiny minority" of Muslims, and that the vast majority are appalled

by what happened. It is important for them to say this to prevent Muslims as a group from becoming targets of hatred. The problem is that dislike and hatred of America and what it stands for are clearly much more widespread than that.

Certainly the group of people willing to go on suicide missions and actively conspire against the US is tiny. But sympathy may be manifest in nothing more than initial feelings of Schadenfreude at the sight of the collapsing towers, an immediate sense of satisfaction that the US was getting what it deserved, to be followed only later by pro forma expressions of disapproval. By this standard, sympathy for the terrorists is characteristic of much more than a "tiny minority" of Muslims, extending from the middle classes in countries like Egypt to immigrants in the West.[14]

The Arab uprising saw Fukuyama, like many others, swing back from that essentialist and demeaning view of Muslims. He suddenly sounded as if he was repudiating what he himself had written over the years. "This change in the Middle East has been incredibly rapid, and it has trumped, for now, old verities about the supposed passivity of Arab culture and the resistance of Islam to modernization", he asserted in March 2011.[15] In a radio interview two months later, he sounded again as if he was recanting his own previous views, yet without acknowledging it, preferring instead to boast that he was proved right after all in his initial universal optimism:

The one part of the world that did not participate in the global resurgence of democracy – that began in the 70s and continued in the 80s and 90s – was the Middle East. A lot of people said that was (because of) culture – that there was something about the nature of Arab culture that made that part of the world *different* – and they would not embrace democracy. If you look at the situation in Tunisia and the way it spread to Egypt and other parts of the region, it turns out people there don't like authoritarian governments that don't respect their dignity any more than people in Eastern Europe or Latin America or India or other parts of the world. The basic impulse to live in a country that respects you by granting you basic political rights is in fact *universal*.[16]

My quoting Fukuyama here should not be misconstrued as a tribute to the importance of his thinking for our topic. His relevance is rather due to the fact that, since 1989, he has been particularly successful at expressing the mainstream Western Zeitgeist. The same ingenuous observation offered above was enunciated innumerable times by countless Western commentators during the first months of 2011. Western academia also joined the fray: theories of "Arab exceptionalism" were widely "revisited", while the field of "democratisation theory" and "democratic transition" studies entered a period of severe turbulence.[17]

The truth, however, is that the Arab uprising was not – or not only or even primarily – a "democratic transition". The latter turns into a flawed superficial concept when applied indiscriminately to radically different situations, ranging from instances of mere political change to all-encompassing metamorphoses – even though, at first sight, the outcomes of the various sequences of events under scrutiny can be labelled, in part or on the whole, as "democratisation". There is indeed a huge qualitative difference between processes of political regime adaptation to sustained socio-economic capitalist development eventually requiring and generating a bourgeois-liberal order – such as the processes that took place in Southern Europe, Latin America or East Asia – and a thorough social–political revolution overturning a whole socio-economic order after a protracted state of developmental blockage, such as happened in Eastern Europe.

And yet, the world was stunned by the great smoothness with which, in general, the overturning of the "Communist" bureaucratic regimes in Eastern Europe happened, although it brought about a metamorphosis of the whole region's socio-economic order from state-bureaucratic to market-capitalist. The amazement was made all the greater because this happened after decades during which a certain kind of "political science" had decreed that those "totalitarian" regimes were "irreversible".[18] Thus, when it looked as if the Arab regimes were about to crumble in their turn, by a domino effect similar to the one that was set off by the fall of the Berlin Wall, the lingering memory of the "Revolutions of 1989" led observers and actors alike to believe initially that the "Arab Spring" was going to be similarly brief and "peaceful". *Silmiyya, silmiyya!* shouted hopeful demonstrators in Egypt, as well as in Syria – a rallying cry that Barack Obama cited, along with a quote from Martin Luther King, in the short, lyrical speech he gave on the occasion of Hosni Mubarak's downfall.[19]

Regrettably, however, the happy surprise of relative smoothness in 1989 was not repeated in 2011, in spite of all the wishful thinking. Bitter disappointment soon prevailed. Like pre-1989 Eastern Europe, but for longer and with much more acute tensions, the Arab region had experienced a protracted blockage of economic development, but with much direr social consequences.[20] From that angle, the uprisings that started in 2011 in the Arab region were indeed pointing to the pressing need for a thorough social revolution that would overthrow the whole socio-economic order of the region. Ideally, this would come through radical democratic political change. However, a crucial qualitative difference made it impossible for the Arab uprising to reproduce the pattern of "Velvet Revolution" (as the 1989 revolution in Czechoslovakia was called), which had characterised most of the Eastern European transformation. And that crucial factor is neither religious nor cultural.

The crux of the matter is that the state system that ruled Eastern Europe was very exceptional historically, in that it was dominated not by propertied classes but by party and state bureaucrats, i.e. functionaries and civil servants. The vast majority of those bureaucrats – especially at the lower tiers of the pyramid – could envisage keeping their jobs or finding new ones, and even improving their purchasing power, under market capitalism, while a significant portion of the upper tier could contemplate their own transformation into capitalist entrepreneurs, taking advantage of the privatisation of the economy.[21] Hence the smoothness – astonishing for most observers – with which the socio-economic order was overturned; however, it should not be confused with political democratisation, whose unevenness across the region is determined by a complex set of national and international factors.[22]

Conversely, the pre-2011 Arab region was characterised by the preponderance of patrimonial states in a general economic setting of crony capitalism: not "neopatrimonial" regimes – the mantra of "political science" and international institutions when this concept is correlated with the view that nepotism and corruption are non-intrinsic diseases of Arab governments, which can be cured and replaced with "good governance" without radically transforming the state – but *patrimonial* states indeed, be they monarchical or "republican"; in other words, states that have more in common with the European absolutism of yesteryear, the *ancien régime* in the strict historical sense, than with the modern bourgeois state.[23]

In such patrimonial states – the eight Arab monarchies, along with pre-2011 Libya and Syria – ruling families "own" the state to all intents and purposes; they will fight to the last soldier in their praetorian guard in order to preserve their reign. True, most of the region's other pre-2011 regimes could be labelled neopatrimonial, like a majority of states in developing countries. But the regional preponderance of plainly patrimonial states, along with the rentier character that is widely shared among Arab states, induced the development within the Arab neopatrimonial states themselves of a deeply corrupt trilateral "power elite": a "triangle of power" constituted by the interlocking pinnacles of the military apparatus, the political institutions and a politically determined capitalist class (a state bourgeoisie), all three bent on fiercely defending their access to state power, the main source of their privileges and profits.[24]

Under such conditions, it was perfectly deluded to expect a repetition of the Eastern European pattern of relatively peaceful radical change in the Arab region. This is indeed why I insisted early on that the region was embarking on a *long-term revolutionary process* that would go on for years, even decades, while I anticipated "new episodes of revolution and counter-revolution in the countries that have already experienced upheavals, and in others as well".[25] The fall of the tip of the icebergs in Tunisia and Egypt – Ben Ali's flight to Jeddah and the proclamation of Mubarak's "resignation" by the Egyptian military junta – not to mention the sham of Saleh's handover in Yemen, was in no way comparable to the popular overthrow of the whole socio-political "communist" order to the east of the Iron Curtain. Libya is the only Arab country where, in 2011, the state did disintegrate altogether. However, decades of "divide and rule" and suppression of political freedoms, with the formation of any stable institutions precluded by the extreme political fickleness of a Caligula-like autocrat, made a smooth transition into a new social and political order highly improbable – still less so in a conflict-ridden regional environment.

One Revolution, Two Counter-Revolutions

The situation was considerably complicated by another distinctive feature of the Arab region, a feature that it shared to varying degrees with other Muslim-majority countries. Decades prior to the uprising, the region had witnessed the development of a mass opposition to the regional order in the form of Islamic fundamentalist movements whose deeply reactionary character is most conspicuous when measured by the yardstick of the progressive aspirations of the "Arab Spring".[26] This reactionary alternative to the reactionary order – whose oppressive agenda differs from the latter only in its accentuation of its religious character – is fostered, funded and promoted, not by one state, but by no less than three oil-rich states. The Saudi kingdom, the emirate of Qatar, and the "Islamic Republic" of Iran all compete in supporting various brands of movements covering the full spectrum of Islamic fundamentalism, from conservative Salafism and the Muslim Brotherhood to Khomeinism and fanatical "Jihadism". These three states – the linchpins of regional religion-based despotism, one of them linked to the West, another opposed to it, and the third (Qatar) opportunistically linking up with both sides prior to 2011, before antagonising them both – devised different strategies to exorcise the demons represented by the radical progressive and emancipatory potential manifested in the Arab uprising.

The Saudi rulers carried on with the role they have been playing in Arab politics since the upsurge of the nationalist movement, followed by its leftward radicalisation in the 1950s and 1960s: that of the main regional bastion of Western-backed reaction. They actively supported the old regime at the regional level, except in Libya, Syria and Yemen. In Yemen, they acted as compromise brokers between the two reactionary camps: that of the president and that of the dominant forces in the opposition. In Libya, they had long wished to be rid of the unfathomable Muammar Gaddafi, and hoped that he would be easily replaced with conservative Muslims in the absence of any discernible progressive opposition after decades of totalitarian rule that purported to be "revolutionary". They nevertheless refused to intervene militarily along with NATO in 2011, due to their general reluctance to engage in "regime change" and wariness of the role of Qatar in backing the Libyan insurgency. In Syria, it was out of the question that they would support the Alawite Bashar al-Assad against his mostly Sunni opposition, as that would have clashed with their own fervent Sunni-sectarian Wahhabi ideology and the powerful religious establishment that fosters it in their kingdom. Across the whole region, however, the Saudi rulers reached out systematically to the most conservative Islamic movements, Salafists in particular, increasing their funding to them and prompting them to buttress the existing regimes, or otherwise – in Libya, Syria and Yemen, and likewise in Egypt under Morsi – to reinforce the reactionary wing of the opposition, to the detriment of any progressive forces.

Qatar's emir, in alliance with Turkey's Recep Tayyip Erdogan, bet on the Muslim Brotherhood, whose regional organisation he had been sponsoring for many years, in an attempt to co-opt the Arab uprising for the benefit of all three of them, and that of Washington.[27] Neither Doha nor Ankara hesitated, however, to maintain open channels of communication and occasional facilitation with more radical brands of Sunni-sectarian fundamentalists – up to al-Qaida and even its most dreadful mutant, Abu Bakr al-Baghdadi's "Islamic State".[28] As for Iran, after reacting in unison with Qatar and Turkey in the early weeks of the Arab uprising, its main concern quickly became to shore up Bashar al-Assad's regime against Syria's popular opposition, when the latter joined the regional uprising in its turn. The Iranian rulers espoused Assad's repressive cause all the more resolutely, as they had themselves faced and crushed a popular democratic movement only two years earlier, in 2009. In support of the Assad regime, Tehran mobilised its Shi'i-sectarian fundamentalist satellites and allies in Iraq and Lebanon. The same sectarian logic led it to support the camp of former president Saleh, with whom Iran's Houthi friends allied in Yemen's civil war, which began to unfold in 2014. Thus, Tehran ended up siding with two of the six Arab rulers who had been the target of the 2011 "Arab Spring".

This very complex regional political setting led to the highly convoluted development of the Arab revolutionary crisis, compared to which most other revolutionary upheavals in history look rather uncomplicated. It gave rise to what was potentially, when not immediately, a three-cornered struggle: not a binary confrontation between revolution and counter-revolution, as in most revolutionary upheavals in history, but a triangular conflict between one revolutionary pole and two rival counter-revolutionary camps – the regional *ancien régime* and its reactionary antagonists – both equally inimical to the emancipatory aspirations of the "Arab Spring".[29]

Anyone aware of this complexity should have had no illusion that the Arab uprising might be brief and peaceful. In the absence of forces strong enough organisationally to embody the revolutionary pole and/or able politically to lead a socio-political transformation that would conform with "the people's will" as it was expressed in the squares of Arab cities, the binary clash between the two counter-revolutionary camps was fated to take over, relegating the revolutionary pole to the background. The situation thus created was fraught with the dangerous possibilities represented by two dreadful outcomes: either a repressive backlash driven by the old regime or a descent into bloody mayhem, with each of these two outcomes feeding the possibility of the other. It is in light of this assessment that I concluded *The People Want* in 2012 with a "prophecy" – in the sense emphasised by my good friend, the late Daniel Bensaïd, of announcing not what *will* be but what *might* happen *if*, which he described as the hallmark of strategic discourse.[30] I warned then: "Unless there is a radical turn in the region's political trajectory, one capable of erasing the reactionary developments of the last few decades and reviving progressive social projects on a profoundly democratic basis, the whole region runs the risk of plunging into barbarism."[31]

Alas indeed, in the absence of a radical and sustainable shift in the region's political trajectory, which could only have resulted from the emergence of an organised and determined progressive popular leadership, the euphoria of the "Arab Spring" was soon overwhelmed by the gloom of what was most predictably called an "Arab Winter". Indeed, the later each country joined the regional revolutionary wave, the bloodier were the initial consequences of its upheaval. There is of course a simple logic at work here: that of "snowballing". It played a key role in the spread of the uprising to the whole of the Arabic-speaking region in the manner identified by Huntington when, discussing the "third wave of democratization", he defined "snowballing" as "demonstration effects, enhanced by new means of international communication ... providing models for subsequent efforts at regime change in other countries".[32]

However, all too predictably, lessons from the same "demonstration effects" have also been drawn by the regimes (still) in place: the fall of Ben Ali and Mubarak despite their belated promises of reform was attributed by the other regional despots to the fact that the protesters had not been sufficiently deterred from carrying on their rebellion. There had been no determined attempt at drowning the uprising in a bloodbath when it had begun to unfold in either Tunisia or Egypt.[33] In Yemen, the general armament of the populace, and the fact that the country's dominant political fault-line ran through the armed forces themselves, meant that a frontal military attack on the protesters would have led to a civil war, the consequences of which looked costlier for Saleh at the time than what he hoped to achieve through political manoeuvring. In Bahrain, the uprising was dissuaded from organising its self-defence against brutal state repression by the intervention of troops from the Saudi kingdom and other Gulf monarchies.

In both Libya and Syria, however, the repression of the uprisings was much bloodier from the outset than in any of those four countries: a fact directly related to the patrimonial character of both regimes and their accurate conviction that any substantial compromise – any breach in their armour – would spell their end. Moreover, unlike the Bahraini monarchy, the Libyan *jumlukiyya* (the Arabic popular neologism combining "monarchy" and "republic") that pretended to be a *jamahiriyya* ("state of the masses") was not actively supported by any outside power, be it regional or international. Gaddafi was such a lunatic maverick, indeed, that no influential state was willing to support him. On the other hand, the Libyan opposition seemed so reassuringly conservative that military intervention against Gaddafi's forces came to be seen by the alliance of NATO and the three Arab monarchies of Qatar, the UAE and Jordan as a good opportunity to co-opt the Libyan uprising, and thereby to try to hijack the regional uprising as a whole in order to exorcise its emancipatory potential. The Syrian dissidents believed that this UN-greenlighted foreign military intervention against Gaddafi would dissuade the Syrian regime from resorting to full force, and that it might even push a section of the regime to remove Assad, just as the Egyptian military had removed Mubarak, rather than take the risk of a war like the one that had erupted in Libya.

The persistence of the Libyan uprising, thanks partly to Western support, the successful insurrection in the capital, Tripoli, in August

2011 and the speed at which it led the Libyan state apparatuses to collapse – taking NATO itself by surprise – with the final exit of Gaddafi himself in October, all served strongly to galvanise the Syrian uprising. But the eventual fate of the Gaddafi family and their cronies also convinced the Assad family and their cronies that it was for them literally a matter of life or death. From November 2011 onwards, the Syrian regime went on a full-scale offensive, starting with its onslaught on the city of Homs. Backed by Russia and Iran, unlike Gaddafi, the Assad clan knew that the odds were very poor that the United States and its Western allies would intervene militarily in Syria, as they had in Libya. The Libyan fiasco – in which direct Western intervention ended with the complete dismantlement of a second Arab (oil) state after that of Saddam Hussein in Iraq, with similarly chaotic results – would soon come to constitute a further reason for Washington not to risk repeating such a mistake in Syria.

The Assad regime's offensive, and its resort to systematic, bloody repression on an increasingly horrific scale, engaged Syria inexorably on the path of a civil war that would soon turn into the most tragic conflict that the world has witnessed since the Rwandan Genocide and the horrendous wars in Central Africa. In response to the regime's murderous escalation, the Syrian insurgency went into high gear, launching a counter-offensive in various regions, with cumulative successes. The regime began to lose ground increasingly to the opposition. By the spring of 2013, signs of regime exhaustion had multiplied: the Assad regime was in dire need of support. At that point, Iran massively stepped up its support to the regime through its regional Lebanese and Iraqi proxies. The tipping point was the al-Qusayr offensive, begun in April 2013, during which Lebanese Hezbollah troops, along with the Iranian-instructed regime's auxiliary militias, called National Defence Forces, played the major role in recapturing this strategic area close to the border with Northern Lebanon. From that moment, the Syrian regime and its allies continued a counter-insurgency campaign that scored several successes – signalling a turning point in the regional momentum, which switched from the initial revolutionary phase to a counter-revolutionary phase, in a reversal soon to be underlined by developments in Egypt.

The two chapters that follow assess the situation that has unfolded since the end of October 2012 – when I completed writing *The People Want* – in Syria and Egypt, the two countries whose trajectories most strongly determine the fate of the regional revolutionary process as a whole. Tunisia, Yemen and Libya – the other three countries where uprisings achieved initial victories, and which remained in turmoil up to the time of writing (unlike Bahrain) – will be briefly discussed in the Conclusion. My aim here is to identify the key issues that made the "Arab Spring" turn into an "Arab Winter", in order to formulate a new forecast, to use a term that fits well with this now ubiquitous seasonal metaphor.

Syria

The Clash of Barbarisms

If one side uses force without compunction,
undeterred by the bloodshed it involves, while
the other side refrains, the first will gain the upper
hand. That side will force the other to follow suit;
each will drive its opponent toward extremes ...

Carl von Clausewitz, *On War* (1816–1830)

My assessment of the Syrian situation in *The People Want* concluded
as follows:

[S]ince there exists no political-military leadership equal to the
task of the Syrian uprising, the sectarian dynamics of the conflict
have inevitably intensified the longer it has gone on. The regime's
increasingly blind, deadly violence and the accumulation of
sectarian massacres perpetrated by its special forces or its *shabbiha*
have begun to provoke reactions of the same general sort from Sunni
fighters, who are, moreover, being egged on by the Saudi Wahhabis'
sectarian propaganda. ...
 The armed Syrian uprising is confronted with two acute problems. The first is the marked superiority of the regime's military
forces ... [This] superiority is being maintained by outside support
– political support and arms from Russia, financial support, arms,
and fighters from Iran and its regional allies. ...
 The Western capitals, with Washington in the lead ... never
ceased to proclaim their unwillingness to intervene. As in Libya,

they have refused to deliver weapons to the combatants out of
fear that those arms will be directed against their interests in the
medium or long term. ...

[Thus] the second acute problem with which the insurrection
is faced [is] money. ... Money is needed to provision the Syrian
combatants, as well as to provide them with the weapons that
they cruelly lack. In this respect, the most privileged of all those
fighting the Syrian regime are the fundamentalist Sunni groups:
funds emanating from the Saudi government or the Wahhabi
religious institution are reaching them. These funds give them an
indisputable advantage over the networks of citizen-fighters who
have declared allegiance to the [Free Syrian Army]. They thus
intensify the potential danger that these fundamentalist Sunni
groups represent for the Syrian uprising as well as for the country's
future in general. From this point of view as well, the sooner the
Syrian regime topples, the better. The longer it lasts, the greater is
the risk that the country will plunge into barbarism.[1]

Written in the autumn of 2012, this prognosis was predicated,
on the one hand, on the fatal dynamics resulting from the lack of a
counterweight to the Syrian regime's military prevalence, enhanced
by Russian and Iranian full-spectrum support, and, on the other
hand, on the reliance of Western powers on Gulf oil monarchies
as funders of the Syrian opposition. In the early period of the civil
war, when the armed force of the mainstream Syrian opposition –
the Free Syrian Army (FSA), linked to the Syrian National Council,
and later to the National Coalition of Syrian Revolution and
Opposition Forces that succeeded the former as the main body of the
mainstream opposition – was still predominant among insurgents on
the battlefield, Washington did not provide it with anything more
than token support. This was despite the fact that this mainstream
opposition, with its dominant mixture of Muslim Brotherhood,
traditional politicians and secular liberal modernists, was quite
compatible with US interests. Later on, when this coalition started
losing ground among anti-regime forces, to the advantage of rival

Islamic fundamentalist forces that were both hostile to the progressive aspirations of the 2011 uprising and ideologically inimical to the West, Washington increased its support to the FSA within limits that remained closer to a symbolic gesture than to real support. The bottom line is that Barack Obama has persistently denied the Syrian opposition the defensive weapons it has most crucially needed – and insistently requested – in order to circumscribe the regime's military advantage: first and foremost, advanced anti-aircraft weapons.

The Abandonment of the Syrian People

A monopoly of air power and full control of the air above Syria have, of course, provided the Assad regime's most decisive military edge. The regime felt safe enough in that respect to indulge in cheaper and more murderous (i.e. more "cost-effective") low-altitude strikes: since the summer of 2012, the Assad regime has resorted increasingly to using helicopters as bombers, loading them with rudimentary but hugely and indiscriminately murderous and destructive "barrel bombs".[2] To curtail this edge, the Syrian opposition did not, and could not, request large surface-to-air missiles of the kind that requires sophisticated military capabilities for its handling and use. It requested advanced portable missiles (known as man-portable air-defence systems – MANPADS), such as the US-made FIM-92H Stinger-RMP missile, a weapon whose market unit cost is less than $45,000.[3] Turkey could easily have supplied such MANPADS with Gulf states' funding, as it is itself involved in the production of the Stinger systems.[4] However, the US vetoed early on any such deliveries.

> To keep control of the flow of weapons to the Syrian rebels, Turkey, Saudi Arabia and Qatar formed a joint operations room early this year [2012] in a covert project US officials watched from afar.
> The US has limited its support of the rebels to communications equipment, logistics and intelligence. But US officials have

coordinated with the trio of countries sending arms and munitions to the rebels. The Pentagon and CIA ramped up their presence on Turkey's southern border as the weapons began to flow to the rebels in two to three shipments every week.

> In July, the US effectively halted the delivery of at least 18 MANPADS sourced from Libya, even as the rebels pleaded for more effective anti-aircraft missiles to counter regime airstrikes in Aleppo, people familiar with that delivery said.[5]

Up to the time of writing, the Syrian opposition, all tendencies included, possessed mostly antiquated Soviet-made anti-aircraft weapons, including shoulder-fired missiles, seized from the Syrian army's stocks.[6] The supply of a few Chinese-made MANPADS (FN-6) to Syrian rebel groups in 2013 enabled them to shoot down two Soviet-era helicopters (Mil MI-8), a feat that they celebrated with much fanfare.[7] (Although this supply was shrouded in secrecy as it circumvented the US veto, the *New York Times* reported that they were sold by Sudan's government to Qatar, which arranged their delivery through Turkey.[8]) These were no state-of-the-art MANPADS (the Chinese equivalent of the FIM-92 is the more advanced FN-16), and most of them did not even work.[9] And yet, the very fact that such achievements remained exceptional, and were celebrated each time accordingly, only illustrates the scarcity of such weapons in the hands of the Syrian opposition.

In the summer of 2013, when the Syrian regime was mounting a full-fledged counter-offensive, with the support of Iran and its regional proxies – when the situation was indeed "at the tipping point" in the words of a Western official quoted by the *Wall Street Journal* – General Salim Idris, then FSA's chief of staff, requested in a "desperate plea" (the journal's phrase) 100 shoulder-fired missiles.[10] To no avail. Similar requests had been made to Washington since the previous summer. "But proposals to arm the rebels, advocated by then-Central Intelligence Agency chief David Petraeus and then-Secretary of State Hillary Clinton, ran into opposition in the White House from Mr Obama."[11] The conspicuous contrast between the scale of US support to the Syrian opposition and Russian support to the regime has been aptly emphasised by Muhammad Idrees Ahmad:

> The conflict in Syria is often described as a "proxy war" between the US and Russia. Syrian rebels are rarely mentioned without the obligatory prefix "US-backed". (The regime army on the other hand isn't often described as "Russian-backed".) The backing, though tangible, takes distinctly different forms; and the support that the contending parties have received reflects the character of their patrons.
>
> Not used to doing things by half, Russia has supplied the Syrian regime with bombers, gunships, armour and missiles. The US, on the other hand, has spent many years trying to ensure that no anti-aircraft weapon would reach Syrian rebels lest it affect its ally Israel's ability to bomb Syria with impunity. Instead, its support has taken the form of non-lethal aid, such as night-vision goggles and satellite phones. It took many years before it supplied outdated TOW anti-tank missiles but has refrained from passing on any game-changing technology.[12]

Had the attitude of the Obama administration been simply one of "non-intervention", it could have been seen as catering to American public opinion against US involvement in yet another military venture – although there is no indication that the public would have objected to US support to the Syrian insurgency short of direct military involvement. But the administration did actually intervene quite decisively in the Syrian events by preventing its regional allies from providing the Syrian opposition with the qualitative weapons that it needed, thus increasing the imbalance resulting from Russian and Iranian intervention on the side of the Syrian regime.

In order to justify his lack of effective support to the Syrian moderate opposition, one of Barack Obama's arguments – not to say pretexts – was that it lacked the necessary manpower to handle the

weapons that it requested. Thus, on 19 June 2014 – in response to a
journalist asking him: "The United States has been slow to provide
significant weapons and training directly to the Syrian opposition.
Has the expansion of the Syria war into Iraq changed your mind
about the type of weapons and training we're now willing to give
the opposition there?" – the US president argued the following:

> The question has never been whether we thought this was a serious
> problem. The question has always been, is there the capacity of
> moderate opposition on the ground to absorb and counteract
> extremists that might have been pouring in, as well as an Assad
> regime supported by Iran and Russia that outmanned them and was
> ruthless.
>
> And so we have consistently provided that opposition with
> support. Oftentimes, the challenge is if you have former farmers or
> teachers or pharmacists who now are taking up opposition against a
> battle-hardened regime, with support from external actors that have
> a lot at stake, how quickly can you get them trained; how effect-
> ive [sic] are you able to mobilise them. And that continues to be a
> challenge.[13]

When trying to justify the same lack of support, US vice president
Joseph Biden argued exactly the contrary in a famously gaffe-ridden
performance at Harvard University, on 2 October 2014: "The fact
of the matter is the ability to identify a moderate middle in Syria
– there was no moderate middle, because the moderate middle
are made up of shopkeepers, not soldiers. They are made up of
people who in fact [are] ordinary elements of the middle class in
that country."[14] Thus, in short, the Obama administration did not
give effective support to the Syrian opposition because (1) it is
composed of "farmers or teachers or pharmacists" instead of soldiers
(Obama), and (2) there were no "shopkeepers" or "middle class"
among them but only soldiers (Biden). The flagrant contradiction
between the president's and his deputy's statements betrays the
vacuity and falsity of such pretexts. Rather than a lack of confidence

in the opposition's military skills, there are some grounds to believe that Washington did not seriously support any particular group of the Syrian opposition because it could not guarantee their loyalty to US interests. As then-chairman of the Joint Chiefs of Staff General Martin Dempsey wrote in August 2013 in response to a formal query from a member of the US Congress: "Syria today is not about choosing between two sides but rather about choosing one among many sides. *It is my belief that the side we choose must be ready to promote their interests and ours when the balance shifts in their favor. Today, they are not.*"[15]

In tune with this political distrust is the argument that the Syrian opposition could not be trusted to keep US weapons from falling into the wrong hands – the hands of terrorist groups that are fiercely hostile to the United States and the West, such as al-Qaida. This was indeed the key pretext invoked by the Obama administration to justify its refusal to deliver anti-aircraft weapons to the Syrian dissidents, as well as its refusal to allow the United States' regional allies to provide them with such weapons, even if not US-made. When Washington's Arab allies – dismayed by the escalation in Tehran's backing of the Assad regime and disappointed by the failure of Moscow to exert firm pressure on the regime for a compromise at the Geneva talks (Geneva II Conference on Syria, January–February 2014) – requested anew from the Obama administration that it allow them to deliver anti-aircraft weapons to the Syrian opposition, their request was met with rejection all the same. The *Wall Street Journal* reported:

> Saudi Arabia has offered to give the opposition for the first time Chinese man-portable air defense systems, or MANPADS, and anti-tank guided missiles from Russia, according to an Arab diplomat and several opposition figures with knowledge of the efforts. Saudi officials couldn't be reached to comment.
>
> The US has long opposed arming rebels with anti-aircraft missiles for fear they could fall into the hands of extremists who might use them against the West or commercial airlines. The Saudis have held

off supplying them in the past because of US opposition. A senior Obama administration official said Friday that the US objection remains the same. "There hasn't been a change internally on our view," the official said.[16]

Faced with similar pressure from the United States' Arab allies, the White House leaked information aimed at giving the impression that it had weighed very carefully the option of providing anti-aircraft weapons to the Syrian insurgents. *Time* magazine carried an article on this issue, in which the view attributed to "an Arab official" that "the introduction of MANPADS could be a game changer in Syria, like it was in Afghanistan in the 1980s with Stinger missiles" is countered with a belittling of the potential impact of such weapons on the conflict, along with the adumbration of a catastrophic scenario of global economic disruption by terrorism: "A 2005 Rand Corp. study found that the shooting down of a civilian airliner might temporarily freeze air travel worldwide and produce total economic losses of more than $15 billion."[17] The article concluded: "Even [US Senator John] McCain seems to acknowledge that MANPADS would have a primarily humanitarian use, as a defense against helicopter-borne barrel bombs. And for now at least, that's not reason enough for Obama to risk a $15 billion nightmare."

Leaving its cynicism aside, this argument does not even hold water; it is a blatant instance of scaremongering in order to make up a pretext. As Anthony Cordesman, a prominent expert on military and security affairs working for a bipartisan strategic think tank based in Washington, noted in a perceptive and comprehensive assessment of US options in Syria, "the US has now had years in which to modify key weapons like [MANPADS] and ATGMs [anti-tank guided missiles] to limit their active life, the areas in which they can operate, and their vulnerability to US countermeasures."[18] When Washington reluctantly consented to deliver "a small number" of BGM-71 TOW anti-tank missiles to Syrian anti-regime fighters in the spring of 2014, they were "equipped with a complex, fingerprint-keyed security device" controlling who could fire them, according to a security expert quoted by the *Wall Street Journal*.[19] Moreover, it is not as if no MANPADS have ever fallen into the hands of terrorists, or ever been used against civil aviation. According to a 2011 report by the Bureau of Political-Military Affairs of the US State Department, "Since 1975, 40 civilian aircraft have been hit by MANPADS, causing about 28 crashes and more than 800 deaths around the world. ... Thousands of MANPADS ... are believed to be outside of the control of national governments. The United States believes that a number of terrorist organizations, including al-Qaida, have MANPADS in their possession."[20] To this it should be added that "the black market cost of MANPADS can vary widely, ranging from as little as a few hundred dollars to over one hundred thousand dollars, depending on the model and its condition."[21] This is not to argue that MANPADS in the hands of lunatic terrorists are not a serious threat – they definitely are – but to show that the $15 billion scenario is not worth 15 cents. The potential terrorist threat would hardly have increased had the Syrian opposition been provided with MANPADS programmed in such a way that their operational workability would remain under control.

The truth of the matter is that this scaremongering line of argument is simply an attempt to cover what is, in the first place, an unwillingness to help that is predicated on deep human indifference to the fate of the population of an oil-poor Arab country.[22] Barack Obama would not lose sleep over the Syrian people's calamity: hundreds of thousands of Syrians killed and maimed (let alone the millions turned into refugees) were tolerable in his view, as long as they were slaughtered by "conventional" bombing. Only the use of chemical weapons constituted a "red line" – and that was because it might endanger Syria's neighbours, starting with Israel. The US president's own enunciation in August 2012 of the rationale of his position on "humanitarian assistance" and on a chemical "red line" speaks for itself:

What we've said is, number one, we want to make sure we're providing humanitarian assistance, and we've done that to the tune of $82 million, I believe, so far. And we'll probably end up doing *a little more* [sic] because *we want to make sure that the hundreds of thousands of refugees that are fleeing the mayhem, that they don't end up creating – or being in a terrible situation, or also destabilizing some of Syria's neighbors.* ...

I have, at this point, not ordered military engagement in the situation. *But the point ... about chemical and biological weapons is critical. That's an issue that doesn't just concern Syria; it concerns our close allies in the region, including Israel. It concerns us.* We cannot have a situation where chemical or biological weapons are falling into the hands of the wrong people.

We have been very clear to the Assad regime, but also to other players on the ground, that a red line for us is [if] we start seeing a whole bunch of chemical weapons moving around or being utilised. That would change my calculus. That would change my equation.[23]

In the second place, the Obama administration's scaremongering line of argument about weapons delivery to the Syrian opposition was a cover for the true central political rationale of its disinclination to intervene: the obsession with securing an "orderly transition" and avoiding the repetition of the Iraqi debacle by preserving the bulk of the Syrian state apparatus, as I emphasised on several occasions since 2011.[24] This assessment has been fully confirmed by Hillary Rodham Clinton's testimony in her 2014 memoirs, where she asserts that, despite the differences within the administration on the course of action in Syria, they all "agreed that it was important to *maintain the integrity of the Syrian state and its institutions*, particularly enough of the security infrastructure to prevent the kind of chaos we had seen in Iraq after the fall of Saddam Hussein and the disbanding of the Iraqi Army and government"[25]

The then-secretary of state was so dedicated to that supreme consideration that – as she herself explains somewhat ingenuously – when she, along with then-CIA director and former US commander in Afghanistan and Iraq, David Petraeus, advocated training and equipping a Syrian rebel force, "*the goal was not to build a force strong enough to defeat the regime.*" Rather, "the idea was to give us a partner on the ground we could work with that could do enough to convince Assad and his backers that a military victory was impossible."[26]

This same central rationale stands behind the very unimpressive manner in which Barack Obama handled the "chemical weapons" crisis in August 2013, when – exactly one year after he had declared the use of such weapons to be a "red line" – he was confronted with the most murderous chemical attack perpetrated by Assad regime forces until that day, in the Ghouta suburb of Damascus. Obama delayed action by seeking a highly hazardous authorisation from Congress – "in a move that surprised many in Washington", according to Hillary Clinton.[27] Soon after, Clinton's successor as secretary of state, John Kerry, suggested to Moscow publicly, albeit indirectly, that the administration would be satisfied with a deal whereby Damascus would relinquish its chemical arsenal and turn it over to "the international community". Moscow immediately seized upon this suggestion – and so did the Assad regime. The latter cowardly surrendered right away its single deterrent weapon of mass destruction, although Israel – which Damascus is purported to be bravely "confronting" according to its own propaganda and that of its regional allies and supporters – is heavily armed with the full spectrum of such weapons.

The actual reason for the amazing alacrity of all parties in striking the chemical deal was nothing other than their common concern to avoid the Syrian regime's sudden collapse. Indeed, a Damascus-based correspondent of mine, a former army officer, told me at the time that Washington's threat to launch cruise missiles against Syrian regime targets had provoked a wave of panic engulfing the regime's military apparatus. This was in spite of the insistence of Obama administration officials – in their attempt to mollify US domestic opposition to the bombing – that the planned attack was going to be very limited. My correspondent assured me that, had the attack been launched, the regime's armed forces would have instantly faced a risk of mass desertion and disintegration.

It is for exactly the same reason that, when it started bombing the "Islamic State in Iraq and al-Sham" (ISIS, sometimes designated as ISIL[28]) in both Iraq and Syria, with official approval from Baghdad and tacit approval from Damascus, the United States took special care not to hit any target related to the Assad regime. And when, in December 2014, Washington finally launched a $500 million program to train and equip a US-controlled Syrian "moderate" force, the key condition it defined for its recruitment was that it should fight exclusively against ISIS. No wonder it turned into a farcical failure, as Barack Obama acknowledged candidly at a press conference in October 2015:

> The training-and-equip program was a specific initiative by the Defense Department to see if we could get some of that moderate opposition to focus attention on ISIL in the eastern portion of the country. And I'm the first one to acknowledge it has not worked the way it was supposed to ... And part of the reason, frankly, is because when we tried to get them to just focus on ISIL, the response we'd get back is, how can we focus on ISIL when every single day we're having barrel bombs and attacks from the regime? And so it's been hard to get them to reprioritise, looking east, when they've got bombs coming at them from the west.[29]

The result of all this care not to harm the Syrian regime was indeed that "confident of American inaction, Mr Al Assad killed three times as many civilians in the 28 months after the chemical attack as he had in the 28 months before."[30] Having given the Assad regime a de facto licence to kill with "conventional weapons", Barack Obama would go down in history as the US president who bears a key responsibility for the destruction of Syria and its people, in the wake of three presidents who bear chief responsibility for the destruction of Iraq and its people. The difference is that, whereas the three previous presidents devastated Iraq by way of direct US military aggression, Obama contributed to the devastation of Syria by letting its dictatorial regime achieve it.

The failure of the duty to rescue a person in peril – when the potential rescuer is able to act without harming themselves or others – is punishable in the penal code of several countries. From a moral standpoint, the failure to rescue an entire population in peril is a crime of much bigger scope; it can indeed amount to tacit complicity in a crime against humanity. And yet, this crime is not inscribed as such in international law, which only provides for a "Responsibility to Protect" (R2P) when it suits a consensus among the UN Security Council's permanent members.[31] Washington, of course, does not wait for a UN green light in order to intervene when it deems that its interests are at stake. It bombed Serbia in 1999 and invaded Iraq in 2003 without UN approval. From that angle, Washington's crime against Syria is no less reprehensible than the one it committed against Iraq.

The Making of the Syrian Disaster

The symmetry between George W. Bush and Barack Obama – their production of similar results in opposite ways: military aggression in Bush's case and denial of assistance in Obama's – does not stop at the devastation of both the countries affected. It also concerns one of the dreadful consequences of this devastation: whereas the Bush-run US invasion of Iraq created the conditions that led to the emergence of the "Islamic State of Iraq" (ISI) that al-Qaida proclaimed in 2006, as well as to the expansion of the parent organisation across the Arab region, the Obama-adjudicated denial of crucial support to the Syrian opposition created the conditions that allowed the ISI to develop in Syria and mutate into ISIS in 2013. This was followed the year after by the announcement of the "Islamic State" tout court as a successful franchise, opening branches in its turn all over the Arab region and way beyond.

Robert Ford, who resigned from his position as US ambassador to Syria in February 2014 due to his disagreement with Barack Obama's Syrian policy, very clearly attributed responsibility for this disastrous course of events to the US president. He made his statement in an interview on *PBS Newshour* a few months after his resignation, including a premonitory warning against future attacks on US soil, as was to happen with the San Bernardino ISIS-inspired shooting on 2 December 2015:

> Events on the ground were moving, and our policy wasn't evolving very quickly. We were constantly behind the curve. And that's why now we have extremist threats to our own country. We had a young man from Florida, apparently, who was involved in a suicide bombing, and there will be more problems like that, I fear. Our policy wasn't evolving, and finally I got to the point where I could no longer defend it publicly. ...
>
> We have consistently been behind the curve. The events on the ground are moving more rapidly than our policy has been adapting. And at the same time, Russia and Iran have been driving this by increasing and steadily increasing, increasing massively, especially the Iranians, their support to the Syrian regime.
>
> And the result of that has been more threats to us in this ungoverned space which Assad can't retake. We need and we have long needed to help moderates in the Syrian opposition with both weapons and other nonlethal assistance. Had we done that a couple of years ago, had we ramped it up, frankly, the al-Qaida groups that have been winning adherents would have been unable to compete with the moderates, who, frankly, we have much in common with. But the moderates have been fighting constantly with arms tied behind their backs, because they don't have the same resources that either Assad does or the al-Qaida groups in Syria do. ...
>
> And we can't get to a political negotiation until the balance on the ground compels – and I use that word precisely – compels Assad not to run sham elections, but rather to negotiate a political deal. But the situation on the ground is key.[32]

As was the case for Iraq, many actors and observers in Washington itself have been warning the White House all along of the calamitous consequences of its course of action – or rather inaction, in Syria's case – just as Robert Ford did. Anthony Cordesman hit the nail on the head when he wrote in 2013:

> The failure to act decisively when the more moderate rebel forces in Syria seriously threatened Assad, and at the crest of rebel success, has not made anything better or brought Syria one step closer to a negotiable outcome. The pendulum in US politics seems to have swung from the ideologically-driven overreaction and strategic absurdist optimism of the Bush Administration to its exact opposite. ...
>
> If anything, the Administration's failure to act ... has systematically empowered both Iran and the Hezbollah while simultaneously empowering Al Qa'ida and Sunni Islamist extremist[s] – not only in Syria, but Lebanon and Iraq. ...
>
> No action the US takes in regard to Syria is without risk. ... Any "success" at the military level means a new Syrian government whose structure is unpredictable, a legacy of enduring political problems, and tensions throughout the region. ...
>
> Inaction, however, is also a form of decision-making, and exaggerating costs and risks has consequences. The US is already watching arms flood into the region, Iranian influence grow, and a major rise in Sunni and Shi'ite/Alawite extremism.[33]

Washington's responsibility in this post-2011 turn of events has been similarly confirmed by two key members of the Obama administration, even though they stood on opposite sides of the debate on Syria that split the administration. In the edifying interview she gave to the *Atlantic*'s Jeffrey Goldberg, which was published on 10 August 2014, former US Secretary of State Hillary Clinton had this to say on the issue of Syria:

> [Y]ou have more than 170,000 people dead in Syria. You have the vacuum that has been created by the relentless assault by Assad on

his own population, an assault that has bred these extremist groups, the most well-known of which, ISIS – or ISIL – is now literally expanding its territory inside Syria and inside Iraq. ...

I know that the failure to help build up a credible fighting force of the people who were the originators of the protests against Assad – there were Islamists, there were secularists, there was everything in the middle – the failure to do that left a big vacuum, which the jihadists have now filled.

They were often armed in an indiscriminate way by other forces and we had no skin in the game that really enabled us to prevent this indiscriminate arming.[34]

The second confirmation came from US vice president Joseph Biden. During his above-mentioned gaffe-ridden performance at Harvard University on 2 October 2014, he made a statement that was intended as a rebuttal of Hillary Clinton's criticism, but in fact confirmed her main argument:

[O]ur allies in the region were our largest problem in Syria. The Turks were great friends ... the Saudis, the Emiratis, etc. What were they doing? They were so determined to take down Assad and essentially have a proxy Sunni–Shia war. What did they do? They poured hundreds of millions of dollars and tens, thousands of tons of weapons into anyone who would fight against Assad – except that the people who were being supplied were Al Nusra and Al Qaeda and the extremist elements of jihadis coming from other parts of the world. ... So now what's happening? All of a sudden everybody is awakened because this outfit called ISIL which was Al Qaeda in Iraq, which, when they were essentially thrown out of Iraq, found open space and territory in eastern Syria, worked with Al Nusra who we declared a terrorist group early on and we could not convince our colleagues to stop supplying them.[35]

Biden's statement was extensively quoted by jubilant supporters of the Assad regime as confirmation of what was hardly a secret:

the fact that Turkey and the oil monarchies were backing Sunni fundamentalist forces among the Syrian insurgents. In doing so, those enthusiastic supporters overlooked the fact that the vice president's statement was above all a refutation of what they themselves had been claiming since the beginning of the Syrian uprising, namely that it is essentially a US-backed insurgency against a Syrian regime deemed "patriotic" (*watani*) by its Arab fans, or "anti-imperialist" by its Western "left" supporters. These Assad enthusiasts ignored the obvious truth that the situation on the ground would have been completely different had the US been seriously backing the opposition, as they claimed. The regime would not have been able to carry on slaughtering the population and destroying the country, as it managed to do owing to its monopoly of air power and heavy weaponry, supplied by Russia and Iran.

It is actually the lack of US support to the mainstream Syrian opposition from the early stage of the civil war that allowed the Syrian situation to end up being caught between the hammer of an increasingly murderous regime backed by increasingly sectarian Lebanese and Iraqi Shi'i fundamentalist proxies of Iran,[36] and the anvil of increasingly sectarian and fanatical Sunni-fundamentalist anti-Assad regime forces. Indeed, here lies the Obama administration's primary responsibility in producing the worst of all possible outcomes – not only for the Syrian people, but even for US imperialism itself, in the same way that the Bush administration's inept mishandling of Iraq led to what is undoubtedly the biggest strategic failure in US imperial history until now, one that is combined, alas, with an ongoing human tragedy among the worst since the end of the Cold War. When disastrous failures of imperialism happen at the cost of terrible human tragedies, there can be no schadenfreude from a truly humanist anti-imperialist perspective.

The Assad regime was initially confronted with a peaceful uprising led by Coordination Committees (*tansiqiyyat*) mostly composed of young people sharing the same aspirations for freedom, democracy and social justice that inspired all those who initiated what was called the "Arab Spring" in 2011.[37] In December 2012, the editor-in-chief of the pro-Damascus Hezbollah-linked Lebanese newspaper *Al-Akhbar* reported that none other than Bashar al-Assad's official deputy, Syrian vice president Farouk al-Sharaa, told him that "at the beginning of the events, the government was begging [*tatawassal*] to see a single armed man or sniper on the roof of a building."[38]

The interview was meant to show that Sharaa, who was believed to be under house arrest, was free to speak. The circumstances described in the interview itself rather indicated that it was an exercise in controlled freedom, like so many interviews of personalities under house arrest in countries with murderous regimes. It was quite important, nevertheless, in revealing that there had been a major disagreement at the top of the Syrian state on the way to tackle the crisis, pitting against those who advocated a political settlement those – starting with Assad himself – who wanted to terminate it by the use of force:

> The decline in the number of peaceful protesters led in some way or another to an increase in the number of armed men. It is true that the provision of security to the citizens is a duty of the state, but this is different from opting for a security solution to the crisis. ...
>
> Those who are able to meet the president will hear him say that this is a long struggle, and that it is a big conspiracy with many participants (terrorists, bandits, traffickers). He does not hide his desire to use military force in order to achieve complete victory on the ground; political dialogue would then become possible. [On the other hand] many in the [ruling Baath] Party, the [Baath-led National Progressive] Front and the armed forces have believed from the beginning of the crisis until now that there is no alternative to the political solution, and no return backwards.[39]

The regime chose to face the peaceful protests of the first months of the uprising with increasing violence, trying at first to deter them from carrying on their struggle and then doing its best to turn it into an armed confrontation, so as to feel free to use the full range of its weapons.[40] It also did its best to bring about the "self-fulfilling prophecy" that it had intensively propagated from the very beginning of the movement in March 2011 – namely, that the uprising was but a "Takfiri" Salafi-jihadist armed conspiracy.[41] Muammar Gaddafi resorted to exactly the same type of lies at the beginning of the Libyan uprising, when he claimed that it was orchestrated by al-Qaida. The main purpose of the fabrication in both cases was to dissuade the West from lending any form of support to the uprising.

In the Syrian case, it had the additional purpose of scaring the country's religious minorities, as well as the better-off layers of its Sunni majority.[42] In order to push the insurgents to resort to arms in self-defence, and thus confirm its claims and justify a further escalation of its ruthless violence, the Assad regime relied on the inevitable effect of the murderous escalation of its crackdown, combined with highly cynical measures such as surreptitiously providing weapons to dissidents.[43] In order to promote the rise of Salafi-jihadists within the opposition, the regime went so far as to release from its jails prominent militants belonging to this category, several of whom were to become key leaders of various jihadist groups.[44] This happened in the second half of 2011, at a time when the regime was arresting thousands upon thousands of democrats involved in the peaceful protests. Martin Chulov described this process in the *Guardian*, in one of the best investigative articles written about ISIS. The story he tells is very revealing as to the metamorphosis of the Syrian uprising:

> By the time another young jihadi, Abu Issa, was freed from Aleppo's central prison in late 2011, the Trojan horse act that was ISIS was well under way – fuelled by Turkey's porous borders, the savagery of the Syrian regime, feckless attempts to organise opposition fighters into a cohesive force, and the release of militant prisoners like himself. A Syrian with historical links to the group's earliest incarnation, al-Qaida in Iraq, Abu Issa was released along with dozens of men

like him as part of an amnesty given by Assad to Islamist detainees, which was touted by the regime as a reconciliation with men who had long fought against them.

Most of the accused al-Qaida men had been in the infamous Syrian prison system for many years before the uprising against Assad began. "We were in the worst dungeons in Syria," said Abu Issa, who was a member of the various forerunners of ISIS, and fought against the US army in 2004 and 2005 before fleeing Baghdad in 2006. "If you were charged with our crimes, you were sent to Political Security prison, Saydnaya in Damascus or Air Force Intelligence in Aleppo. You could not even speak to the guards there. It was just brutality and fear."

But several months before Abu Issa was released, he and a large group of other jihadis were moved from their isolation cells elsewhere in the country and flown to Aleppo's main prison, where they enjoyed a more communal and comfortable life. "It was like a hotel," he said. "We couldn't believe it. There were cigarettes, blankets, anything you wanted. You could even get girls." Soon the detainees were puzzled by another prison oddity, the arrival of university students who had been arrested in Aleppo for protesting against the Assad regime. ...

Abu Issa and the other Islamist detainees soon formed the view that they had been moved to the Aleppo prison for a reason – to instil a harder ideological line into the university students, who back then were at the vanguard of the uprising in Syria's largest city.

On the same day that Abu Issa and many of his friends were released, the Lebanese government, which is supported by Damascus, also freed more than 70 jihadis, many of whom had been convicted of terrorism offences and were serving lengthy terms. The release puzzled Western officials in Beirut who had been monitoring the fates of many of the accused jihadis in Lebanon's jails for more than four years.[45]

Like the Abu Issa described by Martin Chulov, many of the jihadists released in 2011 had previously fought in Iraq – with the Syrian

regime's connivance. During the initial years of the US occupation
of Iraq, the Assad regime, true to its Machiavellian character, had
indeed allowed Syrian and foreign jihadists to infiltrate into Iraq
across its long shared border with Syria.[46] It had also allowed former
loyalists of Saddam Hussein to take refuge in Syria and support the
Sunni-sectarian insurgency across the border. The Syrian regime had
already released jihadists from its own jails to send them to Iraq, as
Syrian lawyer and human rights activist for the organisation Swasia,
Catherine al-Talli, told the US embassy in Damascus, on the basis
of her investigation of the circumstances surrounding the bloodily
repressed Saydnaya prison riots in 2008–09:

> According to Talli's contacts, after the US invasion of Iraq, the SARG
> [Syrian Arab Republic government] offered Seidnaya inmates the
> opportunity to receive military training in Syria and then travel to
> Iraq and fight coalition forces ... Talli had no additional information
> on how many inmates joined or at what times they were sent to Iraq.
> She did report, however, that of those who returned from Iraq to
> Syria, some remained at large (but in contact with the regime),
> others were sent to Lebanon, and a third group were re-arrested and
> remanded to Seidnaya prison. ...
>   Talli's reporting adds to the mounting evidence that the SARG
> allowed Seidnaya prisoners to train in Syria for combat operations
> in Iraq.[47]

In the 2005 quasi-official biography that Bashar al-Assad
induced David Lesch to write about him as part of a charm offensive
towards the West – thereby following in the footsteps of his father,
who relied on Patrick Seale for the same purpose[48] – there is a
clumsy attempt at selling the idea that Syrian facilitation of and
support to the jihadi insurgency next door was beyond Assad's
personal control. In essence, we are told, "Bashar was not yet able to
crack down on the porous Syrian border or those elements linked
with the regime behind the exchanges and associations with Iraqi
insurgents ... "[49]

However, after Nouri al-Maliki, a close ally of Tehran and long-time friend of Damascus, was made prime minister in Baghdad in May 2006, the Assad regime had to stop playing the deadly game of exporting jihadists to Iraq, as it became inimical to its regional alliances to carry it on, especially since the situation there had slipped into a sectarian war in which it was no longer in the Syrian regime's interest to strengthen the Sunni camp. Damascus stepped up the (re)incarceration of jihadist returnees. "The group of returned foreign fighters in Seidnaya felt the SARG, by sending them back to prison, had cheated them, Talli explained. The inmates had expected better treatment, perhaps even freedom, and were upset over prison conditions." This led them to stage "a riotous protest over prison conditions".[50]

The Assad Regime's Preferred Enemy

But what on earth, one might wonder, could persuade a supposedly "secular" – even "socialist" (as the Baath Party officially calls itself) – regime to facilitate a jihadist armed insurgency in the country next door, and then invite it to play on its own turf? The answer lies in the same logic that governed both cases: the Assad regime's intense repugnance towards the contagious potential of democracy. Bashar al-Assad's father, Hafez, had supported and joined the US-led war against Iraq in 1991, when its goal was limited to ejecting Iraqi forces from Kuwait, thus preventing the Syrian regime's Baathist "twin enemy" from acquiring renewed stamina after its exhaustion in its eight-year war against Iran. The 2003 invasion of Iraq was a different matter altogether: although Tehran, the Syrian regime's ally, tacitly approved this US war as it had the previous one – knowing that it was best poised to fill the vacuum created by the fall of Saddam Hussein's regime and the collapse of its state apparatus – Bashar al-Assad could not follow suit.

The precedent of a US-led overthrow of a Baathist regime next door, however inimical it was to Syria's own Baathist regime, was too dangerous to condone. It was all the more dangerous in that the Bush administration deceitfully portrayed its invasion of Iraq as the prelude to installing a model liberal democracy in that country. When the US occupation was eventually forced to deliver on the promise of electoral democracy by the pressure of the Shi'i mass movement that built up in 2004, leading it to allow the organisation of two free elections in Iraq in 2005, the Syrian regime's stake in the failure of this experience became crucial.[51] The development of a jihadist insurgency in Iraq overwhelmed by al-Qaida and its ISI served Damascus's purpose in buttressing its claim that the only alternative to Baathist dictatorships among Sunnis in that part of the Arab world was jihadist Salafism of the terrorist type. Indeed, Iraq's Arab Sunni Baathists themselves ended up joining al-Qaida's ranks en masse, whether as individual converts or by decision of the underground Baathist leadership, when, unable to swim against the current, it chose to swim with it. In that, it was assisted by Damascus.[52]

Damascus stopped fostering al-Qaida across its border at a time when the Iraqi regime was clearly taking on an increasingly authoritarian, corrupt and Shi'i-sectarian shape, with Maliki at the helm and under Tehran's thumb. It could thus no longer represent an inspiring model for the Syrian population. Syria's former support for Iraqi Sunni jihadism had in fact suited Tehran in that, like Damascus, it had a stake in the predictable outcome of the rise of sectarian tensions in Iraq. The exacerbation of sectarianism buried the prospect of a Shi'i-majority liberal-democratic government in Baghdad – a prospect that is as repulsive to Iran's Islamic Republic as it is for Syria's Baathist dictatorship. By the same token, the rise of sectarian tensions in Iraq contributed tremendously to enhancing Tehran's clout in that country by enabling the rise of a kindred Shi'i-sectarian authoritarian government in Baghdad.

Syria's intelligence services nevertheless maintained their connections with the Iraqi jihadists, in line with their long-established custom of "embedding" themselves in jihadist groups. Syrian General Intelligence Director (GID) General Ali Mamlouk boasted of the expertise thereby acquired to a US delegation led by coordinator for counter-terrorism, Daniel Benjamin, on a visit to Damascus in February 2010:

> The GID Director said Syria had been more successful than the US and other countries in the region in fighting terrorist groups because "we are practical and not theoretical." He stated Syria's success is due to its penetration of terrorist groups. "In principle, we don't attack or kill them immediately. Instead, we embed ourselves in them and only at the opportune moment do we move." ...
>
> According to Mamlouk, Syria's previous experience in cooperating with the US on intelligence "was not a happy one." ... Alluding to the "wealth of information" Syria has obtained while penetrating terrorist groups, Mamlouk declared "we have a lot of experience and know these groups. This is our area, and we know it. We are on the ground, and so we should take the lead."[53]

When the democratic uprising started in Syria itself, the Assad regime resorted to the same trick it had used to subvert the democratic experience that had unfolded next door under US occupation (actually, in spite of it) by fostering jihadism of the worst and most repulsive kind. As Peter Neumann explained in a remarkable article on the role of the Assad regime in that regard, there was a direct continuity with the fact that, since 2003,

> Assad allowed the jihadists in his country to link up with [Abu-Mus'ab al-] Zarqawi [the leader of al-Qaida in Iraq, killed in 2006] and become part of a foreign fighter pipeline stretching from Lebanon to Iraq, with way points, safehouses and facilitators dotted across the country. With the active help of Assad's intelligence services, Syria was opened to the influx – and influence – of experienced and well-connected jihadists from Libya, Saudi Arabia, Algeria, Tunisia, Yemen and Morocco, who brought with them their contact books, money and skills. Within a few years, the country ceased to be a black spot on the global jihadist map: by the

late 2000s it was familiar terrain to foreign jihadists, while jihadists from Syria had become valued members of al-Qaida in Iraq, where they gained combat experience and acquired the international contacts and expertise needed to turn Syria into the next battlefront. When the current conflict broke out, it was hardly surprising that jihadist structures first emerged in the eastern parts of the country, where the entry points into Iraq were located, and in places like Homs and Idlib, which were close to Lebanon; or that it was jihadists – not the Muslim Brothers – who could offer the most dedicated and experienced fighters with the skills, resources, discipline and organisation to hit back at the government. They were also the ones who found it easiest to prevail on international networks of wealthy sympathisers, especially in the Gulf, to supply weapons and funding.[54]

Iraq's al-Qaida was actually allowed to set up a franchise in Syria. According to the founder of the Free Syrian Army, Riyad al-Asaad, himself a former colonel in the Syrian Air Force, Syria's Air Force Intelligence had maintained connections with al-Qaida's branch inside Iraq, the self-proclaimed Islamic State of Iraq (ISI). Interviewed in the spring of 2012, when al-Qaida had just emerged in the open on the Syrian side of the border, al-Asaad affirmed categorically that this could only have happened with the connivance of Air Force Intelligence.[55] The ISI first launched the al-Nusra Front (Jabhat al-Nusra li-Ahl al-Sham) as an autonomous Syrian branch, before deciding to merge both branches across the border under the name of ISIS in 2013. This provoked a split within al-Nusra, which was soon to be followed by a full break between ISIS and the post-bin Laden global al-Qaida network led by Ayman al-Zawahiri, who repudiated ISIS. The Iraqi militants played a decisive role in this development.

By April 2013, the number of Iraqis fighting in Syria had reached at least 5,000 and was growing daily. Iraqi veterans of the fight against the US occupation, and the sectarian war against the Shias, had

crossed the border and were taking leadership positions in a new
group that would soon subsume the most organised and capable
jihadi outfit in Syria, Jabhat al-Nusra. ...

Within months, the pieces were sufficiently in place for
Baghdadi to start his move. He announced in April that Jabhat
al-Nusra, the al-Qaida-aligned jihadi group, would be subsumed by
the newly named ISIS. That same afternoon, Baghdadi's men, most
of them Iraqis like Abu Ismael, rode into central Aleppo and kicked
al-Nusra members out of their main base in the city's eye hospital.
They then painted it black and took it over.

Across northern Syria, the scene was repeated with ruthless
efficiency.[56]

The regime's collusion became blatant after the split between
the Iraqi-dominated organisation with which the Assad regime had
a long record of connivance and the Syrian-dominated group that
kept working under the name of al-Nusra. The latter is naturally
keener on fighting the Assad regime, and has been competing with
the rest of the opposition in that respect.[57] It has been helped by
Qatar – with Al Jazeera offering a broadcast platform to al-Nusra
and its leader, Abu Muhammad al-Julani, as it has been doing over
the years for Osama bin Laden, Ayman al-Zawahiri and the global
al-Qaida – as well as by Turkey, while both countries maintained an
ambiguous attitude towards ISIS until 2014.[58]

For its part, ISIS engaged in trade with the Assad regime,
including oil, gas and electricity deals – a lucrative business in which
a prominent and typical figure of the Syrian state bourgeoisie,
George Haswani, the boss of HESCO Engineering & Construction
Co., has played a key role.[59]

ISIS seized control of three dams and at least two gas plants in Syria
used to run state electricity. Rather than risk blowing out swaths of
the power grid, Damascus appears to have struck a deal.

"ISIS guards their factories and lets state employees come to
work," Mahmoud says. "It gets to take all the gas produced for

cooking and petrol and sell it. The regime gets the gas needed to power the electrical system, and also sends some electricity to ISIS areas."

Not only does the Assad government pay the gas plant staff, but workers say it sends in spare parts from abroad and dispatches its own specialists to the area for repairs.[60]

For all the reasons explained above, ISIS is indeed by far the Assad regime's "preferred enemy". When it achieved its stunning breakthrough in Iraq in the summer of 2014, the Assad regime's complicity was flagrantly exposed by the fact that ISIS was able to move an impressive convoy of vehicles at the beginning of its offensive without fearing the regime's air force. Shortly before his death, Hassan Abboud – the leader of the Salafi and Muslim Brotherhood-related Ahrar al-Sham,[61] who was killed in a bomb attack along with twenty-seven other commanders of his jihadist organisation on 9 September 2014 – expressed to Yvonne Ridley the view common to most fractions of the Syrian opposition in this regard:

"[F]or us fighting on the ground we know you cannot emerge and grow and develop without entering into a conflict with the Assad regime."

The Syrian government, he pointed out, has targeted many rebel groups but it seems that ISIS has not engaged in any frontline fighting with Assad nor has it ever been targeted by the president.

"For instance, even if there are three cars travelling in the countryside Assad's air force will strike them in the belief that it must be a convoy. Now you tell me, when movement is coming under such intense scrutiny how was ISIS able to move a convoy of 200 vehicles from one province to another and finally into Iraq without coming under one single attack or meeting resistance at any regime checkpoints?"[62]

However, when ISIS, through its sweeping extension into Iraq, became a threat to Iran's interests there, drawing Tehran into de facto alliance with Washington to counter it, Damascus – which had become entirely dependent on Iran since 2013 – had to adapt its game, exactly as it had had to adjust it when Iran gained the upper hand in Iraq's government after 2006. It initiated a token confrontation with ISIS, while concentrating incomparably more serious effort against the rest of the opposition, backed by Doha and Riyadh. Eventually, sooner rather than later, the Assad regime reverted to its collusion with ISIS, helping its offensive against the rest of the opposition in the spring of 2015.[63] A former US intelligence officer aptly summarised the situation:

> The main threat to the regime comes not from the ISIS strongholds in eastern and central Syria, but from the kludge of rebel groups that pose a growing danger in western areas key to the regime's survival, especially northern Latakia, Idlib, north Hama, and south of Damascus. Indeed, the regime has never made ISIS its top priority for military operations, at various times cooperating with or fighting the group based on pragmatic assessments of the military situation at the time.[64]

The Syrian regime will fight ISIS only if, and to the extent to which, it believes that it enhances its position in the fight against its main enemy: the mainstream opposition backed by Turkey and the Gulf monarchies.

Turkey's and the Gulf Monarchies' Preferred Friends

Paradoxically, ISIS also benefitted from the Turkish state's benevolent laissez-faire approach, despite the profound enmity that had built up between Damascus and Ankara since 2011. This improbable convergence was due to the fact that ISIS was clashing simultaneously with the Syrian enemies of Damascus and the

Kurdish enemies of Ankara. A major concern of the Turkish state is indeed to counter the prospect of the three Kurdish cantons within Syria's borders (Rojava, or Western Kurdistan, as the Kurds call them) falling durably under autonomous rule by the Democratic Union Party (PYD, in the Kurdish acronym), the de facto Syrian branch of the Kurdistan Workers' Party (PKK, in the Kurdish acronym). This would provide the latter with a "liberated zone" from which it could greatly enhance its bid for devolution in Turkey's Kurdish territories. This is why Ankara pretended to adopt a stance of "a plague on both your houses" in the battle of Kobani, which started in the autumn of 2014, rejecting both sides of the conflict – the PYD-PKK and ISIS – as equally "terrorist".

In reality, Ankara's attitude was helping ISIS by preventing reinforcements from reaching Kobani across the Turkish border. When the United States, irritated by Turkey's attitude, started airdropping weapons to the Kurdish fighters defending the canton, Ankara immediately changed its stance and allowed reinforcements to go through – provided that they included fighters from both the FSA and Iraq's Kurdish Regional Government (the famous *peshmerga*), both close allies of Turkey. It was only in July 2015 that Ankara started to bomb ISIS, bowing to US pressure at long last for fear of being left aside in the wake of the "nuclear deal" struck between Washington and Tehran on 14 July. But Ankara attacked ISIS while simultaneously attacking – much more forcefully and resolutely – the PKK, its Kurdish nemesis.

Since intense repugnance towards democratic contagion afflicts the Arab regional *ancien régime* in its entirety as much as it afflicts the Assad regime, it was only natural for the region's most reactionary linchpin, the Gulf oil monarchies, to contribute massively to fostering Islamic fundamentalism within the Syrian opposition by funding all sorts of groups that raised a religious banner. They thus objectively colluded with the Syrian regime in swamping the secular-democratic networks that had launched the Syrian uprising with Islamic fundamentalist Sunni-sectarian forces – forces motivated by a type of ideology much more reassuring to

them than that of the former networks. Whereas the two main
regional players among the Gulf oil monarchies, the Saudi kingdom
and the emirate of Qatar, held antithetic positions in countries like
Egypt and Tunisia – where the kingdom supported the old regime
while the emirate tried to co-opt the uprising in collaboration
with the Muslim Brotherhood – their interests fundamentally
converged in Syria, despite minor rivalry and frictions. Support for
the Assad regime was out of the question for the Saudis, due to its
Alawite-sectarian character, as well as its alliance with Tehran; the
only counter-revolutionary option was therefore for Riyadh to co-
opt the uprising along with Doha.

In tandem with its closest regional state partner, Recep Tayyip
Erdogan's Turkey, and with Western backing, Qatar took the lead
in fostering the formation in 2011 of the Syrian National Council
(snc), based in Istanbul, in which the Syrian Muslim Brotherhood
was the dominant force.[65] The situation changed in 2013, when the
Saudis gained the upper hand within the National Coalition that
replaced the snc as the mainstream representative of the Syrian
opposition. Meanwhile, the Saudis funded Salafist competitors to
the snc-sponsored Free Syrian Army. Qatar reciprocated mainly
through Islamic groups linked to the Syrian Muslim Brotherhood,
while entertaining a relationship with al-Nusra, the official Syrian
branch of Riyadh's rebellious child, al-Qaida. But the fundamental
Saudi–Qatari convergence over Syria made it possible for the major
Islamic fundamentalist organisations, other than al-Nusra and isis,
to regroup under the Islamic Front in 2013.[66]

Other Gulf monarchies joined Qatar and the Saudi kingdom
in their funding spree, with a similar view to exorcising the
democratic potential of the regional uprising and turning it into a
sectarian issue. Last but not least, throughout the Gulf monarchies,
networks of private donors and fundraisers, as well as institutional
religious networks, contributed to tilting the balance among the
Syrian dissidents in favour of whoever would wave an Islamic
fundamentalist and Sunni-sectarian banner, including al-Qaida
and isis. As a matter of fact, adopting an Islamic fundamentalist

profile and growing beards – often for purely opportunistic reasons – became the easiest way to secure funds on the side of the Syrian opposition, resulting in the proliferation of Islamic fundamentalist groups in its midst. As Hassan Hassan and Michael Weiss have noted, "A little-explored facet of the Syrian Civil War was how a highly competitive bidding war for arms [and funds, they should have added] by fighters naturally inclined toward nationalism or secularism accelerated their radicalization, or at least their show of *having been* radicalised."[67]

The Assad regime was very careful to develop and exacerbate the sectarian potential thus created.[68] Given that the surest and most effective way to foster oppositional sectarian violence is, of course, to commit sectarian violence, the Assad regime had no shortage of thugs for such a purpose, and no qualms about letting them perform it:

Inside Syria, [a trend of fighters drifting to extremist groups] existed since mid-2012, when reports of civilians being slaughtered by pro-Assad militias became international news. The impact of those massacres on the psyche of anti-regime Syrians was also immense. Those conscious of their own radicalization typically point to the Houla and al-Bayda and similar massacres as the reason for their turn to Islamist and jihadist rebel factions closer to the end of 2012. However, native Syrians tended to enlist with homegrown extremist factions rather than the more foreigner-friendly ISIS. Even still, ISIS benefited from the Assadist massacres in another respect: for one, the gruesome manner in which they were carried out helped create some level of tolerance for beheadings, which was accepted by many Syrians as retribution against the regime and its Iranian-built militias.

The most notorious regime massacres typically occurred in areas where Alawite, Sunni, and Ismaili (another Shia offshoot) villages and hamlets adjoined one another, the better to encourage sectarian reprisal bloodlettings. They also followed a pattern of assault: a village would be shelled overnight by the Syrian Arab Army, and the next morning, militiamen from nearby would storm it. Armed with knives and light weapons, they would go on killing sprees, slaughtering men, women, and children. The killing was portrayed as systematic and driven by sectarian vigilantism. Videos of torture also showed shabiha or popular committees, the precursors to the National Defense Force, taunting Sunni symbols and forcing victims to affirm al-Assad's divinity and make other sacrilegious statements.[69]

According to a 2015 survey of sectarian and "ethnic cleansing" killings published by the Syrian Network for Human Rights, until June 2013 only Syrian government forces and their paramilitary allies had perpetrated massacres involving a majority of unarmed civilians, with a significant number of women and children among them.[70] According to the same source, a total of fifty-six sectarian massacres had been perpetrated by June 2015, forty-nine of which were the responsibility of Syrian government forces and their allies, while the remaining seven were committed by various opposition forces, including al-Nusra and ISIS. Whichever macabre accounting one takes as accurate, it is obvious that the prognosis with which I ended my assessment of the Syrian situation in October 2012, quoted at the beginning of this chapter – that "the longer [the Syrian regime] lasts, the greater is the risk that the country will plunge into barbarism" – has proved only too true, alas. Sadly, Syria has already arrived at that condition. With the barbarism of the Assad regime fostering the emergence of that of ISIS, Syria has become a major theatre of that dreadful dialectic that I termed the "clash of barbarisms", whose dynamics I analysed in the aftermath of the 9/11 attacks of 2001.[71]

At that time, I assessed those terrible attacks as one spectacular moment in a fatal dialectic of which the original and major impulse was the huge qualitative escalation in US imperial violence in the Middle East, represented by the US-led onslaught on Iraq in 1991. Following the same line of argument, five days after the fall of Baghdad to US troops in 2003, I predicted the following:

As it extends its presence in the Arab world further and further, the US is stretching its troops too thin. The hatred that it evokes in all Middle Eastern countries and throughout the Islamic world has already blown up in its face several times; 11 September 2001 was only the most spectacular, deadliest manifestation so far of this hatred. The occupation of Iraq will push the general resentment to extremes; it will speed up the decomposition of the regional order backed by Washington. There will be no Pax Americana. Rather there will be another step downward towards barbarism, with the chief barbarism of Washington and its allies sustaining the opposite barbarism of religious fanaticism – as long as no new progressive forces emerge in this part of the world.[72]

In the face of the overwhelming barbarism of the US occupation, the counter-barbarism of al-Qaida managed to take hold in Iraq's Arab Sunni regions after 2003. Likewise, the gruesome barbarism unleashed by the Assad regime and its allies in Syria since 2011 created the conditions for al-Qaida's barbarism to come to a climax in both Syria and Iraq, in the shape of ISIS. And there is no more striking illustration of the direct relation between the US imperium's original barbarism and that of ISIS than the latter's use of Guantánamo-style orange jumpsuits for its detainees. In the foreseeable future, as long as the civil war rages on in Syria, there will be in that country no way out of the fatal dynamics of the clash of barbarisms and its drive towards extremes, along a Clausewitzian spiral of "primordial violence, hatred, and enmity, which are to be regarded as a blind natural force".[73]

The new progressive forces that emerged in Syria with the beginning of the uprising in 2011 have been suffocated by the dynamics of a civil war for which they were totally unprepared. There are narrow limits indeed to what can be achieved through an improvised network facilitated by the use of social media – especially in a dictatorial country such as Syria, or any Arab country for that matter. The Syrian calamity is simply one more tragic demonstration of the cost of lacking an effective organisation with a sound strategic vision for radical political change. The Local Coordination Committees (LCC) – a prominent component of the larger network of coordination committees (*tansiqiyyat*) that initiated the Syrian uprising and steered it in its first phase – abdicated that role and joined the Istanbul-based Syrian National Council (SNC). The LCC are closely linked to the Democratic People's Party (DPP), which originated from a major split within the Syrian Communist Party in 1972. The SNC is fundamentally an heir of the 2005 Damascus Declaration for National Democratic Change – an alliance of the DPP and other left and liberal opposition groups with the Syrian branch of the Muslim Brotherhood.[74]

As a result of their funding by the oil monarchies, the SNC and its sequel, the National Coalition, underwent the same extremely rapid descent into corruption that the PLO had undergone after 1967 under the impact of similarly co-optive funding – a process that was completed when the PLO was forced into fragmented exile after its expulsion from Lebanon. Palestinian critics of its corruption then called it the "five-star PLO".[75] The SNC and National Coalition are thoroughly deserving of the same nickname – and quite literally, since their meetings are usually held in five-star hotels. When Lebanon's civil war started, in 1975, the corruption at the head of the PLO translated into massive looting and racketeering at the level of its rank and file. The same phenomenon ravaged the Free Syrian Army and other Gulf-funded groups, to a point where, in many instances, more ideologically rigid organisations like al-Nusra and ISIS have been welcomed by local communities as paragons of probity, by contrast. Here, in fact, lies one key reason for the massive failure of the FSA. Matters could have evolved differently, as they had indeed begun to early on.[76]

The Syrian Predicament

The huge difference made by the existence of an effective progressive organisation has been demonstrated in the Syrian case by the achievement of the Kurdish PYD and its armed wing, the People's Protection Units (YPG) and Women's Protection Units (YPJ). They managed to become the dominant force in most of the Kurdish-majority areas of north and north-east Syria (Rojava). Without falling into what David Harvey rightly called "the romance that some people on the left in Europe and North America may have that, 'oh well, this is the place, finally!'",[77] it is hardly disputable that the autonomous administration created by the PYD in Syria's three Kurdish-majority cantons since 2012 – if not the beacon of radical democracy that some wishful Western observers believe it to be[78] – is, from a social and gender-relations perspective, the most progressive experience to emerge to this day in any of the six countries that were scenes of the 2011 uprising.

One consequence of this was that, when the US-led coalition started bombing ISIS in the summer of 2014 to halt its advance towards Kurdish areas in Iraq and Syria, as well as Arab Shi'i areas in Iraq – to the great relief of all Kurdish forces and of Baghdad and Tehran, and with the tacit approval of the Assad regime itself – much less noise was heard on the side of the knee-jerk "anti-imperialist" left than when a similar US-led coalition started bombing Gaddafi's forces in Libya to halt their advance towards the city of Benghazi. The same "anti-imperialists" uttered incoherent mumblings or fell into embarrassed silence in the face of US airstrikes aimed at breaking the ISIS siege of the Kurdish city of Kobani, along with US airdrops of weapons to the PYD defenders of the city. No outcry was heard from them when the PYD leadership and the Kurdish local authority in Kobani warmly thanked the US government and the US-led coalition.[79]

When the population of Benghazi cried for international air support in order to prevent Gaddafi's planes and troops from crushing their city and massacring them in March 2011, and when the peaceful Syrian demonstrators requested the same shortly thereafter to prevent the destruction of their country and people, they were met only with scorn and harsh condemnation by the same knee-jerk "anti-imperialist" left. Likewise, when the Syrian mainstream opposition and insurgent population begged for much-needed defensive weapons, they were yet again denounced as "imperialist stooges" and other such epithets.

The only logic at work here is that this kind of "anti-imperialist left" is able to show some understanding for a population in peril, desperate for help from whichever side it may come, only when that population is led by people who share its own ideology.[80] And that is not to mention the fact that this "anti-imperialist" left remains silent, when not approving, in the face of Russian imperialism's involvement in support of the Assad regime in the Syrian conflict, which far exceeds Western involvement in support of the Syrian opposition. The same goes for the Iranian Khomeinist Islamic fundamentalist regime's involvement on the side of the Assad regime, which dwarfs the Saudi and Qatari Wahhabi Islamic fundamentalist regimes' involvement on the side of the Syrian opposition.

This said, the sad truth is that the Rojava experience reverberated more within the Western Left than within the Arab Left. Carried on almost solely by the Kurdish national minority and restricted to its own areas, the impact of events in Rojava is much bigger on Turkey's and Iraq's sections of Kurdistan than it is on the rest of Syria, ethnic affinities and acrimony playing a major role in that regard. This fact puts a tight limit on the Rojava experience's ability to offer inspiration to the Syrian uprising as a whole, not to mention the other theatres of the Arab uprising. In fact it places such a limit even on the PYD's ability, if not willingness, to play a major role in the fighting against ISIS much beyond the territory it controls – despite the US-sponsored creation for that purpose of multi-ethnic Syrian Democratic Forces under the PYD's hegemony.[81] This is compounded by the fact that the PYD has maintained relations with both sides in the Syrian civil war, as well as with both Washington and Moscow, playing on their rivalries in order to widen its own margin of manoeuvre and drive a wedge between Turkey and Russia, as well as between Turkey and the United States.[82]

In any event, it is now much too late for the rise of a similar progressive armed self-rule to occur among Arab Syrians. The logic of the war makes it hardly conceivable that an armed progressive alternative could emerge between the two jaws of the crusher constituted by a tyrannical regime backed by Russia and Iran, on one side, and an opposition dominated by reactionary forces and backed by Gulf oil monarchies, on the other. In order for any progressive potential to materialise in an organised political form among the Syrian people at large, the precondition at this stage is for the war to stop. In that regard and given the abysmal situation that has arisen in Syria after four years of war, the appalling level of killing and destruction, and the immense human tragedy represented by the refugees and displaced persons (about one half of Syria's population), one can only wish for the success of the international efforts presently being deployed to reach a compromise between the Syrian regime and the mainstream opposition.

The situation has evolved in such a way that even a settlement keeping Assad himself in power for a period said to be transitional – an idea that has been floated increasingly often in Western capitals – would seem today like a lesser evil; if it had any chance of success, that is. In the words of one of those heroic medics who attend the wounded in makeshift clinics in war-torn areas, Dr Adnan Tobaji, a resident of the Damascus suburb of Douma quoted by the *New York Times*, "The fate of Assad for us is nothing compared to the fate of Syria the country, the people and the children."[83] This would be even less than the scenario sought by Barack Obama early on – namely, the "Yemeni solution", a negotiated compromise that would retain the bulk of the Baathist state and of the Assad clan's power base in place, while Assad himself would step down and hand power to a figure in the regime more agreeable to the opposition. The National Coalition of the Syrian opposition endorsed this scenario long ago, on the condition that it clearly included Assad's exit from his post.

Rather than creating a situation conducive to its implementation, Washington's specific policy for pursuing this "Yemeni solution" has so far, in fact, been instrumental in delaying any prospect of it, and prolonging the tragedy. As explained above, this is because this policy was accompanied from the start by a refusal to provide the FSA with the defensive means it required. The "Yemeni solution" might have been implemented significantly earlier in Syria, and at a much lower cost, had the Obama administration enabled the Syrian opposition to represent enough of a threat to the Baathist regime that the latter would have felt compelled to seek a compromise. However, with the tragedy largely consummated after four terrible years of war, the same "Yemeni solution" has come to the fore as a result of the shared exhaustion of the Syrian regime and opposition against the backdrop of Syria's devastation.

With no positive scenario left in view, the "Yemeni solution" has come to be seen as the least bad option – even though Yemen itself collapsed in 2014, plunging in its turn into civil war. Currently, no better prospect remains, however unlikely it may be to succeed, since the Syrian state's collapse in response to the growing dominance of Islamic fundamentalist militias in the opposition could only bring dreadful results, including the further fragmentation of the country. But the truth is that the odds in favour of the success of a transitional scheme in preserving a functioning state in Syria are now much longer than they were in the first couple of years of conflict. The official state apparatuses are in advanced decay, after more than four years of devastating and murderous war, while the regime has done its best to destroy any democratic alternative to its administration.[84] The Assad regime, moreover, has developed auxiliary forces that are no better than the worst opposition forces that have emerged from the mayhem. As Anthony Cordesman put it in September 2015, "This is no longer 2012. That real time window to support the moderates is not only closed, it is bricked over."[85] Indeed, under the present conditions, "Syria will at best be the land of least-bad options, and least bad is likely to be really bad for at least the next half decade."[86]

The likelihood of that least-bad scenario successfully preventing the worst-case one from unfolding further is itself quite limited, to be sure. In Syria today, a compromise would only occur and have the slightest chance of being implemented if it were cosponsored by all of the United States, Russia, Iran, Turkey and the Gulf monarchies.[87] Washington has been deploying efforts in this direction in higher gear since the conclusion of its "nuclear deal" with Tehran. In all this, it has been taking advantage of the strong economic pressure exerted on Russia and Iran through the "oil price war" waged by the Saudi kingdom since 2014.[88]

However, the acute problem faced by Western countries in 2015, as a result of the surge in the number of Syrian refugees crossing to Europe, led the Obama administration to panic about the situation in Syria, and talk increasingly of the necessity of accommodating Bashar al-Assad. The obvious truth that only knee-jerk and one-sided "anti-imperialists" ignore was revealed to CBS in no uncertain terms by none other than the Russian ambassador to the UN, Vitaly Churkin:

> I think this is one thing we share now with the United States, with the US government: They don't want the Assad government to fall. They don't want it to fall. They want to fight [ISIS] in a way which is not going to harm the Syrian government. On the other hand, they don't want the Syrian government to take advantage of their campaign against [ISIS]. But they don't want to harm the Syrian government by their action. This is very complex. ... To me, it is absolutely clear that ... one of the very serious concerns of the American government now is that the Assad regime will fall and [ISIS] will take over Damascus and the United States will be blamed for that.[89]

The statement of Iranian president Hassan Rouhani to CNN's Christiane Amanpour on 2 October 2015 fully concurred with Churkin's assurance. This is indeed the impression that Washington conveyed to both Moscow and Tehran:

> Well, you see, when in Syria, when our first objective is to drive out terrorists and combating terrorists to defeat them, we have no solution other than to strengthen the central authority and the central government of that country as a central seat of power.

So I think *today everyone has accepted that President Assad must remain so that we can combat the terrorists*. However, as soon as this movement reaches the various levels of success and starts driving out the terrorists on a step-by-step basis, then other plans must be put into action so as to hear the voices of the opposition as well.

Those who are in opposition but are not terrorists must come to the table of talks and negotiations, talk to various groups, including government representatives, and then reach a decision, make a decision, and implement that decision for the future of Syria.[90]

Russian Intervention and Western Wavering

Washington's obvious disarray opened the way for Russia to enhance significantly its direct military presence in Syria, as well as its military support to the Syrian regime. This was done with Washington's tacit, if not explicit, approval according to Rouhani, who, in the same interview, said that Putin told him "that he had even spoken with Mr Obama about this topic and he would like to renew his commitment to the fight and the defeat of Daish or ISIS". Putin also told him, said Rouhani, that "Mr Obama welcomed that analysis and that plan. So even previously the United States of America was made aware." All this happened in the name not only of fighting ISIS, but also, and much more importantly, of preventing a Libyan-like collapse of the Syrian state – a priority that Washington could only share. As the BBC's Mark Urban rightly put it in an analysis posted on 23 September 2015:

The Kremlin's objective, stated plainly, has been to prevent an implosion of the Syrian state – or what's left of it. Mr Putin last week said he intended to prevent a complete implosion of government authority of the kind that happened in Libya, following NATO's 2011 intervention there. It's a smart message, that taps into Western guilt about what has happened since Colonel Gaddafi's overthrow.

What's more, the idea of preserving the Syrian armed forces and security agencies, while working towards a transitional government or peace process finds some support in Western countries, and indeed the American line has shifted significantly in recent days to allow President Assad to remain in power for the time being, making his removal subsidiary to the aim of crushing Islamic State.[91]

Unsurprisingly, the Russian military intervention in the Syrian war – Moscow's first direct foreign intervention since the Soviet invasion of Afghanistan – targeted the mainstream Syrian opposition forces in order to stop their continuous erosion of the regime's position, and open the way to a counter-offensive aimed at rolling them back. Two weeks into the Russian bombing campaign, the Syrian regime embarked on a large-scale offensive with enhanced Iranian participation.[92] Their goal was to recover in full and consolidate what Bashar al-Assad called in the widely discussed speech he gave on 26 July 2015 "the important regions": "regions onto which the armed forces hold so that they do not allow the other regions to fall – the importance of these regions is defined according to several criteria: they could be important from the military perspective, or the political one, or from that of the economy and services."[93] Two months earlier, a regime insider had informed Agence France Presse (AFP) about this "de facto partition", whereby Damascus would cling only to a "useful Syria":[94]

People close to the regime talk about a government retreat to "useful Syria."

"The division of Syria is inevitable. The regime wants to control the coast, the two central cities of Hama and Homs and the capital Damascus," one Syrian political figure close to the regime said.

"The red lines for the authorities are the Damascus–Beirut highway and the Damascus–Homs highway, as well as the coast, with cities like Latakia and Tartus," he added, speaking on condition of anonymity.[95]

It was obvious that the Russian intervention – happening as it was at a time when the Assad regime was in retreat under increasing pressure, and not when ISIS spectacularly extended its territorial control, in the summer of 2014 – would not be about fighting ISIS, but primarily and fundamentally about shoring up the regime against the whole opposition.[96] As Kremlin spokesman Dmitry Peskov himself bluntly acknowledged at the beginning of the Russian strikes, their targets "are chosen in coordination with the armed forces of Syria" and their aim was "to help the Syrian army where it is weakest".[97] The *Guardian*'s Middle East editor, Ian Black, summarised very well the true circumstances that led to Russia's direct intervention:

Officials and analysts say Moscow decided to deepen its involvement after the fall of the northern towns of Idlib and nearby Jisr al-Shughour in May served as a "wake-up call" about the parlous state of the Syrian army. ...

Russia's move was prompted in part by Assad's other main ally, Iran, which plays a powerful though discreet role in Syria but is usually reluctant to commit its own forces. "The Iranians told the Russians bluntly: if you don't intervene, Bashar al-Assad will fall, and we are not in a position to keep propping him up," said a Damascus-based diplomat.

The strength of the regular Syrian army is estimated to be down from a pre-war figure of 300,000 to between 80,000 and 100,000. Fatigue, desertions and losses have taken a heavy toll, as has the sectarian nature of the conflict. That means once-loyal Alawites – the Assad family's minority sect – are no longer ready to fight for Sunni areas but only to defend their own homes.

"Idlib fell very quickly because Syrian soldiers were simply not prepared to fight," said one Syrian expert. "Ahrar al-Sham [one of the rebel groups] were surprised how quickly the regime defences crumbled."

Assad's forces are badly overstretched. In the Damascus area the Fourth Division of the elite Republican Guard, commanded by the president's brother Maher, has failed to take back rebel-held territory such as eastern Ghouta, which was hit by a ferocious bombardment that killed some 240 people in mid-August.[98]

Against all this evidence, the Obama administration displayed an amazing degree of complacency and wishful thinking. In his statement to the UN Security Council on 30 September 2015, John Kerry actually gave advance legitimacy to Russian strikes on targets unrelated to ISIS by equally welcoming strikes on al-Nusra, although the latter was allied until late October 2015 with key components of the rest of the Syrian opposition in a single military coalition, the Army of Conquest (Jaysh al-Fath), whose forces intermingled on the ground:

> The United States supports any genuine effort to fight ISIL and al-Qaida-affiliated groups, especially al-Nusrah. If Russia's recent actions and those now ongoing reflect a genuine commitment to defeat that organization, then we are prepared to welcome those efforts and to find a way to de-conflict our operations and thereby multiply the military pressure on ISIL and affiliated groups. But we must not and will not be confused in our fight against ISIL with support for Assad. Moreover, we have also made clear that we would have grave concerns should Russia strike areas where ISIL and al-Qaida-affiliated targets are not operating. Strikes of that kind would question Russia's real intentions [of either] fighting ISIL or protecting the Assad regime.[99]

This prompted John McCain, chair of the Senate Armed Services Committee, to declare indignantly in an official statement: "Unfortunately, it appears 'deconfliction' is merely an Orwellian euphemism for this administration's acceptance of Russia's expanded role in Syria, and as a consequence, for Assad's continued brutalization of the Syrian people."[100] The fact of the matter, however, is that the Obama administration did indulge in wishful thinking about Moscow and Tehran helping it out of its Syrian

quandary by convincing Assad to step down.[101] In an interview for
MSNBC, John Kerry even sounded as if he was betting on Assad's
own good will! The bottom line, he explained – in tune with signals
given by Washington and its allies that they were ready to accept
Assad remaining in position, but only for a "transitional" period
– is not Washington's rejection of Assad, but his rejection by "the
Sunnis":

> *Question*: Given what you know, though, about President Assad and
> the way he's behaved even just over the last three to five years, what
> makes you think that he will be managed out of power?

> *Secretary Kerry*: Well, we don't know that. We honestly don't know
> that. But Assad himself has said on several occasions recently that if
> the people of Syria don't believe I should be there in the future, then
> I would step – I would leave. He has said it. He has, on occasion,
> hinted that he wants a political settlement of one kind or another.
> I think it's up to his supporters, his strongest supporters, to make
> it clear to him that if you're going to save Syria, Assad has made a
> set of choices – barrel bombing children, gassing his people, tor-
> turing his people, engaging in starvation as a tactic of war. I mean,
> all of these things that he has done, there's no way even if President
> Obama wanted to just play along that you could actually achieve
> peace, because there are 65 million Sunni in between Baghdad and
> the border of Turkey, Syria, and Iraq, who will never, ever again
> accept Assad as a member – as a legitimate leader. They just won't
> accept it. It doesn't matter what we're thinking.[102]

The summary of the Syrian situation offered by Barack Obama
himself at a press conference on 2 October 2015 reveals his
thinking very clearly. The only pledge the US president had to
offer in response to Russia's direct involvement in the Syrian war
alongside the Assad regime was that the US would not cooperate
with Moscow in the destruction of Assad's opponents!

Well, first and foremost, let's understand what's happening in Syria and how we got here. What started off as peaceful protests against Assad, the president, evolved into a civil war because Assad met those protests with unimaginable brutality. And so ... this is a conflict between the Syrian people and a brutal, ruthless dictator.

Point number two is that the reason Assad is still in power is because Russia and Iran have supported him throughout this process. And in that sense, what Russia is doing now is not particularly different from what they had been doing in the past – they're just more overt about it. They've been propping up a regime that is rejected by an overwhelming majority of the Syrian population because they've seen that he has been willing to drop barrel bombs on children and on villages indiscriminately, and has been more concerned about clinging to power than the state of his country.

So in my discussions with President Putin, I was very clear that the only way to solve the problem in Syria is to have a political transition that is inclusive – that keeps the state intact, that keeps the military intact, that maintains cohesion, but that is inclusive – and the only way to accomplish that is for Mr Assad to transition, because you cannot rehabilitate him in the eyes of Syrians. This is not a judgement I'm making; it is a judgement that the overwhelming majority of Syrians make.

And I said to Mr Putin that I'd be prepared to work with him if he is willing to broker with his partners, Mr Assad and Iran, a political transition – we can bring the rest of the world community to a brokered solution – but that a military solution alone, an attempt by Russia and Iran to prop up Assad and try to pacify the population is just going to get them stuck in a quagmire. And it won't work. And they will be there for a while if they don't take a different course.

I also said to him that it is true that the United States and Russia and the entire world have a common interest in destroying ISIL. But what was very clear – and regardless of what Mr Putin said – was that he doesn't distinguish between ISIL and a moderate Sunni opposition that wants to see Mr Assad go. From their perspective, they're all terrorists. And that's a recipe for disaster, and it's one that I reject.

So where we are now is that we are having technical conversations about de-confliction so that we're not seeing [Russian] and American firefights in the air. But beyond that, we're very clear in sticking to our belief and our policy that the problem here is Assad and the brutality that he has inflicted on the Syrian people, and that it has to stop. And in order for it to stop, we're prepared to work with all the parties concerned. But we are not going to cooperate with a Russian campaign to simply try to destroy anybody who is disgusted and fed up with Mr Assad's behavior.[103]

The tragedy here is that Washington's wavering attitude, far from accelerating a compromise, will only make it more difficult to attain. The same logic has been at play from the start: in order for the regime to be willing to compromise, it needs to feel threatened in its very existence – or else to be put under firm pressure by its sponsors, who would do so only if they feared that the alternative was the regime's collapse. By condoning Russia's reinforcement of the regime, and showing more and more inclination to retreat from previous Western insistence that Assad must step down and cede power as an indispensable precondition for a political settlement – a trend that increased significantly in the wake of the Paris ISIS attacks of 13 November 2015 – Washington and its Western allies are only encouraging Assad to stick to his post, and Russia and Iran to stick to Assad. As Neil Quilliam has rightly written: "While Western leaders have very few levers to pull, acquiescing to Russia's insistence that Assad be part of the transition means that they will ultimately be complicit in prolonging the conflict and, at the same time, risk broadening the appeal of ISIS."[104]

Whither Syria?

It must be obvious to everyone that no significant section of the Syrian opposition could accept any compromise that would be so "compromising" as to give up the central demand of the opposition and the original popular uprising – namely, Assad's departure from power. Any settlement that does not include that central demand will be overwhelmingly rejected by the armed factions, all the more so because they are constantly poised to outbid each other. Hence, it will not stop the ongoing tragedy. In order to achieve this extremely urgent goal, nothing short of a transitional compromise predicated on Assad's resignation will do.

The shift from the SNC to the National Coalition in November 2012 went along with Washington's enhanced involvement in trying to steer the Syrian opposition. This translated into the appointment as head of the National Coalition of Moaz al-Khatib, former imam of the Umayyad Mosque in Damascus, a follower of the Qatar-based Yusuf al-Qaradawi and a partisan of the "Yemeni solution" advocated by Washington. Five months later, Moaz al-Khatib resigned, dismayed by Washington's refusal to allow the Syrian opposition to acquire the necessary means to fight the Assad regime efficiently.[105] Since then, he has been pursuing efforts towards a negotiated end to the war while building up links across the spectrum, from Moscow and the conciliatory wing of the Syrian opposition (the National Coordination Committee of Democratic Change Forces) to Salafist-jihadist components of the mainstream opposition, such as those with whom he met in Istanbul in May 2015 at the invitation of the Syrian Islamic Council. Given his popularity among Syrians, Moaz al-Khatib is the kind of opposition figure who may prove central to a compromise transition.

One can also safely bet that large segments of the now-jihadist groups, and even more of their members individually, will shift away from jihadism when it stops providing a way of making a living. It has already been noticed how the meeting of the Syrian opposition convened by the Saudis in Riyadh in early December 2015 – in preparation for the impending political process that received a decisive boost from the meetings of the so-called International Syria Support Group, held in Vienna in October and November, and more decisively from UN Security Council Resolution 2254, adopted unanimously on 18 December 2015 – led to a softening of the stance of a number of jihadist groups, most visibly that of Ahrar al-Sham.[106]

On the regime's side, Assad's vice president, Farouk al-Sharaa, is quite likely to play a central role. Early on, Sharaa expressed his support for a political settlement. In his above-quoted December 2012 interview, he declared:

> Neither the National Coalition, nor the Istanbul Council, nor the Coordination Committee as a multipolar internal opposition, and none of the peaceful or armed opposition groups with their well-known foreign links, can pretend to be the sole legitimate representative of the Syrian people. Likewise, the existing government with its doctrinal army and its Front-member parties – in the first place, the Socialist Arab Baath Party, with its long experience and its deep-rooted bureaucracy – cannot alone, after two years of crisis, implement change and evolution without new partners partaking in preserving the homeland's fabric, its territorial unity and regional sovereignty. ...
>
> The solution must be Syrian, but through a historic settlement that includes the major states of the region and members of the [UN] Security Council. This settlement must comprise, first of all, a cessation of violence and a ceasefire simultaneously and the formation of a national unity government with broad prerogatives.[107]

If any such transition ever sees the light of day, it would still be very optimistic to bet on its durability and eventual success in stemming the tide of the catastrophe. But one thing is certain: it will fall very far short of fulfilling the aspirations of those who initiated the uprising in 2011. It might, however, start to recreate the conditions under which a progressive alternative to both camps – the Assad regime and the armed opposition with all its ills – might re-emerge. For, against all odds, the potential for such an alternative still exists in Syria. It exists in the vast number of progressive-minded young people who took to the streets in 2011 and are still alive, many having fled into exile. The remarkable Syrian democratic experience of 2011–12 – when local councils were set up in order to make up for the paralysis or collapse of local state authorities and public services – has not completely vanished. Frederic Hof, who served as a special adviser for transition in Syria at the US State Department in 2012, recently acknowledged this potential in terms that sound more like the wishful thinking of an overenthusiastic partisan of self-management than the sober, realistic assessment of a former diplomat:

> There are today hundreds of local councils throughout non-Assad parts of Syria. Some operate clandestinely in areas overrun by the so-called Islamic State. Some operate in areas where the Assad regime – with Iran's full support – unloads helicopter-borne "barrel bombs" onto schools, hospitals and mosques. Some operate in neighborhoods subjected to Iranian-facilitated starvation sieges. These local councils are supported by a vast network of civil society organizations ... All of this is new to Syria. It is the essence of the Syrian Revolution.
>
> This combination of local councils and civil society organizations is a cocktail of bottom-up, localised efforts. The women and men risking all for their neighbors are heroes. Yet these heroes are literally unsung. Everyone in Syria knows of Assad and his rapacious family. Many in Syria know the names of exiled opposition figures and leaders of armed groups inside the country. Yet those who represent Syria's future political elite are largely unknown.[108]

The seemingly quite idealistic Hof mistook the bottom-up social organisation that he described for a feature of "Western democracies". He thus naively called upon the United States and its partners to champion this "alternative to Assad [that] is arising from Syria's grass roots", while expressing his bewilderment at "concerns vocalised by Obama administration officials that Assad – the mass murderer – may fall too quickly".[109] The fact, however, is that, were a radical democratic experience of that sort to prevail and threaten to spread from Syria to neighbouring countries, it would constitute a much bigger challenge to the US-dominated regional order than anything represented by ISIS.

Egypt

The "23 July" of Abdul-Fattah al-Sisi

> Hegel remarks somewhere that all facts and
> personages of great importance in world history
> occur, as it were, twice. He forgot to add: the first
> time as tragedy, the second as farce.
>
> Karl Marx, *The Eighteenth Brumaire
> of Louis Bonaparte* (1852–1869)

The above epigraph is one of the best-known and most often repeated and mimicked quotations from Karl Marx.[1] Commenting on the coup d'état that Louis-Napoléon Bonaparte (the future Napoleon III) led on 2 December 1851, thus ending the short-lived French Second Republic (1848–51), Marx was comparing it with the coup led by Louis-Napoléon's uncle, the famous Napoléon Bonaparte (the future Napoleon I) on 9 November 1799 – 18 Brumaire Year VIII of the French revolutionary calendar.[2] What Marx's ironic comment overlooked, however, is that the "farce" itself can be quite tragic – what the French call *farce tragique*. Alfred Jarry's play *King Ubu* (*Ubu Roi* in the original – a partial parody of Shakespeare's *Macbeth*) is regarded as this genre's founding text.[3] From it, the French derived the adjective *ubuesque*, which refers to grotesquely cruel despotism.

Of course, 23 July is the date of the coup that Egypt's Free Officers, led by Gamal Abdel-Nasser, executed in 1952, overthrowing the Egyptian monarchy. On 3 July 2013, Abdul-

Fattah al-Sisi led a coup toppling Mohamed Morsi, and ending the short-lived Egyptian Second Republic (2011–13). Without any fear of ridicule, Sisi's coup was travestied ad nauseam by its enthusiasts as a second iteration of what, in Egypt, is referred to as the "23 July Revolution". The truth, however, is that Louis-Napoléon Bonaparte's coup had much more in common with his uncle's – they were both essentially *reformist* coups, ending a phase of revolutionary turmoil in order to carry through a major stage of France's bourgeois transformation – than Abdul-Fattah al-Sisi's coup has with the one led by Nasser. The latter was a textbook case of a *revolutionary* coup d'état, whereas the coup executed on 3 July 2013 was definitely a *reactionary* one that restored Egypt's old regime – indeed, with a vengeance.[4]

When I finished writing *The People Want*, at the end of October 2012, the chairman of the Muslim Brotherhood's Freedom and Justice Party, Mohamed Morsi, had been president of Egypt for only four months. His co-thinkers were celebrating his success in imposing civilian control over the military – as demonstrated in their eyes by Morsi's sending into retirement of the two most senior members of the Supreme Council of the Armed Forces (scaf), on 12 August 2012 – and the global media overwhelmingly shared their assessment. Against this widespread view, I emphasised that *"the army's power and privileges have by no means diminished under Morsi in comparison with what they were under Mubarak.* Egypt has seen nothing even remotely resembling the events in Turkey ... that put a real end to the military's tutelage over the Turkish political authorities."[5]

With regard to the economic and social perspectives, I asserted that, by following the neoliberal prescriptions, "Morsi, his government and, behind them, the Muslim Brothers are leading Egypt down the road to economic and social catastrophe." The political and social instability engendered by the uprising made the prospect of growth led by private investment in conformity with the neoliberal credo still more improbable, "and one has to have a strong dose of faith to believe that Qatar will make up for the penury of public investment in Egypt ... "[6] As a result of this failed economic policy continued by Morsi, social turmoil was on the rise: I quoted data showing that the number of social protests and strikes had increased in Egypt during the first one hundred days of Morsi's presidency. "Managerial and state authorities reacted to this resurgence of struggles with repressive measures, including a sizeable number of individual and collective dismissals. But none of this has been or will be any use ... "[7]

Indeed, both crucial problems crippling Morsi's tenure – the army's tutelage, albeit initially muted in the aftermath of Morsi's election, and the social turmoil – continued to worsen week after week.

How the Muslim Brotherhood's Bid for Power Unfolded

Through the emirate of Qatar's mediation, Washington had bet on the Muslim Brotherhood in Egypt and at the regional level as a way to co-opt the 2011 revolutionary shockwave and steer it towards results compatible with US interests.[8] As emphasised in the introduction above, this led to a triangular contest between one revolutionary pole and two rival counter-revolutionary camps, both equally antithetical to the emancipatory aspirations of the "Arab Spring". The weakness and/or inaptitude of the revolutionary pole allowed the confrontation between the two other rival camps to predominate, and after a while become the primary concern of each of them. Egypt provides a very clear illustration of this unfortunate development.

As it officially joined the mass mobilisation in Cairo's Tahrir Square on 28 January 2011, the Muslim Brotherhood offered its counter-revolutionary services to the Egyptian army, the backbone of the post-Nasserist mutant regime, which was deployed in the capital in the evening of that same day. From that moment until the Muslim Brothers' betrayal of their pledge not to seek control of parliament by limiting the number of their candidates to the elections, they worked hand-in-glove with the military. In an unholy alliance with the *fulul* (the old regime's "debris" or remnants) and the Salafists, they campaigned for the Yes vote in the SCAF-sponsored constitutional referendum of 19 March 2011.

This was in tune with the tradition established since Sadat's release of the Muslim Brothers from Egyptian jails in the 1970s: their strategy had been consistently predicated upon collaboration with the regime in a bid to exert their moral–cultural influence on the society and polity until such time as they were in a position to accede to political power – a typical strategy of "war of position" preparing the ground for a "war of manoeuvre" in due time. These military concepts are known to have been borrowed by Antonio Gramsci in his discussion of hegemony and counter-hegemony. What is original in the Muslim Brotherhood's case, however, is the fact that the reactionary ideology it propagated could actually be regarded by the regime as serving its own hegemony to a large extent. Both Sadat and Mubarak were happy to let the Brotherhood play an ideological role in the face of the left and liberal oppositions, provided it did not overstep its role by trying to interfere with political power. Both presidents repressed the Brotherhood every time they felt it had crossed the line.

But the Muslim Brotherhood's rapid expansion under the new conditions created by the 2011 uprising – its ability to act freely and take advantage of Qatar's financial support and television promotion (through Al Jazeera) and its attraction of a vast proportion of the middle classes seeking an alternative enforcer of law and order after the apparent demise of the old regime – led it to become increasingly assertive and ambitious. The Muslim Brothers' collaboration with the SCAF started seriously unravelling when the parliamentary election held between late November 2011 and early January 2012 gave them a large plurality of seats in the People's Assembly. They demanded the dismissal of the SCAF-appointed Kamal al-Ganzouri's cabinet, and asserted their right to form a new one. They thereby put themselves on a collision course with the military.

There was no way that the Egyptian military would allow the Brotherhood to hold both legislative and executive power, thus challenging their own control of the state. The Muslim Brothers' constant reference to AKP-run Turkey as a model was not made to appease the SCAF's worries, either. The dismantling of the Turkish army's tutelage over the state and the humiliating purge and imprisonment of its top brass by an AKP government availing itself of the parliamentary majority were for the Egyptian military a nightmarish scenario that it was not going to allow at home. This required thwarting the Brotherhood's plan to design a Turkish-like parliamentary system for Egypt and secure its domination over it by way of its powerful electoral machine. Accordingly, the Egyptian judiciary – another unscathed institution of the old regime, complicit with the military – challenged the new parliament's constitutional prerogative, and put the very existence of the People's Assembly in doubt by questioning its constitutionality in February 2012 (due to a defect in the electoral law that had been promulgated by the SCAF itself). In April, the judiciary imposed a thorough modification of the composition of the Constituent Assembly that the parliament had elected.

The Brotherhood's countermove consisted in betraying yet another of its initial pledges: it decided to aim at the top executive position, and field a candidate to the presidential election in the person of its key leading member, Khairat al-Shatir, a wealthy businessman known to play as important a role in the organisation, if not more, as that of the General Guide, Mohammed Badie, himself. This bold decision, taken at the end of March 2012, sharply contrasted with decades of circumspection on the part of the Brotherhood. It was far from unanimous within the movement's 108-member Consultative Council (Majlis al-Shura), which split in half over the issue, those in favour outnumbering those opposed by only four. The Brotherhood's youth activists, in alliance with the hardliners led by Shatir, had managed to tip the balance.[9] The critics warned of the dire consequences likely to result from a head-on clash with the army.[10]

This move accelerated the chess game between the SCAF and the Brotherhood, with each side manoeuvring to prevent the other's best candidate from running. The electoral commission disallowed Shatir's candidacy, along with that of the ultra-populist Salafist Hazim Abu Isma'il. In order to give this double elimination a semblance of fairness, Omar Suleiman's improbable candidacy was likewise rejected. Mohamed Morsi – the Brotherhood's "spare wheel", as he was nicknamed by Egyptian public opinion – replaced Al-Shatir, while the Brotherhood's attempt to block through parliament the candidacy of former commander-in-chief of the Air Force and last Mubarak-designated prime minister Ahmed Shafiq was dismissed.

When it became clear, after the first round of the presidential election on 23–24 May 2012, that the Brothers' candidate stood a good chance of winning the second round despite everything, the intensity of the tug-of-war between them and the military increased dramatically. At the very end of the second round, held on 16–17 June, the SCAF seized upon the ruling by the Constitutional Court that the parliamentary election completed in January had been unconstitutional, in order to formally dissolve the law-making lower house of parliament, the People's Assembly, and issue a "complementary constitutional declaration" on 17 June. By virtue of this decree, it took legislative power back into its own hands, granted itself the power to form a new constituent assembly if the existing one proved unable to achieve its mission and curtailed the constitutional prerogatives of the soon-to-be-elected president.

The Brothers feared that the state apparatuses were going to rig the presidential election. They made sure to enlist Washington's blessing of their presidential bid and its firm opposition to fixing the election's results. On 22 June, the *Wall Street Journal* published a long interview by a member of its editorial board with Khairat al-Shatir, "the millionaire businessman" whom the article accurately described as the head of "the dominant conservative wing of the Brotherhood – also known as the 'Persian Gulf' crowd" and "the boss, in a Chicago machine sort of way, of the Muslim Brotherhood"

– a man who "if the Brotherhood came to power ... would be in charge".[11] Shatir told the journal's editor most bluntly that *"the priority* [for the Brotherhood] *is a close 'strategic partnership' with the US,* which the group expects to help it unlock credit markets and gain international legitimacy".[12]

Eventually, having granted themselves "legal" means to block the new president's action if necessary, the military let the electoral commission release the election results and proclaim Morsi's victory. Indeed, this was the smartest thing for them to do. They had lost a lot of credit running the country by default since February 2011, and were not in a position to risk a major clash with a still popular Muslim Brotherhood – whose candidate has been anointed by Washington, to boot. It was much wiser to let the Brothers burn their fingers in turn by handing them the very hot potato of governing a country in revolutionary turmoil. Morsi was therefore confirmed as president of Egypt. The Brotherhood were in charge of the civilian government thereafter, but without holding real power. The latter, in Egypt more than in most countries, grows not out of the ballot box but "out of the barrel of a gun", as Mao Zedong famously put it.

Neither Lion Nor Fox

Yet political power is an equation in which force is not the only factor; the ability to achieve consent is certainly crucial as well. The prince must be both lion and fox, in Machiavelli's famous prescription. Furthermore, political shrewdness can lead to the acquisition of force, whereas force cannot lead to the acquisition of shrewdness. Morsi's tenure, lacking the lion's force, miserably failed in achieving consent by want of the fox's talent. His first major blunder – or that of the Muslim Brotherhood's leadership, which pulled the strings behind him – was to overlook that he had won the election in the second round thanks to the votes of millions who had not chosen him in the first round. The majority that elected

him was thus composite, and his government ought therefore to
have reflected this fact by seeking the largest possible consensus.
Instead of that, in July 2012 Morsi formed a cabinet headed by
Hisham Qandil, a Brotherhood sympathiser, bearded like himself,
who had been a member of the outgoing Ganzouri cabinet. The
only adherents of political parties among the cabinet members
belonged to the Muslim Brothers' Freedom and Justice Party (FJP)
and two of their friendly splinter groups. However, the "sovereign
ministries" (as they are called in the Arab region) of defence,
interior and foreign affairs remained firmly in the hands of men
carrying on in their posts from the Ganzouri cabinet (except for
the new interior minister, a security general, who had been assistant
minister in the outgoing cabinet). They guaranteed that the bulk
of the old regime continued unabated. The minister of finance and
two other lesser members of the Ganzouri cabinet (the only two
women ministers out of thirty-five) were also kept in post. The
remaining cabinet members included a number of "technocrats",
and men who had served under the old regime.

In *The People Want*, my general assessment of the 2011 upheaval
was that

> In Egypt, as in Tunisia, a broad segment of the political component
> of the power elite was swept aside, as was the fraction of "politic-
> ally determined capitalism" most closely affiliated with the former
> ruling family. The structure of the capitalist class that was to blame
> for the social explosion – a state bourgeoisie and a market bour-
> geoisie in a framework of neoliberal inspiration – has nevertheless
> survived the earthquake. So has the state's repressive hard core: the
> army and the principal paramilitary corps.[13]

Here was the Muslim Brotherhood signifying to Egypt's
core state apparatuses and the bulk of its capitalist class, state
bourgeoisie included, that it was essentially aiming at acting in
symbiosis with them, and replacing only that part of "the political
component of the power elite" that had been discarded by the

uprising. Accusations surged from various quarters of the left and liberal opposition, and even from the Egyptian Current founded by dissident members of the Brotherhood's youth, that the Muslim Brotherhood was thus helping to restore the old regime. For its part, the Salafist Nour Party, which had refused to take part in the new cabinet unless it received a significant number of portfolios, blamed the Brotherhood for reneging on their promise to enforce the Sharia (including the replacement of "principles" with the more restrictive "rules" – *ahkam* – in the famous Article 2 of Egypt's constitution, which says: "The principles of the Islamic Sharia are the chief source of legislation").

Morsi demonstrated his intention to carry forward the purge of members of "the political component of the power elite" and replace them with people loyal to the Muslim Brotherhood by decreeing sweeping changes in the top management of the publicly owned media under a minister of information who was himself a prominent member of the Brotherhood. The next spectacular measure, the replacement of Hussein Tantawi and Sami Anan, at the head of the SCAF, with Abdul-Fattah al-Sisi and Sedki Sobhi, on 12 August 2012, was definitely not a change of course, as I explained in *The People Want*, except in relation to the hypocritical way in which it was orchestrated so as to give the lie to the opposition's accusations and show Morsi in a "revolutionary" light – a posture that did not fail to irritate the military.[14]

But Morsi's other move on that same 12 August was a much more serious challenge to the military: he cancelled the "complementary constitutional declaration" that the SCAF had promulgated shortly before his election and gave himself the full range of legislative and executive powers that the SCAF had held by virtue of the constitutional declaration of 30 March 2011. It was not that the military wanted to retain constitutional and legislative power, but they were apprehensive of seeing the Brotherhood dominate all branches of government. They feared that it would use these powers to shape a constitution that would increase and perpetuate its political role, while cutting down the prerogatives that the army had previously enjoyed. The same move was likewise a challenge to judicial authority, which Morsi had already tried once to bypass when he attempted to reinstate the People's Assembly shortly after his inauguration – only to backtrack the next day. In October 2012, he tried again to twist the arm of the judiciary by dismissing the prosecutor general, backpedalling once again soon after.

The various actors in this political drama regarded the constitutional process as the most crucial issue, all other powers being provisional. This process turned sour in November: Morsi and the Brotherhood could not reach an agreement with the left and liberal opposition on a consensual draft constitution. Protesting against the determination of the Islamic fundamentalist majority to impose its views and tailor a constitution to its taste, both the opposition and the representatives of Egypt's churches boycotted the Constituent Assembly thereafter. Sensing that the latter might be dissolved by the Supreme Constitutional Court, to which its case had been referred on 23 October, the Muslim Brothers decided to go one step further in encroaching on the judiciary.

To ensure Washington's support in this escalation, Morsi made several gestures of good will with regard to Israel. On 17 October, the new Egyptian ambassador to Israel handed then-Israeli president Shimon Peres a letter from Morsi in which the Egyptian president addressed his counterpart as "my great and dear friend", expressed his "strong desire to develop the affectionate relations that fortunately bind our two countries", and wished Israel "prosperity".[15] This was followed in November by Morsi's performance of a key role in brokering a ceasefire between Gaza's Hamas government and the Israeli government, thus ending Operation Pillar of Defense, which the Israeli armed forces had launched on Gaza on 14 November (generating a death toll of over 170 Palestinians and six Israelis). The ceasefire was announced jointly in Cairo on 21 November by Secretary of State Hillary Clinton and the Egyptian minister of foreign affairs. Clinton declared that "Egypt's new government is assuming the responsibility and leadership that has long made this country a cornerstone of regional stability and peace."[16]

As the Associated Press aptly put it, "after winning US and worldwide praise, Morsi immediately cashed in on his new political capital by seizing more power at home."[17] Indeed, emboldened by Clinton's praise, Morsi issued the very next day, on 22 November, a new constitutional declaration in which he proclaimed that all his constitutional declarations, laws and decrees – from the time he had taken office until a new constitution was approved and a new People's Assembly elected – were "final and binding and cannot be appealed by any way or to any entity. Nor shall they be suspended or cancelled and all lawsuits related to them and brought before any judicial body against these decisions are annulled."[18] The declaration also shielded the Constituent Assembly from potential dissolution by any judicial body, and gave Morsi the power to appoint the prosecutor general, which he had failed to achieve the previous month. The opposition unanimously cried foul, accusing Morsi of having enthroned himself as "new pharaoh of Egypt", with an unprecedented range of powers going far beyond those that had been enjoyed by Mubarak.

Morsi's "white coup", as it was widely called, prompted the opposition to form a National Salvation Front (NSF), regrouping the left and liberal parties with people who had collaborated with the old regime – a coalition well represented by its three main figures: the Nasserist Hamdeen Sabahy, the liberal Mohamed El-Baradei and the member of the establishment under Mubarak, Amr Moussa.[19] The NSF organised days of street protests, with hundreds of thousands rallying once again in Tahrir Square, calling for Morsi to "leave" (*irhal*) and chanting "the people want to overthrow the regime". Clashes soon erupted between Morsi's supporters and opponents. The Brotherhood-Salafist Constituent Assembly rushed to complete a draft constitution before the end of November. Then, on 2 December, Morsi announced that a referendum on the new constitution would be held in less than two weeks, on 15 December, further aggravating the tension. On the same day, the Muslim Brotherhood rallied its partisans outside the Supreme Constitutional Court to block judges from entering, and thus prevent them from ruling against the Constituent Assembly.

On 4 December, more than 100,000 anti-Morsi protesters marched on the presidential palace of Al-Ittihadiyya, demanding the cancellation of the referendum and the drafting of a new constitution. Over the next two days, bearded members of the Muslim Brotherhood and allied groups attacked the peaceful anti-Morsi sit-in outside the palace, provoking street battles that left eleven dead – mostly killed by live bullets.[20] Despite this climax in political tension, a two-phase constitutional referendum was held on 15 and 22 December, with some of the opposition calling for a No vote and others for a boycott. The constitution was approved by a majority of 63.8 per cent. With only 17 million votes cast in total (compared with 25.5 million in the presidential election six months earlier), little over one-fifth of Egypt's eligible voters had approved the document.

The new constitution included a number of articles potentially restricting the rights of women and religious minorities, and it enhanced parliamentary power in comparison with the preceding constitution of 1971. Reflecting the Muslim Brotherhood's desire to appease the SCAF, it also significantly enhanced the Egyptian military's prerogatives, with the creation of a National Defence Council "responsible for matters pertaining to the methods of ensuring the safety and security of the country and to the budget of the Armed Forces". The military retained the right to put civilians on trial before military courts "for crimes that harm the Armed Forces". Unsurprisingly, the NSF declared that the constitution lacked legitimacy because of the lack of consensus about it.

Far from facilitating a compromise, Morsi reshuffled his cabinet in early January 2013 so as to increase the number of ministers belonging to the Muslim Brotherhood's FJP from five to eight. He thus further corroborated the accusation that the Brotherhood was extending its stranglehold on the state (what the Egyptians called "brotherhoodisation" of the state: *akhwanat al-dawla*). Morsi also replaced the interior minister, who had shown reluctance to repress the opposition's protests, with the deputy minister, Mohamed Ibrahim, who seemed more inclined to fulfil this role. From 25 January onwards, the second anniversary of the initial 2011 uprising, the situation deteriorated seriously. On that day, hundreds of thousands of demonstrators held rallies against Morsi in Tahrir Square and across Egypt, with clashes erupting in many places. On 27 January, the violent repression of a mass protest in the city of Port Said – against a court ruling that had sentenced to death twenty-one local soccer fans arrested during a stadium riot a year before – killed several dozen people, with Morsi praising the police for their brutal crackdown. Protests went on in Port Said and other cities during February and March, with dozens more killed.

Anti-Brotherhood sentiment was sharply rising across Egypt, provoking clashes between supporters and opponents of the president and attacks on FJP offices. Morsi was rapidly losing control of the situation, while the military were increasingly distancing themselves from his government. Meanwhile, the domestic security establishment suspected the president of wanting to replace their heads of department with officers favourably inclined towards the Brotherhood. Morsi attempted to convene a national dialogue, but only the broad spectrum of Islamic parties – from the liberal former Muslim Brother Abdel Moneim Aboul-Fotouh to hard-line Salafists – attended.

The NSF demanded as a prerequisite that the Brotherhood agree to amend the constitution's controversial articles and form a national unity government. On this last demand, the Front was soon joined by the Salafist Nour Party, a move that the SCAF (and the Saudi kingdom) had certainly encouraged. In early April, Morsi turned down a compromise with the NSF that had been submitted to him by the European Union's foreign policy chief, Catherine Ashton. In exchange for the formation of a "technocratic" cabinet and the amendment of the electoral law along the lines required by the Constitutional Court, the opposition was willing to recognise Morsi's legitimacy and take part in the forthcoming parliamentary election.[21] The Brotherhood rejected the offer.

Morsi initiated a new confrontation with the judiciary over his attempt to hold the parliamentary election in April – only to backtrack yet again. On 7 May, in a further cabinet reshuffle, three more Brotherhood-FJP members were given ministerial portfolios, bringing the total to eleven – close to one-third of the cabinet. As if to add fuel to the fire, on 17 June Morsi appointed seven Brotherhood members among sixteen new provincial governors (out of a total of twenty-seven). The appointments provoked protests and clashes between Brotherhood supporters and opponents in several governorates. Clashes likewise multiplied in response to the opposition's growing campaign to unseat Morsi. The whole country was reaching boiling point. Attacks on Copts and Shi'is failed to replace political tension with sectarian antagonism, which would have better suited the Brothers and their allies.

Incensing the Country

The extremely inept handling of the political situation by Morsi was incensing a country made highly inflammable by deteriorating economic and social conditions. His handling of the economy only made things worse.[22]

International Monetary Fund (IMF) approval was the pivot of the Qandil cabinet's economic strategy, as it had been for successive governments in Egypt since the time of Anwar al-Sadat. Underlying this continuity, Qandil's first finance minister had been reappointed from the Ganzouri cabinet. In August 2012, Morsi requested from IMF managing director Christine Lagarde, on a visit to Cairo, a $4.8 billion loan, up from the $3.2 billion that had been under negotiation with the SCAF. Reneging on the conditions that the FJP itself had put forward for accepting the loan when it was in opposition,[23] the Muslim Brotherhood was betting in its turn on the Fund's help in designing ways to decrease the budget deficit, stem the haemorrhage of foreign currency reserves, and attract foreign investment.

Morsi needed to show to all potential donors, lenders and investors – whether international, Western or Arab – as well as to Egypt's capitalist class and its military–industrial complex, that he could deliver where previous governments had failed in meeting the IMF's stringent conditions. He believed he could perform this feat thanks to his being backed by a massive political machine with popular roots. He would thus prove to the various actors mentioned above that the Muslim Brotherhood could be of crucial use to Egypt's capitalism. On 9 December 2012, a few days after reducing subsidies on butane gas and electricity, Morsi approved sweeping increases in sales taxes on a host of goods and services, including cigarettes and shisha (water pipe) tobacco, cooking oil, mobile phone calls, fertilisers, pesticides and alcoholic and soft drinks.

As expected, the announcement led to a huge popular outcry, and the Brotherhood proved unable to dampen the discontent. Morsi's own FJP co-thinkers had to disavow his decision and demand its suspension: they were dismayed at its unbelievably clumsy timing, six days ahead of a referendum on their controversial draft constitution. The way Morsi backpedalled for the umpteenth time on his decree is the stuff of comedy or political satire. He suspended the decree with a short update to his public Facebook page a few hours after issuing it, at 2 a.m. Giving assurances that he did not want to impose extra burdens on Egypt's citizens without their consent, he declared that he was therefore postponing his decisions until they were accepted by the public. Still, a "summer of discontent" loomed on the horizon, as Dina Ezzat aptly stressed, by the end of 2012:

"The ship is cracking, but neither the president nor the Muslim Brotherhood wants to admit it, and are thus not acting to fix the cracks," said an independent economic source.

According to this source, whether Morsi and the Guidance Bureau likes it or not, economic hardship is heading Egypt's way, and fast.

"This coming summer would be for sure the summer of discontent. Scorn would not just be about increased prices of commodities and services, but also about declining quality of services and maybe scarcity in some commodities," the same source said.

"We are expecting to see electricity and water outages that would last for long hours in Cairo and the big cities. The only way to help save the situation is to adopt very fast an effective economic scheme. But this cannot be done if the Muslim Brotherhood continues to manipulate power," said a retired source at the finance ministry.

"It looks like they think they can fix the situation. But what we have seen so far suggests that they are only making things worse. If they continue with the same performance they will completely wreck the boat," the source added.[24]

The truth is that Morsi's first presidential summer had already been a "summer of discontent". He had been in post for barely two weeks when he was faced with a strike by the 24,000 textile workers of Mahalla, the main hotbed of Egyptian workers' activism. Not only had they not yet obtained the wage increases they demanded; they were also deeply frustrated by the suppression of three annual bonuses that they had previously received. The workers saw in this retribution by Morsi for the poor score that Mahalla had given him in the presidential election. They also saw in it a betrayal of Morsi's electoral promises, which led them to chant slogans demanding his resignation – barely a fortnight after his inauguration![25]

The Mahalla workers were only the crest of a wave of workers' struggles that kept rising, sweeping all economic sectors and beating, under Morsi, all previous records of "industrial action".[26] According to the data gathered by the Egyptian Center for Economic and Social Rights (ECESR), the number of *social* protests of all sorts increased dramatically in 2012 from July onwards – that is, after Mohamed Morsi's investiture. From 157 in June, their number soared to 566 in July and remained at a very high level until the fall of Morsi, reaching an all-time record of 4,682 protests during the twelve months from July 2012 to June 2013, including strikes by police units across the country.[27]

From a score of 1,969 for the whole year 2012, the number of *workers'* protests reached 1,972 during the first half of 2013 alone (2,239 for the whole year). These figures should be compared with the total score of 3,313 for the eleven years from 2000 to 2010, and about 1,400 workers' protests in 2011, the year of the uprising.[28] This was in spite of various attempts by the Morsi-Qandil government to repress workers' struggles both legally and physically. One peak of this repression was reached in April 2013, when the government resorted to using the army to quell a major strike by over 70,000 railway workers and employees, conscripting hundreds of drivers to work under military command.

In this respect, the Center for Trade Unions and Workers Services (CTUWS) issued in June 2013 a damning report on the condition of workers under Muslim Brotherhood rule. The report denounced the betrayal by Morsi and the Brothers of all their electoral promises with regard to the workers, accusing them of being only concerned with extending their control over the state. It censured them for unprecedented violation of workers' rights and unprecedented violence in confronting strikes, especially by letting bosses hire thugs to attack workers – with firearms, in some cases. The report blamed Morsi and his co-thinkers for using mosques' pulpits in addition to the publicly owned media in order to incite feeling against the workers. It denounced "the Brothers' plan to quell the independent unions and take control of the official trade union federation by removing Mubarak's men and replacing them with the [General] Guide's men ... "[29]

The blatant failure of Morsi and the Muslim Brotherhood to restore "law and order" and reboot the economy, including their failure to deliver the neoliberal economic reforms requested by the IMF, along with their incredibly short-sighted and crass attempt to get their hands on one segment of the state after another, in a headlong rush against the dwindling tide of their popularity – all this led the SCAF to lose patience, and gradually abandon its wait-and-see attitude. Morsi's appropriation of "pharaonic" powers on 22 November set the military off on an independent and increasingly defiant course.[30] It confirmed what their colleagues in the security apparatus had been trying to convince them of:

> "The army like many people who have not dealt directly with the Brotherhood and seen their dirtiness wanted to believe that they have something to offer to Egypt [a senior security officer said]. But for us it was a waste of time."
>
> Officials in the Interior Ministry warned the military that Mursi's manoeuvrings were merely a way to shore up his power. The Muslim Brotherhood, they told their army colleagues, was more interested in creating an Islamic caliphate across the region than serving Egypt.
>
> "The Brotherhood have a problem with the Egyptian state," said the state security officer. "I am certain that Mursi came to implement the plan of the Brotherhood ... They don't believe in the nation of Egypt to begin with."
>
> Over time, middle-ranking Interior Ministry officers became more vocal with the military. The message got through at the highest level.[31]

On 8 December 2012, in the wake of the deadly clashes near the Ittihadiyya presidential palace, the SCAF called for a national dialogue conference to foster an agreement on the constitution between the Muslim Brotherhood, the Nour Party and the NSF, one week ahead of the referendum. This call was initially made with Morsi's approval, but had to be cancelled after the president changed his mind due to opposition from the Muslim Brotherhood. Morsi now declared that it was his prerogative to convene such a meeting, despite the NSF's refusal to accept his invitation unless prior conditions were fulfilled. A few days later, Sisi issued a decree in his capacity as minister of defence prohibiting the sale of land in Sinai (a militarily sensitive zone) to non-Egyptians, thus thwarting a Palestinian–Qatari scheme to buy territory in the peninsula with the blessing of the Brotherhood's Guidance Bureau.[32]

When riots erupted in Suez Canal cities in the wake of the sentencing to death of Port Said football fans in late January 2013, Morsi appeared on television to declare a state of emergency and impose a night-time curfew. The army was deployed in the cities to stop the violence. In fact, however, it stood between the police and the protesters, allowing the latter to defy the ban openly. This was depicted by the military as belonging to the same pattern of behaviour that had led the army to protect the protesters in Tahrir Square in January–February 2011 – a pattern that would be repeated still more spectacularly in June 2013. At the same time, the tension continued to increase between the military and Morsi on the issue of the smuggling tunnels between Sinai and Gaza, which the army had started to destroy in the belief that it could help stem the rising jihadist militancy in Sinai.

In addition to all that, another red line for the SCAF was crossed when the Egyptian military academy announced in March 2013 that a few Muslim Brothers' sons, including the president's nephew, were among its new trainees.[33] It had been traditional in the past for the military to exclude applicants whose vetting showed any political or parental connection with opposition currents. The rule could obviously no longer be applied to the Brotherhood, since it was now in government. Contradicting an anxious public rumour that then still held that Sisi was in bed with the Brothers, this development could only worry a man like him, who had headed military intelligence before heading the SCAF. He and his colleagues knew only too well that the Muslim Brotherhood might finalise its seizure of the Egyptian state if allowed to infiltrate and eventually control the army. They strongly resented this perspective.

The military were now determined to end Morsi's presidency, but they needed to find the best way of achieving this goal. Mustafa Bakri, a journalist and former member of parliament close to the SCAF, published a book on relations between the military and the Brotherhood in April 2013 – three months before the final

showdown.[34] The book offered an assessment of the military's
options, which no doubt reflected their own thinking – so much so
that its central scenario reads now almost like the roadmap that the
military did in fact follow. The best-case scenario depicted by Bakri
would have been a consensual intervention, the army deploying
troops on the streets to restore law and order while the Brotherhood
agreed to hold new presidential elections in the near term (under
the pretext that a new constitution had been adopted).[35]

In the next-best case (all other options being based on
catastrophic scenarios), the army would need to "assume
government for a limited period, in order to restore security and
stability in the country, until new presidential elections are held ..."
It would therefore inevitably be confronted with opposition from
the Muslim Brotherhood; "however, this opposition will not go to
the extreme of declaring civil war, but will seek an understanding
on the conditions of the next period." For the Brothers – or so
Bakri and his military friends believed – were "pragmatic when it
comes to dealing with military or security force, and their tactics
are always to avoid confrontation", especially when they had lost
popular support.[36]

If this were to happen, the Arab regimes would welcome the
army's move with relief – especially the Gulf monarchies, which
would act swiftly to support the economy and thus consolidate the
military takeover. Western reactions would be divided between
discretion, especially from France and Germany, and temporary
condemnation from the United States, though without breaking
relations.[37] Bakri then described the conditions for a new military
takeover on the model of that of February 2011:

> In case of repetition of the model of popular revolution that the
> country witnessed on 25 January, and its persistence for a while in
> the streets and squares and around the various institutions, the army
> will find itself part of the equation. It will be deployed on the streets
> and repeat the previous military command's plan of protecting the
> demonstrators and their security, and siding with their legitimate

demands. In that case, the army will be able to impose its conditions on the president of the republic – either ceding power for a limited transitional period to a presidential council headed by the army commander and composed of a number of influential civilian figures, or holding an early presidential election … In that case, the international community will regard the army's intervention and its decisions as acceding to the people's will, which is the source of legitimacy, exactly as occurred during the 25 January Revolution.[38]

Here, then, was a SCAF confidant envisaging a repetition of the "25 January Revolution" as a prelude to a second edition of the 11 February coup. The plot had to be the same, but two of the collective actors needed to exchange roles – as in that famous direction of Shakespeare's *Richard II*, where two actors alternate the roles of King Richard and Bolingbroke (who ends up overthrowing Richard II and seizing the throne). On Egypt's throne this time stood Mohamed Morsi, representing the Muslim Brothers who had contributed to Mubarak's overthrow and incarceration. In their turn, Mubarak's former partisans stood this time in the ranks of the opposition that would gather in Egypt's streets and squares. Two other actors kept their role unchanged: the liberal-left opposition, in the forefront of the mobilisation against one president-pharaoh after the other, and the military, still acting as ultimate arbiter and kingmaker.

Enter Tamarrod

Tamarrod, the anti-Morsi "campaign", whose name is Arabic for "rebellion", was founded in late April 2013 by five young people who had been active in the Kefaya movement, well known for the key role it had played in the political struggle against Mubarak's regime. The five were Nasserists: they belonged to the ideological current that venerates a sanitised image of Nasser's progressive legacy – a mixture of Arab-Egyptian nationalism and socialist populism – and constitutes the main form of popular left consciousness in

Egypt. It is this same ideological current that manifested itself in the first round of the 2012 presidential election in the surprisingly massive vote for Hamdeen Sabahy, a most congenial proponent of an updated democratic version of Nasserism. In his words:

> Of all leaders, Nasser was the most dedicated to his nation in our recent history. We observe the nostalgia for Abdel-Nasser these days: no portrait other than that of Gamal Abdel-Nasser was carried in Tahrir Square, and the same happened in Tunisia and Yemen. Abdel-Nasser was a man of his time, and his time was one of mobilisation through the single party. But had he lived in our time, he would have talked of democracy, pluralism, civic and political freedoms and rights, multiparty system and fair elections.[39]

Asked by a delegation of the Carter Center in June 2012 how he viewed the role of the military, Sabahy emphasised the "qualitative difference" between the revolution led by the Free Officers in 1952 and that accomplished by the "free masses" in 2011. He stated that he opposed any interference by the military in internal politics, and believed that their role should be limited to that of defending Egypt against its external enemies. The military institution, he added, should abide by the constitution and have no prerogatives above those of elected institutions, lest Egypt fall back into a situation similar to that of Turkey.[40] In short, as Ekram Ibrahim aptly put it in explaining Sabahy's electoral score, "Being Nasserist, pursuing a socialist agenda with social justice at its heart, committed to personal freedoms and promising a national agenda against all foreign intervention makes Sabbahi appealing to many revolutionaries. Sabbahi's presidential program could be summarised in the slogan of the revolution; 'bread, freedom, dignity and social justice.'"[41]

The five Nasserist activists who founded Tamarrod had all been dedicated to that same perspective. They had been actively involved in all episodes of the revolutionary process inaugurated on 25 January 2011, including the battles against the SCAF. Some had even voted for Morsi in the second round of the 2012 presidential election, in order to block the old regime's candidate from winning. In common with hundreds of thousands of like-minded young men and women, these activists quickly found themselves engaged in a bitter fight with Morsi's government and the Muslim Brotherhood. Sensing that the rejection of Morsi had attracted mass support, they had the brilliant idea of launching a petition in favour of Morsi's recall (by a proclamation of no confidence) and early presidential elections. For the launch of their campaign, they symbolically chose Labour Day, 1 May 2013. The petition invoked the problems of security, poverty, national sovereignty, dignity, the economy and the vindication of the martyrs. It stressed that none of the revolution's objectives – bread, freedom, social justice, national independence – had been realised under Morsi.

Tamarrod was thus reviving a tradition with deep historical roots in Egypt – in the Wafd's countrywide collection of signatures authorising Saad Zaghloul and his companions to demand complete independence from Britain on the eve of the Egyptian Revolution of 1919. To be sure, the tiny group of young activists of 2013 could hardly be compared to the Wafd's prominent figures and their political network. However, they made up for the lack of a physical network by their intensive use of the virtual network of social media – an art in which Egyptian activists have been excelling since the launch of the "6 April" (2008) and "Kulluna Khalid Sa'id" (2010) Facebook pages that were a salient component of the prelude to the 25 January 2011 uprising. Through social media, Tamarrod disseminated the petition's image file, inviting people to print multiple copies of it in order to collect signatures in their neighbourhood. The campaign set itself the goal of gathering 15 million signatures – more than the votes that Morsi had obtained in June 2012 – with the ultimate goal of staging a gigantic mobilisation on the first anniversary of his investiture on 30 June.

Hundreds of thousands of people joined the Tamarrod network, from every position on the political and social spectrum of opposition to the Muslim Brotherhood. Vast numbers of ordinary people participated in the collection of signatures, many thereby engaging in their first ever political activity beyond marching in a demonstration. The NSF endorsed the campaign, and political parties of a range extending well beyond the boundaries of the NSF – to its left, up to the radical left, as well as to its right, up to *fulul* circles – offered their offices and services.

Left critics of the NSF such as the 6 April Youth Movement and the Revolutionary Socialists (RS) joined the campaign. On 19 May 2013, the latter issued a statement announcing "resolutely" their "full participation in the campaign". Their assessment was that

> what is new and completely different in this campaign is that it stems from a popular initiative and opens a space for revolutionary action from below, and therefore the theoretical and practical possibility of starting a grass-roots opposition movement that goes beyond the narrow opportunistic horizon of the reformist front [the NSF] and contradicts completely the plans of the *fulul*, who hate democracy infinitely more than they hate the Brothers.

The RS called upon all activists to join "this battle that will necessarily prepare the ground sooner or later for a second popular uprising against this dictatorial regime with all its interests and biases, and replace it with majority rule in the interest of the majority."[42]

Read in hindsight, this statement may sound like all-too-familiar radical-left wishful thinking. Yet, although it did indeed indulge in a wishful assessment of the *actual* balance of forces, it was in fact not far off the mark with regard to the *potential* of the campaign. Indeed, there can be no doubt that the Tamarrod campaign was the most massive involvement of people in a methodical action in pursuit of a single practical political objective – collecting signatures in order to get rid of a head of state – in Egypt's history, and certainly one of the most massive in world history. The sad fate of that gigantic mobilisation should not obscure its importance: it deserves to be considered a landmark in the history of social movements.

The Tamarrod campaign involved not only hundreds of thousands of activists in political action – some of them seasoned, but most of them complete novices; it also incorporated the independent labour movement in what undeniably represented a zenith of workers' class struggle. Heba El-Shazli summarised this latter dimension as follows:

So workers collected hundreds of thousands of signatures, endorsing the call for early presidential elections. The Center for Trade Union and Worker Services, a mainstay in the independent labor movement since its establishment in 1990, used its six offices around the country to collect the Tamarod petitions. The Egyptian Federation of Independent Trade Unions (EFITU) and the Egyptian Democratic Labor Congress (EDLC) both actively encouraged their members to come out and protest on 30 June. Meetings were held at their respective headquarters, provincial trade union federations, and local union offices, all to encourage members to show their support for Tamarod Campaign principles and protest former President Morsi's rule.

Even before the appointed day of 30 June, workers' protests were already taking place. For example, in al-Mahalla al-Kubra, after the first shift at Ghazl al-Mahalla textiles factory on 27 June, thousands of workers went out on a protest march. They were outraged at the speech that former President Morsi had given on 26 June, and at the general policies of the Muslim Brotherhood, and its political arm the Freedom and Justice Party (FJP). They chanted that Morsi should "leave" (*irhal*). The same day, FJP member Mohamed al-Ganayni called for the dismissal of the head of the board of directors of the Ghazl al-Mahalla company, Engineer Mohamed Ibrahim, for not stopping the march.

Before 30 June, the major players in the independent workers' movement: EDLC together with CTUWS and EFITU set up "operation centers" in their offices to monitor workers' presence in the protests and any incidents of violence or harassment. These operation centers were also in direct communication with the Tamarod Campaign headquarters, in order to coordinate activities such as meeting points for workers to begin to march towards Tahrir Square, and to al-Itti-hadiyya Presidential Palace. In addition, tents were set up for workers at each protest location. These served as resting stops as well as meeting points for protesters to get news updates.[43]

On the other end of the wide spectrum of early Tamarrod supporters, drawn from the broad opposition to the Muslim Brotherhood, stood members of the business and political wings of the old regime's power elite, most of whom had had a discordant relation with Mubarak. Those were former members of Mubarak's "loyal opposition" and members of the liberal faction of the market bourgeoisie (in contrast to the crony-capitalist state bourgeoisie).[44] Hisham al-Bastawisi, the vice president of the Court of Cassation and the 2012 presidential candidate of Mubarak's loyal left-wing opposition (al-Tagammu') provided Tamarrod with its headquarters in Cairo, while the Coptic neoliberal tycoon Naguib Sawiris offered it the use of all the offices and material means of the party he had founded after the 25 January uprising, the Free Egyptians. More importantly, Sawiris backed the campaign with the influential TV network (ONTV) and the daily newspaper (*Al-Masry al-Youm*) that he owned. Some of the most popular private Egyptian TV channels likewise supported the campaign. The construction entrepreneur Mamdouh Hamza, a man who had objected to Mubarak's nepotistic practices, funded the printing of millions of Tamarrod petition forms.[45]

As the campaign gathered momentum, the range of participants and backers went beyond those who, like those mentioned above, had supported the 25 January Revolution. It started to involve diehard *fulul* of the Mubarak regime, including members of the repressive apparatus: "At first [Tamarrod] was not taken seriously. But as it gathered signatures, Egyptians who had lost faith in Mursi took notice, including interior ministry officials. Some of those officials and police officers helped collect signatures and joined the protests."[46] The participation in the signature-gathering campaign of former members of the ruling party that had been dissolved in

2011 became increasingly noticeable, as was the involvement of the security services.

As the movement grew and called for mass demonstration on June 30, the first anniversary of Morsi's inauguration, new, less familiar recruits permeated its branches.

One Tamarud activist who spoke to Reuters said she resigned three days before the giant protest because she was concerned that the secret police and former Mubarak supporters were infiltrating the movement.

"Suddenly, the faces had changed," said B.A., who asked not to give her full name for fear of retribution from the security services. "Many of the people I'd worked with left, and some of the new faces I knew were *felul* (remnants), nostalgic for Mubarak, or justifying the work of state security."[47]

This was not one more of those cases of infiltration by *mukhabarat* to which Egypt has been accustomed ever since its security apparatus was moulded in the Stalinist tradition by the East German Stasi (Staatssicherheit), as were the Assad regime's *mukhabarat* in Syria later on. It was, rather, an instance of open collaboration, as asserted by one of Tamarrod's key organisers who boasted to a French journalist, a few days after Morsi's overthrow, that the campaign had succeeded in reconciling "the *fulul* and the revolutionaries", who had both understood that "the real problem is the Muslim Brothers."[48] The NSF and Tamarrod openly welcomed the support of prominent representatives of the *fulul*, including Ahmed Shafiq himself, as long as they had not been convicted or prosecuted in relation to their role under Mubarak.

Most importantly, the very backbone of the old regime, the army, played a pivotal role in the success of the gigantic anti-Morsi mobilisation on 30 June 2013. The closer the deadline of Tamarrod's petition campaign approached, the more open the military's support for the mobilisation became. One week prior to the long-planned climax, Abdul-Fattah al-Sisi proclaimed loudly and clearly that the military would protect the nationwide demonstrations and rallies – this a few days after the Muslim Brotherhood, on 15 June, had ominously flexed its muscles by staging a massive rally in Cairo in solidarity with the Syrian uprising, on an openly Sunni-sectarian and jihadist platform. Morsi addressed the rally in person, announcing the severance of diplomatic ties with Damascus and calling for a no-fly zone over Syria.

On 23 June, Sisi declared demagogically, in the name of the "eternal" and unbreakable link between the army and the people, that the military's mission was to protect "the people's will", and that they would not allow any aggression against it. The armed forces, he said, would not "keep silent in front of those who frighten and scare our Egyptian people".[49] The army offered to supervise a compromise whereby a new national unity cabinet would be formed, headed by the SCAF's last prime minister, Kamal al-Ganzouri, in order to organise new elections. This offer, which was subject to an ultimatum ending on 30 June, was rejected by the Muslim Brotherhood.

On 26 June, the army began to deploy armoured vehicles across Egypt, in an operation called Will (*Irada*), in line with Sisi's speech.[50] On the same day, the NSF, Tamarrod and allied groups such as Kefaya announced the constitution of a 30 June Front. They called for Morsi to be replaced by the president of the constitutional court in a temporary and honorary presidential role, while executive power would be entrusted to the head of a cabinet formed of personalities representing "the Revolution's line".[51] They also advocated the suspension of the constitution adopted six months earlier, and the designation of a committee of experts in order to draft a new one to be put to a referendum. Two days later, on Friday 28 June, against the backdrop of tensions and fierce clashes between the two camps in various parts of Egypt, the Muslim Brotherhood and its allies initiated an open mass sit-in in defence of "legality" in Rabi'a al-'Adawiyya Square, in Cairo's Nasr City – a place named after a mosque dedicated to a famous mystic woman of early Sufi Islam (quite remote from the brand of Islam upheld by the Brotherhood).

On the eve of 30 June, Tamarrod announced that it had collected over 22 million signatures, far above its target of gathering more signatures than the 13.2 million votes that Morsi had obtained in the second round of the 2012 presidential election. Even though this figure cannot be taken as accurate, as there was not and could not be any independent verification of the signatures, there is little doubt that a popular majority against Morsi had built up in Egypt. He had received, after all, only 5.8 million votes in the first round in 2012, while 17.5 million votes had gone to his various rivals.

For the same reason, even though it is impossible to verify the figure of 14 million demonstrators on 30 June that the military announced as a result of estimates based on helicopter observation, there is no doubt that the mobilisation on that day was larger than any Egypt had seen since 25 January 2011, and hence in its entire history. The squares and streets of Cairo and other Egyptian cities were filled with the people who had made the 25 January Revolution, except for the Muslim Brothers and their sympathisers. This last crowd was replaced, however, by a much larger number of people who had not joined the 2011 uprising, either because they were partisans of the old regime or because of their wariness of the Muslim Brotherhood's accession to power. A number of police officers even took part in the demonstration.[52]

On 1 July, Sisi gave Morsi a second and final ultimatum of 48 hours to meet "the people's demands" – in other words, to appoint an interim cabinet and open the way to popular consultation on his presidency by referendum, or to a snap presidential election. Abiding by the decision of the Muslim Brotherhood's Guidance Bureau, Morsi replied on the next day by stubbornly rejecting any such moves, arguing that he was the legitimate, democratically elected president. He later conceded that a referendum on his presidency could be held, but only after the parliamentary elections that he had planned to hold in September, notwithstanding the opposition's decision to boycott them.[53] This was in spite of the fact that he had now been disowned by all other major political forces, including the Salafist Nour Party.

Hours before the ultimatum expired on 3 July, two of Tamarrod leaders – including the young man who emerged as the central figure of the movement, Mahmoud Badr – were invited to meet Abdul-Fattah al-Sisi. Badr would later boast about his role on that day in "convincing" the commander-in-chief to implement the coup option:

> On the day the army stepped in to remove Morsi last week, Badr and his two twenty-something co-founders of the "Tamarud–Rebel!" movement got a phone call from a general staff colonel, inviting them to meet the armed forces commander-in-chief.
>
> Speaking to Reuters in a bare suburban high-rise apartment lent to his protest movement by an obscure political party, Badr said it was their first contact of any sort with the military.
>
> They had to borrow a car to drive – unwashed and unshaven – to military intelligence headquarters, where they were ushered into a room with generals, a grand sheikh, the Coptic pope, a senior judge and political opposition leaders.
>
> Far from being overawed, Badr was soon arguing with General Abdel-Fattah El-Sisi about the military's roadmap for a political transition, and rejecting his suggestion that Morsi should call a referendum on his continued rule.
>
> Millions of people were demonstrating for the recall of the president, not for a referendum, the activist told Sisi.
>
> "I tell you, sir, you may be the general commander of the Egyptian army but the Egyptian people are your supreme commander, and they are immediately ordering you to side with their will and call an early presidential election," he said.[54]

If that was indeed Badr's first meeting with the military, there had definitely been coordination all along between the NSF and the SCAF – coordination in which all NSF leaders were involved, including the Nasserist Sabahy, with whom the founders of Tamarrod identified most.[55]

Nasserist Illusions

Like them, Hamdeen Sabahy and his comrades in the Karama Party, as well as the much larger sphere of his Nasser-nostalgic sympathisers, had taken part in all episodes of the struggle to advance the revolutionary process in Egypt since 25 January 2011, including the fight against the SCAF in the period ahead of the 2012 presidential election. In a trajectory that is typical of the behaviour of most of the organised left involved in the Arab uprising, Sabahy had started by allying himself with the Muslim Brothers in the first phase of "the Revolution", carrying on from his cooperation with them in the preceding years. The political links he had forged with the Brotherhood prior to 2011 were older and closer than those embodied in the broad alliance founded in 2010, which included the Brotherhood and his own party, along with the full spectrum of left and liberal actual (as distinct from "loyal") opposition to Mubarak: the National Association for Change, whose central figure was Mohamed El-Baradei.

Sabahy and his Karama Party went so far in this cooperation in 2011 as to enter the parliamentary elections of November–December as part of the Muslim Brotherhood–dominated Democratic Alliance for Egypt. They did so in spite of the vanguard role they had played in the left opposition to Mubarak and in the building of the independent workers' movement. Like the biblical Esau, they thus sold their birthright for a mess of pottage: they won six seats out of the Alliance's 235, of which 213 (over 90 per cent), went to the Brotherhood. Besides, both the Muslim Brothers and Sabahy contributed initially to fostering illusions about the armed forces' alleged support for "the Revolution", albeit for very different reasons. For the Brothers, it was opportunistic cowardice and a strategic wager on their ability to share power with the military over a transitional period, if not in the long run; for Sabahy, it was rather a matter of naive belief in the power of Nasserite nostalgia among the military.

In the face of the repressive escalation led by the SCAF against revolutionary street mobilisations, which reached its peak in late

2011, Hamdeen Sabahy injected a measured dose of criticism in his benevolent attitude towards the military. In a long interview with the London-based daily *Al-Hayat* in January 2012, he blamed the SCAF for its management of the post-Mubarak transition and refusal to prosecute and sanction those who were responsible for the killing of protesters. "The army generals must ask themselves for what reasons did the youth's slogan 'The people and the army are one hand' turn into 'Down with the military rule'."[56] The blame remained coupled with friendly advice to the SCAF on how to achieve "exit" from government; although, to be fair, Sabahy made a point of speaking of an "equitable exit" that included the implementation of transitional justice against those responsible for brutal repression, as distinct from a "safe exit".

Then, in the months leading up to the 2012 presidential election, Sabahy broke with the Muslim Brotherhood due to their high-handed behaviour in parliament – especially after they decided to run their own presidential candidate at the end of April. He had hoped in vain until then that he could win their support for his candidacy, or else agree with them and other potential candidates on uniting in a "presidential council" representative of the Revolution. It was at this juncture, in the weeks prior to the first round of the election, that Hamdeen Sabahy came to embody most prominently an independent revolutionary stance equally opposed to both wings of the counter-revolution: the *fulul* represented by Ahmed Shafiq, and the Brothers represented by Morsi. Sabahy was thus incarnating the political line summarised in a key revolutionary slogan that emerged at the same time: "Neither *fulul* nor Brothers, the revolution is still in the square" (*La fulul wa la ikhwan, lissah al-thawra fil-maydan*).[57]

Sabahy's profile was considerably enhanced by his new political salience, an impressive number of prominent intellectuals and activist groups declaring their support for his candidacy. Initially regarded as a third-rate candidate, he rose sharply in the opinion polls in the very last days before the first round. And yet the score he achieved proved much better than most expectations, including those that had been revised upwards at the last minute: 20.7 per cent of the votes (including a plurality in the two main urban concentrations of Cairo and Alexandria), against 24.8 per cent for Morsi and 23.7 per cent for Shafiq – a feat achieved with ridiculously limited financial, media and organisational means in comparison with those of the other two, who were backed by the powerful Brotherhood and *fulul*. It was hence for good reason that Sabahy felt deeply frustrated that he could not make it to the election's second round in spite of his stunning popular success. It is very plausible that, had he proceeded to that second round, he would have won against either competitor, as most of those who would not have voted for the latter in the first round would have voted for Sabahy in the second.

The Nasserist leader stuck to his third-camp position, explaining that he personally would not vote for either of the two men who disputed the second round. He did not advocate abstention, though, leaving it up to his supporters to decide individually. Building upon the momentum of the first round's result, he sought to unify the Nasserists, calling for the establishment of a new movement, named the Popular Current, that would include his comrades, sympathisers and allies (an invitation that most of the radical left shunned out of narrow-mindedness). He also advocated the formation of a democratic coalition of left and liberal forces equally opposed to both SCAF and Muslim Brotherhood control of the state. Sabahy immediately became the target of abusive attacks from Muslim Brotherhood circles, while he stood out as one of the most vocal critics of their government and its extension of control over the state.

The Popular Current's first statement was issued in reaction to the swearing-in of the first Qandil cabinet on 2 August 2012. It blamed Morsi for not installing a consensual "patriotic" cabinet (*hukuma wataniyya*) led by an independent personality, observing that the new cabinet "fully confirms that there is no real or essential conflict between the Muslim Brotherhood and the SCAF with regard to the management of the country and public policies".[58] However,

Sabahy's participation with Mohamed El-Baradei in the creation of the NSF, along with Amr Moussa and other *fulul* in November 2012 – in reaction against Morsi's "pharaonic" constitutional declaration – represented a first serious departure from this "third camp" line. It went along with a shift in attitude towards the SCAF in the name of countering the Muslim Brotherhood's creeping extension of its control over state institutions at a time when the military were increasingly entering into open dissent against Morsi.

A long, four-part interview of Hamdeen Sabahy, published in *Al-Hayat* on the eve of 30 June 2013 (25–28 June), provides a good snapshot of his thinking at that time. In this interview, Sabahy did not recant his assessment of the SCAF's post-Mubarak rule. He reiterated that "the military mismanaged the transitional period" and that the SCAF had "implemented practices that led to bloodshed and made martyrs [and] created an enmity with the young revolutionary forces that demanded retribution for their martyrs fallen under Mubarak's regime only to find that more martyrs were falling under the SCAF". However, said Sabahy, "we also, as revolutionaries, were so naive as to set ourselves a trap: 'down, down with military rule' [*yasqut, yasqut hukm al-'askar*]. This was ... one of the main tactical mistakes made by the revolutionaries because this slogan created the climate that enabled the 'Brothers' to concur with the SCAF." The more the slogan gained ground, "the more the 'Brothers' presented themselves as a popular alternative supportive of the military institution against revolutionaries intent on destroying it and falling upon its commanders in order to punish them."[59]

The SCAF's choice of cooperating with the Muslim Brothers was facilitated moreover by the fact that, in the absence of a political party of its own, "it found a ready-to-use organisation highly disciplined, implementing compliance and obedience, called the 'Brothers', who offered their services in supporting it ... "[60] In other words, Sabahy was regretting here that the revolutionary camp had not competed with the Brothers in trying to seduce the SCAF! What is more, he criticised the use of the derogatory term *fulul* to describe the old regime's grass-roots partisans, inviting them to join the "revolutionary camp" against the Brotherhood:

It is no longer appropriate for a revolution fighting for its completion to cooperate with elements who were part of Mubarak's regime ... Instead of longing for the restoration of the old regime, I call on them to let their partisans choose between standing with the "Brothers" or with the revolution. For the country is now divided into three camps: the revolution, the "Brothers", and the old regime, by size order, in the sense that the revolution's camp is the largest, followed by the "Brothers" and their allies, and lastly the old regime's camp, whose followers among the masses are victims of its leaders who are linked to that regime unlike the masses.[61]

Here again, the logic was quite odd. Rightly emphasising that, whereas the old regime's ruling party had close to 3 million members, only a small minority of them would be indicted in relation to their abuse of power and money by a transitional justice system, Sabahy was strangely calling on that minority of former power holders to "let their partisans" join the revolution. He was thus, in fact, displaying much more naivety than he attributed to himself for having called for the downfall of the military. This naivety was all the more improbable in that Sabahy stressed the class continuity between Morsi and the old regime:

Nothing changed under Morsi in comparison with Mubarak's period with respect to his economic policy views, the mechanisms of the open market, the connection with the world market and its major ruling institutions such as the International Monetary Fund, the World Bank, the World Trade Organization, and the allegiance to globalisation ... All this is still the same, and the concentration of fortune in the hands of a small minority is still the same, with a shift of the "cronies" from the leaders of the National Party [Mubarak's ruling National Democratic Party, dissolved in 2011] to the leaders of the "Brothers". I believe that there are joint economic interests

between the two groups on the basis of partnerships and extortion.
The poor are still poor, and Morsi did not offer any vision or project
and took no measures with regard to poverty, the most important
issue for Egyptians, which was one of the reasons for the Mubarak
regime's downfall.[62]

Add to this contradiction the fact that, on these key issues,
most of Sabahy's allies within the NSF were much more tied to
the continuity of basic class rule from Mubarak to Morsi than to
the aspirations of Sabahy and the revolutionary youth. Crowning
these inconsistencies, the supreme illusion consisted of the fact
that Sabahy deluded himself into believing that the military were
"an authentic patriotic force", and would content themselves with
unseating Morsi from the presidency and participating in ruling the
country once again for a limited transition period of no more than
six months, until free and fair elections were held.[63]

Faced in 2011 with a popular uprising against the regime of
which they were a part, the military brass kept political power in
their hands for almost a year and a half, relinquishing it only very
reluctantly to a group they could not fully trust. It went beyond the
rational to expect that, this time, after being requested to intervene
by another popular uprising against that same group, they would
hand over political power to someone like Sabahy, who represented
the aspirations of the revolutionary youth – aspirations whose
fulfilment they dreaded immeasurably more than they had the rule
of the Muslim Brotherhood. Here was a textbook instance of the
sort of wishful thinking for which rebel movements have paid a
huge price throughout history.

And yet, here it was again, replicated for the umpteenth time
in one more illustration of the reason why realism, which is quite a
banal value in private life, is regarded as a precious virtue in politics.
Mahmoud Badr may have naively believed that he had "convinced"
Sisi to carry out a coup. The truth is much more probably that
Abdul-Fattah al-Sisi had Badr brought in as a representative of the
vox populi, of the "people's will", so that he could "convince" the

commander-in-chief of the armed forces, in the presence of a wide array of witnesses, to carry out a coup. In other words, Sisi used Badr in order to legitimise the coup that he was about to carry out in the same way that he had used him and his comrades to create the "repetition of the model of popular revolution that the country witnessed on 25 January" (in Mustafa Bakri's phrase), which he needed in order to get rid of Morsi – all for a purpose that had little in common with the original aspirations of the Tamarrod movement.

Others were used for the same purpose. Mona Makram-Ebeid, who resigned from the upper house of parliament shortly before 30 June, narrated how, on the morning of that day, prior to the gigantic demonstration, she was summoned by members of the old regime – including Fuad Allam, former deputy chief of the dreaded State Security Investigations Service (Mabahith Amn al-Dawla), a man who had been involved since Nasser's time in the repression of the Muslim Brotherhood – to a meeting of personalities at the house of a former minister who had served for sixteen years under Sadat and Mubarak. There, they were told that the army wanted them to issue a plea for its intervention, in fulfilment of its pledge to prevent a bloodbath. They drafted the statement, had it signed by several other personalities who they reached over the phone, and delivered it to the military.[64]

The Military's Second Hijacking of the People's Will

It could be said, however, that the coup executed on 3 July 2013 by the SCAF under Sisi, was in many respects simply a re-enactment of the one carried out on 11 February 2011 by the same SCAF under Sisi's predecessor, Tantawi. Yet, on the face of it, there was a major difference between the two cases in relation to the legitimacy of the president being unseated and of the constitution being suspended. Whereas the president and constitution of 2011 were the product of decades of authoritarian rule, those of 2013 reflected a free and relatively fair electoral process. Hence the embarrassment of Western governments, most of all Washington, when confronted with the coup. Hence, likewise, the outcry of a wide range of liberals for whom democracy was primarily an electoral procedure in which the mandate given by the electors to the elected represented a contract more binding for the former than the latter.

This is indeed the substance of "free representation", which was "peculiar to the modern Western world" in Max Weber's time, and is still currently described as "Western democracy" even though it has spread to all continents. "The representative ... is not bound by instruction but is in a position to make his own decisions. He is obligated only to express his own genuine conviction, and not to promote the interests of those who have elected him." Thus, "the representative, by virtue of his election, exercises authority over the electors and is not merely their agent."[65] This so-called representative democracy consists essentially in "deciding once in three or six years which member of the ruling class [is] to misrepresent the people", in Marx's famous words.[66] In contrast to this, and short of the full ideal type of "direct democracy", the most elementary tool in empowering the electorate – i.e. in ensuring that the "legitimate functions" of government power are "wrested from an authority usurping pre-eminence over society itself, and restored to the responsible agents of society"[67] – consists of the right of the electors to call for an early election or a referendum by collecting a determined number of signatures on a petition.

As Weber put it, "The governing powers of representative bodies may be *both limited and legitimised* where direct canvassing of the masses ... is permitted through the referendum."[68] More comprehensively, both recall elections – the right to try to remove elected officials from office by way of an early election, giving them a "liability to recall at any time"[69] – and the referendum in the sense of "the right reserved to the people to approve or reject an act of the legislature"[70] are the basic means by which electors can exert control over the elected and hold them accountable for fulfilling the electoral promises on the basis of which they were elected, as well as for promoting their electors' interests in general.

When these prerequisites of a democracy that conforms to the etymology of its name as people's power are not enshrined in the constitution, and when the elected refuse to take into account a petition that has obviously gathered a compelling number of signatures, then the people "have no other remedy" than to "appeal to heaven", in Locke's famous term[71] – an unwitting echo of the ancient Chinese idea that the ruler may lose the Mandate of Heaven. When the people, or a portion of them, believe that their rights are being violated by the ruler, they usually start by demonstrating the popular will in the streets, in the expectation or hope that the ruler will address their concerns, lest insurrection become for them "the most sacred of rights and the most indispensable of duties".[72]

A crucial touchstone of a ruler's sense of democracy is their readiness to put their legitimacy to free electoral test when challenged by a significant portion of the population. In 1968, when Charles de Gaulle faced a massive workers' and student protest, and a general strike paralysed France, he called for snap parliamentary elections, and held them even though his supporters managed to gather more people in the streets than his opponents, and although he enjoyed the support of the armed forces. In the Egyptian case, the apparatuses embodying the "monopoly of the legitimate use of physical force" were not even favourable to the ruler that the rebellion sought to unseat.[73] They were actually commanded by men who also wanted to unseat him, albeit for different reasons.

This makes Morsi's refusal to call for an early presidential election or referendum on his presidency not only undemocratic, but also foolish. The gigantic mobilisation of 30 June had most clearly shown that an impressive proportion of the Egyptian population, if not an overwhelming majority, wanted him to step down from the presidency. The counter-mobilisation that his co-thinkers had pre-emptively called for on 28 June, and the sit-in that followed, had proved no match at all. And yet, in the name of his "legitimacy" (shar'iyya), based on the fact that he had been

democratically elected one year before – in a second round, after
having obtained less than one-quarter of the votes cast in the first
round – Morsi stubbornly refused to accede to popular pressure,
despite the fact that such pressure also enjoyed the backing of the
military. He would have been well advised to remember what he
himself had said in the speech he gave on 29 June 2012 in Tahrir
Square, when he addressed the huge crowd that came to celebrate
his election, in a gesture intended to match the substance of the
speech, his first after the proclamation of his victory:

> I came to you because you are the source of power and legitimacy
> that stands above any other legitimacy. You are the owners of
> legitimacy, its source and it most powerful location. Whoever seeks
> protection from any other than you loses, and whoever follows your
> will succeeds. ... I declare it very loudly: "There is no power above
> this power." You are the holders of power, the holders of the will,
> the source of this power. You confer it on whoever you wish and
> withhold it from whoever you wish ... [74]

There was nothing wrong with the progressives striving to
mobilise the people in order to dismiss the president, even though
he had been democratically elected. Since their ability to achieve this
goal depended logically on the extent to which the president had
managed to alienate the people's majority, including a large fraction
of those who had voted for him, this was nothing but an exercise in
basic democracy. The problem arose, however, when the Egyptian
progressives *asked the army* to remove the president by carrying
out a second coup, and hence seizing power for themselves. When
Abdul-Fattah al-Sisi read to the media his communiqué announcing
the removal of Morsi, standing behind him were not only the grand
imam of al-Azhar and the pope of the Coptic Church, as well as the
general secretary of the Nour Party, but also Mohamed El-Baradei,
representing the NSF, and Tamarrod's Mahmoud Badr.

Even if the army was arguably the sole force able to depose
Morsi in the teeth of the Muslim Brotherhood's formidable

political machine, the progressives should have carried on their popular mobilisation around strictly democratic demands and by democratic means, such as a general strike. The SCAF would most probably have dispatched Morsi as it had Mubarak, and for the same reason of preventing a further radicalisation of the situation, without the progressives compromising themselves by collaboration with this backbone of the old regime, and hence giving it, *nolens volens*, a blank cheque. This, alas, is what the Egyptian progressives did: both the left and the progressive liberal opposition sang the praises of Sisi and the armed forces, instead of warning against any temptation towards the establishment of military rule in any form.

The predictable result was that, just as the 11 February coup had hijacked the first wave of the revolutionary process that kicked off on 25 January 2011, the 3 July coup hijacked its second wave, which climaxed on 30 June 2013. More accurately, the Egyptian sequence of events can be sketched as follows:

- The revolutionary wave that began on 25 January 2011 was joined soon after by the main reactionary component of the opposition to the established regime, the Muslim Brotherhood, with which the progressive components – left and liberal – had hitherto maintained an uneasy cooperation. The Brotherhood entered the fray as a potential counter-revolutionary alternative, in a bid to help contain the revolutionary process.

- This first revolutionary wave was hijacked by the military on 11 February, in a *conservative coup* aimed at preserving the old regime with the support of the Muslim Brotherhood. Both wings of the counter-revolution – equally opposed to the aspirations of the 25 January Revolution – collaborated, until the rising influence of the Islamic fundamentalist wing drove it to cross the line in seeking to take over the state, thus provoking a bitter rift with the military.

- Meanwhile, the revolutionary process continued its development into a second wave, which manifested itself above all in the peak in workers' struggles, attained before the movement reached its climax on 30 June 2013. As this second wave primarily targeted the Islamic fundamentalist wing of the counter-revolution from the moment its representative took presidential office on 30 June 2012, the revolutionary forces were joined yet again by the main reactionary component of the (recomposed) opposition, i.e. the other wing of the counter-revolution – this time, the bulk of the old regime.

- The second revolutionary wave was hijacked in turn by the military on 3 July, in a *reactionary coup*. It did not take long before the military started to restore the old regime – with a vengeance. The convoluted course of the Egyptian revolution has thus come full circle, in a conclusion of what is merely the first cycle in a long-term revolutionary process.

The old regime's restoration was not immediate, however. The degree of social radicalisation of the second revolutionary wave was such that it needed to be placated before it could be rolled back. This is why the SCAF did not replay the 2011 scenario: having had its fingers burned steering the ship of government in a turbulent sea, it wisely preferred to let civilians confront this perilous task this time around. Moreover, it needed to sustain belief around the country that it was truly fulfilling "the people's will". Sisi therefore went along with the script that the NSF had worked out: he appointed the president of the Supreme Constitutional Court, Adly Mansour, as acting president of the Republic, and an interim civilian cabinet was formed. It was headed by Hazem Beblawi, a liberal reputed to be an enlightened economist, and a founder of the centre-left Egyptian Social Democratic Party, born in the aftermath of the 25 January uprising (one of the deputy prime ministers, Ziad Bahaa-Eldin – also enlightened economist – was another founder of the same party).

Mohamed El-Baradei, whose candidacy for the prime ministership had been vetoed by the Salafist Nour Party, was consequently appointed acting vice president.[75] The most astounding appointment, obviously designed to appease the workers and bring their combativeness down from the peak it had reached at

that juncture, was that of Kamal Abu Aita as minister of labour
(in fact, of "labour force", often also found in English translation
as "manpower") and immigration. After establishing at the end
of 2008 the first independent union since Nasser's time (the Real
Estate Tax Authority Employees General Union), Abu Aita – a
co-founder and prominent member of Hamdeen Sabahy's Karama
Party – had founded at the end of January 2011 the Egyptian
Federation of Independent Workers Unions (known in English
by the acronym EFITU, where T stands for trade).[76] The objection
of the official General Federation of Egypt's Workers' Unions (the
Egyptian Trade Union Federation, ETUF) to Abu Aita's cabinet
nomination was ignored, even though his EFITU did not yet even
enjoy legal status.

These figures of the 25 January Revolution were matched by
several figures of the old regime, some of them carrying on from
the Qandil cabinet under Morsi. To be sure, the real "strongmen"
of the cabinet were the minister of defence, Abdul-Fattah al-Sisi,
and the minister of interior, Mohamed Ibrahim – both members of
the Qandil cabinet, and thus incarnating the basic continuity of the
Egyptian state's hard core since the time of Mubarak. No one failed
to realise that the real holder of power was General Sisi (who later
got Mansour to promote him to the rank of field marshal). And
yet, wishful thinking as to the benevolent character of this de facto
military dictatorship was predominant in the first weeks of the new
political order. Liberal and left currents wished to believe that the
military were going to stick to the proclaimed "roadmap" this time,
relinquishing power once a new constitution had been adopted and
a new president elected.

They did not fully take stock of the fact that, in a sense, military
rule by way of control of a military-appointed civilian government
was worse than direct, temporary SCAF rule. The latter can be
discarded in a clear-cut formal manner, whereas the former is more
insidious, and can therefore prove more complicated to get rid
of. Sisi and the SCAF behind him did not have to choose between
ruling the country and relinquishing that rule. After the 3 July coup,

they instead enjoyed a choice between presiding over the country directly and openly, or continuing to rule it by pulling the strings from Sisi's position of commander-in-chief of the armed forces and minister of defence. The latter option was judged safer, given that the government was facing unceasing social turmoil, though in the absence of an imminent political risk. It was more prudent for the military to let civilians burn their fingers at the red-hot helm of the executive rather than risk burning their own, as had happened to the Tantawi-led scaf when it had assumed executive power.

The Ruthless Rise of Abdul-Fattah al-Sisi

In the initial aftermath of the 3 July coup, the best the scaf could do was indeed to wait and see, and focus on restoring authoritarian law and order. This was achieved to a large extent by the conjunction of two developments. On the one hand, the workers' struggles subsided due to a combination of factors: the expectation of progress from the new government and the illusion that it served the country's best interest, both fostered by the new minister of labour, who tried to obtain a few gains for the workers; but also a crackdown on the struggles and repressive legislation, which the new minister condoned by remaining in post.[77] Thus, workers' protest actions fell sharply from 246 in June 2013 (after a peak of 403 in February) to 48 in July, remaining under 60 for the whole half of the year.[78] Social protests fell from 623 in June (876 in April) to 107 in July, peaking at only 151 (in September).[79]

On the other hand, a fatal and crucial dialectic unfolded between the Muslim Brotherhood and the hard core of the state, which enabled the latter to escalate repression dramatically. Continuing the disastrous political course it had been following under its hardliners' guidance – a course that peaked during Morsi's presidency until his foolish refusal to seize the opportunity of the 48-hour respite that the military had granted him after the 30 June mobilisation – the Brotherhood opted for the no less foolish, indeed quasi-suicidal, posture of demanding that Morsi be reinstated and trying to bring about this outcome through the street mobilisation of its followers and allies. This was all the riskier because the Brothers' allies included unreliable and untrustworthy groups such as hard-line sectarian Salafists. The Brotherhood itself resorted to detestable sectarian demagogy in condemning the coup as Coptic-inspired;[80] indeed, anti-Coptic slogans were a key component of the slogans shouted in the Rabi'a encampment.

Neither did the Brotherhood seize the opportunity offered by the intervention of both the United States and the European Union in order to negotiate a post-coup compromise that would have allowed it to limit the damage, obtain the release of its leaders and members, restore its political rights and carry on peaceful political opposition, in exchange for acknowledging its setback and recognising the new political arrangement. According to a *New York Times* investigative report, al-Shatir, whom the US and EU envoys were allowed to meet in prison, "embraced the need for dialogue, but did not endorse the proposals". Yet the report clearly places the main blame on the new authorities: Beblawi, Sisi and interior minister Ibrahim, the last one being reportedly "convinced that brute force was the only way to break up sit-ins by tens of thousands of Morsi supporters."[81] The Ministry of Interior played a key role in bringing the military to assume full power by pushing the Egyptian state's relationship with the Muslim Brothers to the point of no return. This included their wholesale labelling as "terrorists".[82]

In a gesture typical of *caudillismo*, Sisi invited the Egyptian people on 24 July to take to the streets on 26 July in order to give the military and security forces a "mandate" to confront "terrorism". The SCAF explained that this amounted to a new 48-hour ultimatum given to the Muslim Brotherhood to abide by Sisi's "roadmap" before he changed his strategy in dealing with them – thus implicitly threatening to crush them. Most of the forces and groups that had taken part in the 30 June mobilisation endorsed Sisi's call, starting with Tamarrod and the NSF. Only the radical left, the 6 April Youth movement and Aboul-Fotouh's Strong Egypt Party rejected it. A huge mobilisation took place on 26 July, comparable in scale to that of 30 June. The same night, shortly after midnight, as if to signify the end of the ultimatum, the police perpetrated a massacre against a march of Morsi supporters, killing at least 95 of them (the official figure).

A few days later, interior minister Ibrahim decided to apply "maximum force to get it over quickly" in ending the sit-ins on 14 August – especially at the main encampment in Rabiʿa al-ʿAdawiyya Square.[83] "At least 817 and likely more than 1,000" persons were killed there on that day, constituting what Human Rights Watch described in the report that it published one year later – after a year-long investigation into the slaughters perpetrated during the summer of 2013 – as "one of the world's largest killings of demonstrators in a single day in recent history".[84] Nearly as many were killed on that fatal day alone as during the entire period of the initial uprising from 25 January to 11 February 2011. Two days later, the security forces killed over 120 protesters in the Ramses Square area. The report's overall conclusion is a stinging indictment of the Egyptian government:

> Human Rights Watch's one-year investigation ... indicates that police and army forces systematically and intentionally used excessive lethal force in their policing, resulting in killings of protesters on a scale unprecedented in Egypt. ... Human Rights Watch concludes that *the killings not only constituted serious violations of international human rights law, but likely amounted to crimes against humanity*, given both their widespread and systematic nature and the evidence suggesting the killings were part of a policy to attack unarmed persons on political grounds. While there is also evidence that some protesters used firearms during several of these demonstrations, Human Rights Watch was able to confirm their use in only a few instances, which do not justify the grossly disproportionate and premeditated lethal attacks on overwhelmingly peaceful protesters.

Numerous government statements and accounts from government meetings indicate that high-ranking officials knew that the attacks would result in widespread killings of protesters; indeed, in the single largest incident, the Rab'a and al-Nahda dispersals, the government anticipated and planned for the deaths of several thousand protesters.[85]

Using the mantra of the "war on terror", deployed by the George W. Bush administration as a global pretext for curtailing human rights and committing untold massacres, the Egyptian military-security complex quickly instituted a reign of state terror. In November 2013, the government effectively suppressed the right to protest by adopting a Protest Law ("Demonstration Law" in Arabic), aptly described by Amnesty International as "a fast-track to prison",[86] thus granting the security forces a licence to kill with almost total impunity.[87] Reacting to this, Dina El-Khawaga, a prominent figure on the liberal intellectual scene, noted bitterly that the ongoing coup was "not only against the Brothers, but also against the political principles that made their overthrow acceptable and legitimate and against what made 30 June an alternative scenario for a popular legitimacy preserving us from violations and subjection".[88] Before the end of the year, twenty-four Egyptian human and social rights NGOs were describing the condition of "full security control" attained in Egypt "under the cover of [the state's] war against terrorism" as *worse than the pre-January 25th era*.[89]

Mohamed El-Baradei's resignation from the vice presidency on the day of the Rabi'a mass murder, and his subsequent departure from the country, conveyed the dismay of a major section of the liberals and the left. They had sadly discovered that the evil with which they had allied, believing it was the "lesser evil", proved much more bloodthirsty than the one against which the alliance was sealed. Once again, the inability of progressives to chart an independent course against both wings of the counter-revolution, and not to help any of them get (back) in the saddle while trying to unsaddle the other, proved catastrophic. The most common "lesser evil" argument among liberals and the left in belittling the threat represented by the dictatorial state was characterised by the mislabelling of the Muslim Brotherhood – or their equivalent in other Muslim-majority countries – as "fascist", a misleading analogy that is inaccurate beyond the few similarities it invokes.[90] Referring to this worn-out argument, Karim Ennarah, a researcher on criminal justice and the police, made the following observation – quite perceptive, albeit in hindsight:

> It seems to me that large segments of the public feared fascism (or, to be precise, the fascist aspect of continuous mobilization of one segment of society pitting it against the rest) more than they feared the complete destruction of the newly open political space. It might even be that part of society had become convinced that a free and open political space is the source of the problem.
>
> *To be fair, a large portion of those who took to the streets to protest on June 30 did so only so that they would never have to do it again.*[91]

Indeed, 30 June had seen the most improbable convergence between, on one end of the spectrum, workers, activists and revolutionaries believing that they were scoring a second revolutionary goal after their first one in 2011,[92] and, on the opposite end, bourgeois and petit-bourgeois sectors longing for the restoration of "law and order" after two and a half years of turmoil. Now, think of all that Egypt had gone through since January 2011 and – as Marx sharply observed in his *Eighteenth Brumaire* about the turmoil that affected France from the February 1848 Revolution until the end of 1851 – "you will understand why in this unspeakable, deafening chaos of fusion, revision, prorogation, constitution, conspiracy, coalition, emigration, usurpation and revolution, the bourgeois madly snorts at his parliamentary republic: 'Rather an end with terror than terror without end!'"[93]

'Ali al-Raggal aptly described the situation as follows:

The historical moment of Sisi's ascension and his accession to government was the climax of a massive fear of a possible breakdown and decomposition of the state from the political, economic and social angles. He was thus pushed to the Egyptian scene as a "master" able to stop the flow of history, defeat the revolution, repress the Islamists, and keep the state from collapsing. The wave of 30 June included in its midst a large current opposed to politics, aspiring to wage a politically powerful war – in revolutionary style – in order to put an end to politics, in a contradiction rarely seen in history. Since the January 2011 Revolution, part of the bourgeoisie, along with members of the Egyptian bureaucracy – in particular the conservative layers who constitute a majority within the apparatus – and of the security bureaucracy, as well as a section of their families, were yearning to suppress politics and set the world back to 24 January, when all had seemed stable and under control, and the affairs of these classes seemed in constant improvement, with their paternal, male and class authority stable and safe, and their income blooming.[94]

The fatal dialectic of the clash between the two wings of the counter-revolution led the country to slide back from a peak of active citizen democracy to a low of fundamentally passive authoritarian rule, fully conforming with Juan Linz's classic definition of that category, which was originally inspired by Francoist Spain. Egypt turned into a typical case of those

political systems with limited, not responsible, political pluralism, without elaborate and guiding ideology, but with distinctive mentalities, without extensive nor intensive political mobilization, except at some points in their development, and in which a leader or occasionally a small group exercises power within formally ill-defined limits but actually quite predictable ones.[95]

The logic of the situation made it less and less possible to perpetuate this increasingly authoritarian regime by controlling the government from the back seat of the Ministry of Defence. Moreover, the discrediting of the old regime had been such that none of the men who had been involved in running it was popular enough to beat Hamdeen Sabahy, who hastened to announce his candidacy in the forthcoming presidential election. The popular Nasserist figure believed that, with 30 June 2013, his moment of triumph had come. He was persuaded that the removal of Morsi would be followed by a new presidential election, in which he was assured to accede to the second round this time, with a high probability of winning the election. Hence his collaboration with the military from a pivotal position, through both the NSF and Tamarrod; and hence his praise for them, and for Sisi in particular, in order to reassure them of his amicable intentions were he to become president. For that same reason, Sabahy did not invite his comrade Abu Aita to resign when El-Baradei walked out, even though he himself started to disavow the repression and criticise it openly.

It was, however, out of the question for the military-security nexus to envisage cohabitation with Sabahy as president. Aside from resenting everything he stood for in politics, whether on democratic, social or national issues, they could not imagine him managing to restore law and order where Morsi had failed despite the impressive political machine he had had at his disposal. To the security apparatus, Sabahy was furthermore a potentially dangerous man – the kind of person they have always kept under close surveillance, and occasionally jailed.

The SCAF, moreover, was keen on perpetuating the tradition of the Egyptian republic by which all presidents came from the military, with the exception of one year of Morsi and one interim year of Mansour. The attempt by Mubarak himself to promote his civilian son as his successor had provoked tensions between him and the SCAF – and the first elected civilian president ended up clashing with it. To the military's enormous good fortune, the only man whose popularity was such that he was sure to defeat Sabahy – given the terms of the political debate that Sabahy himself had contributed to defining in a self-defeating way – was a military figure par excellence, the head of the SCAF: Abdul-Fattah al-Sisi.

The Tailoring of Sisi's Presidential Suit

Shortly after the 3 July coup, a campaign started to be orchestrated by the *fulul* and the various apparatuses of the state imploring Sisi to bid for the presidency. It developed into a grotesque Sisi cult that reached abysmal depths of outlandishness of a kind that could have made the late Muammar al-Gaddafi himself jealous. It is worth noting, however, that this campaign was very much in line with the requirements of hijacking the revolutionary wave in general – i.e. that part of the 30 June mobilisation that mingled unnaturally with the counter-revolutionary wave on the same day – and of steeling Sabahy's thunder in particular. The central trick for both purposes was indeed the usurpation and exploitation of the figure of Gamal Abdel-Nasser.[96] Combined portraits of Nasser and Sisi proliferated. Prominent *fulul* on the media scene, who loathed Nasser's legacy, suddenly tried to appropriate his name and image in order to portray Sisi as a second occurrence of the historic leader (forgetting to add: the first time as tragedy, the second as tragic farce).

This claim was preposterous, to be sure: beyond the fact that both were army officers, the two men could hardly have been more different. Nasser led a conspiratorial movement of junior officers who overthrew the military command along with Egypt's *ancien regime*, and implemented soon after a redistributive agrarian reform, before embarking on the nationalisation of foreign interests from a radical anti-colonial perspective. Sisi seized power as head of the old regime's military command in order to restore a neoliberal order of unbridled capitalist exploitation, prioritising the attraction of foreign investment while resting on financial dependence towards the Saudi kingdom. If anything, Sisi was in fact Nasser's antithesis.

During the first six months of Sisi's de facto rule, when he was still hedging his bets about a presidential bid, the SCAF made sure to head off any risk of civilian infringement on military sovereignty. In another development typical of the initial post-2013 coup period, with its heterogeneous combination of concessions made to revolutionary liberal-left aspirations with a counter-revolutionary consolidation of authoritarianism, a committee chaired by Amr Moussa elaborated a draft constitution which, in many respects, was the best improvement on the Egyptian constitution since the uprising. Whereas the draft adopted under Morsi was approved in the December 2012 referendum by 10.7 million votes, the new one was approved in January 2014 by 20 million votes.

In matters pertaining to religion and its role, rights and freedoms in general, and rights of women, religious minorities and media in particular, as well as the limitation of presidential power, the new constitution marked a degree of progress. It even restricted – albeit only slightly – the conditions under which military courts could try civilians, compared with the wording of the 2012 constitution. However, the new constitution went even further than the latter in shielding the military budget from parliamentary scrutiny, and therefore from public scrutiny – a crucial interest of Egypt's military-industrial complex. Whereas the 2012 constitution stipulated that the military budget was to be discussed by a National Defence Council, chaired by the president and composed mostly of the military top brass, without specifying whether the parliament would be authorised to discuss it as well, the new constitution stipulated (article 203) that the military budget be "entered as a single figure" in the state budget. This further anti-democratic restriction was offset only very partially by the inclusion of the heads of the parliamentary commissions on budget and defence in discussion at the National Defence Council.[97]

Furthermore, the pre-eminence of the military and the constitution's conditional and temporary status are nowhere clearer than in "transitional article" 234, about the defence minister. Whereas both the 2012 and 2014 constitutions stipulated that "the minister of defence is the commander-in-chief of the armed forces and is appointed from among their officers", article 234 specified that, during the next two presidential mandates (i.e. eight years), the minister of defence could be appointed only with the approval of the SCAF. In other words, in the event that a Morsi-like situation should arise, with an elected president coming into conflict with the military, there would be no room for that president to change the defence minister and head of the army against the will of the SCAF. The latter would safely continue to nominate its own commander for years to come.

Having thus secured its undemocratic sovereignty during the next two presidential mandates, the SCAF publicly endorsed Sisi's bid for the presidency on 27 January 2014, the day on which the latter chose to have himself promoted to the rank of field marshal. Sisi's first major publicity stunt as potential candidate was the visit he paid to Moscow as minister of defence on 12–13 February – the first of several such visits, as he naturally found strong affinities with Vladimir Putin. The visit was orchestrated as a presidential gesture, including the wide circulation of Sisi's photo in civilian attire on his way to Cairo airport. Putin, in his own name and "on behalf of the Russian people", wished Sisi success in what he described as "a mission for the fate of the Egyptian people".[98]

Unfortunately for the would-be president, the confirmation of his presidential bid did nothing to prevent a sharp resurgence of workers' struggles. Whereas workers' protests had remained below sixty per month during the second half of 2013, they rose above this threshold again in January 2014, and quickly peaked in February with more than 250 protests (with only slightly fewer in March).[99] The struggle was led one more time by the Mahalla textile workers, who went on strike and demonstrated on 10 February against the delay in payment of bonuses due in December. They also demanded the implementation of the minimum wage promised by the government and, a few days later, the resignation of the Misr Spinning and Weaving Company's CEO. Within a few days, the Mahalla workers' example was followed in various other branches of the public sector, including other textile plants, metallurgy (the Helwan Iron and Steel Factory, another traditional stronghold of the Egyptian workers' movement), meat processing, construction, the chemical industry, real estate tax employees, public transport, the postal service and health (including pharmacists, physicians and dentists). This was the most important wave of workers' strikes since May 2013, before the overthrow of Mohamed Morsi.

The Beblawi government, which combined labour minister Kamal Abu Aita's carrot with interior minister Mohamed Ibrahim's stick under Sisi's authority, had blatantly failed to maintain "social peace". It had to be changed: on 24 February 2014, Hazem Beblawi announced his cabinet's resignation. The move was seen as designed to allow Sisi to start his presidential campaign with a clean slate, by shifting the blame for the government's increasing loss of popularity onto the prime minister. Beblawi was replaced by his minister of housing, Ibrahim Mahlab, who was asked to form an interim cabinet until a new president was elected and began his term. The meaning of the cabinet change could not escape anyone: the carrot was discarded while the stick remained in place. Abu Aita was dropped, while Mohamed Ibrahim was reappointed as interior minister. Most importantly, the prime minister was now a man of the old regime, whose designation thus represented a further step in its restoration: Mahlab had been a member of the Higher Commission for Policies in the National Democratic Party, the old regime's ruling party that had been dissolved after Mubarak's fall. He had been one of Mubarak's presidential appointees to the Consultative Council (Majlis al-Shura), the upper house of parliament.

The new cabinet was sworn in on 1 March. Sisi retained his post as head of the scaf, and hence minister of defence, as well as first deputy prime minister, for a few more days, although everybody expected him to resign very soon from all his military and civilian positions in order to prepare his presidential campaign. According to informed sources, including military personnel, quoted by Dina Ezzat, the reason for this further delay was that Sisi was busy

securing his control over the military-security complex by putting
men he trusted in the key positions:

> "The man has still a few things to do before he departs from the
> army to make sure that he is set to rule effectively and without too
> many problems."
> One of the key things that El-Sisi has been doing with the army
> – as with the ministry of interior and intelligence – is to "put the
> right people in the right place" and to send those who "are not fit to
> the next phase" to an early retirement.
> Accounts vary significantly but they all suggest that scores of
> military, police and intelligence men have been offered "generous
> retirement packages" during the past few weeks.[100]

Eventually, Sisi resigned from his positions, bidding officially for
the presidency on 26 March 2014. He did his best thereafter to take
off his dark sunglasses and flash a smile every now and then. (Much
later, one of Sisi's supporters, Yasir Rizq, chair of the administration
board of the Cairo daily *Akhbar El-Yom*, would reveal on television
that the secret of Sisi's permanent wearing of dark sunglasses was
that he needed to hide the tears in his eyes when evoking the fate
of poor Egyptians. This was not said tongue-in-cheek, but most
earnestly!)[101] At the end of a presidential campaign accurately
described by an observer as "the largest promotion of a political
candidate in the country's history",[102] Abdul-Fattah al-Sisi was
elected with 96.9 per cent of the vote. He thus soundly beat the
88.6 per cent "achieved" by Hosni Mubarak in 2005, the two scores
constituting a good-enough indication of the two men's respective
positions on the scale of authoritarianism. The old electoral tricks
of the old regime's political and security machine were back at
full strength – and yet, it proved a "coronation flop", as London's
Economist put it sarcastically:

> Everyone pitched in. The government closed schools two weeks
> early and declared a national holiday. The Morale Department

of the Egyptian army dispatched trucks blaring patriotic songs. Church leaders, mosque loudspeakers and television announcers urged, cajoled and in some cases angrily harangued citizens to do their patriotic duty. Yet, despite a controversial last-minute move by election officials to extend voting into an unprecedented third day, the turnout for the first presidential poll since the military coup last July was lower than its organisers had wished. ...

After three days of voting, the main newspapers said the turnout had been 48 per cent, which was oddly higher than early reports, but still unimpressive. ... Democracy International, an American-based monitoring group that fielded one of the few foreign-observer missions, called the extension "just the latest in a series of unusual steps that have seriously harmed the credibility of the process."[103]

Sabahy had decided, after prolonged hesitation, to stay in the race – a testament to his courage, given the intense flak he had to endure from the Sisi-cult crowd for daring to challenge their idol. He thus came to realise how much his illusions about the benevolence of the Egyptian military command were just that: illusions. As bravely as he could, while taking care not to lend himself too much to demagogic sneers and slanders, he denounced the slide towards authoritarianism and the curtailment of democratic rights – daring even to reject the characterisation of peaceful Muslim Brotherhood protesters as "terrorists" – and warned of the basic continuity between Sisi and the old regime. But it was much too late.

The price Sabahy paid for fostering misconceptions about the military and remaining silent about the security state, when he was focusing short-sightedly on dislodging Morsi from power, was enormous. During the press conference that he gave the day after the three-day election, he stated that the proclaimed figures were "an insult to Egyptians' intelligence", reflecting a widely held opinion. But he had to acknowledge that his defeat was undisputable. Although he most likely received substantially more votes than the 3.1 per cent he was officially credited with,[104] there was no doubt that he had squandered the momentum he had managed to achieve in 2012. Not only did he lose most of the huge popular credibility he had won that year, but a whole section of his own entourage and co-thinkers switched over to the opposite side – starting with Mahmoud Badr and other members of the Tamarrod group, which turned into a cog in the pro-Sisi machine, prompting Sabahy's loyal supporters to split. It is highly probable, moreover, that a large proportion of Sabahy's 2012 voters, especially among the youth, abstained from voting.

The Farcical Aspect of Egypt's Tragedy

By the end of 2015, Abdul-Fattah al-Sisi has been president of Egypt for over one and a half years, and de facto head of the state for thirty months. His most outstanding achievement, to this day, pertains to his expertise as a long-time member of the military-security apparatus. The man boasts a military career spanning thirty-seven years, including two years at the top of Egypt's military intelligence (*al-mukhabarat al-harbiyya*) before his appointment as commander-in-chief of the armed forces in August 2012. Under his authority, Egypt has witnessed a tremendous increase in repression. Altogether, between 22,000 (according to the interior ministry) and 41,000 people (according to the Egyptian Center for Economic and Social Rights) were arrested in less than one year, between the 3 July coup and the inauguration of Sisi's presidency. Most of them are alleged members and sympathisers of the Muslim Brotherhood. The vast majority of them have been kept in custody without due process or sentenced to long-term imprisonment.

Under Sisi, Egypt was transformed from a country in revolutionary turmoil into a truly *ubuesque* state.[105] Second to the bloody episodes of repression in the summer of 2013, the most salient aspect of this metamorphosis was the repressive madness that seized Egypt's judiciary. A special award in the "tragic farce" category is deserved for the provisional sentencing to death, after two speedy mass trials in March and April 2014, of 1,212 persons on charges of killing one and the same policeman in August 2013

(220 of these death sentences were upheld, while close to 500 were converted to life imprisonment). This hitherto unequalled judicial "productivity" continued under the new President Sisi, with the following peaks: the provisional sentencing to death in December 2014 of 188 people accused of attacking one police station (183 of these death sentences were upheld); the sentencing to life imprisonment in February 2015 of 230 people, including prominent figures of the 2011 uprising, accused of rioting, inciting violence and attacking security forces; provisional sentencing to death in May 2015 of former president Morsi and 114 other people on bogus charges related to their breaking out of prison during the uprising of January 2011 (all these sentences were upheld).

Assessing the first year following Sisi's inauguration as president on 8 June 2014, under the expressive title "Year of Abuses Under al-Sisi", Human Rights Watch pointed to other dreadful aspects of this unrelenting record:

> After a period of two and a half years after the 2011 uprising in which Egypt carried out no executions, the authorities have executed 27 people since al-Sisi took up office. Among them, seven had been convicted of murder in connection with political violence, six of them following unfair trials in a military court. The six men were executed despite credible evidence that at least three of them had been in detention at the time of the crimes for which they were accused.
>
> In October 2014, al-Sisi issued a decree expanding military court jurisdiction to all "public and vital facilities" for two years. Since then, prosecutors have referred at least 2,280 civilians for military trial, according to a Human Rights Watch count based on media reports. In May, one of these military courts, in Alexandria, sentenced six children to 15 years in prison, according to the National Community for Human Rights and Law.[106]

In addition to tens of thousands of alleged Muslim Brotherhood members and supporters, the repression also engulfed many of

Egypt's prominent and less prominent young democratic activists – the very same young people who had spearheaded the 2011 uprising:

> The harsh crackdown and arrest campaign that began after the July 2013 coup has sent numerous secular activists to prison, including human rights defenders Yara Sallam and Mahienour al-Masry, April 6 Youth Movement co-founder Ahmed Maher, and blogger Alaa Abdel Fattah. Other secular activists have been sentenced to long prison terms in mass trials. In February 2015, a judge sentenced activist Ahmed Douma, women's rights defender Hend al-Nafea, and 228 others to life in prison for participating in a December 2011 protest.[107]

Amnesty International also commented on the same occasion of the first anniversary of Sisi's presidential investiture, "Egypt's 2011 'Generation Protest' has now become 2015's 'Generation Jail'":

> President Abdel Fattah al-Sisi's government has made it clear that there is no room for further protest or political dissent. ... The authorities have returned to the repressive tactics of a police state, crushing peaceful dissent in the streets, restricting opposition groups and jailing their critics and political opponents.
>
> Today, many of the figureheads of the 2011 uprising that toppled Hosni Mubarak are in prison. However, Abdel Fattah al-Sisi's government must know that they cannot turn back the clock. The police state and repressive tactics are feeding into an atmosphere of dissatisfaction and disenfranchisement.[108]

Indeed, nothing indicated this disenfranchisement better than the very low turnout in the parliamentary election held in October–December 2015: only 28.3 per cent of eligible voters, i.e. 15.2 million (according to the official figures, while some observers believe the actual figure is lower still), whereas the turnout achieved during the 2011–12 parliamentary election was

54 per cent, amounting to 27 million voters. This very poor result occurred in spite of Sisi having personally and repeatedly exhorted the population to vote, while the grand imam of Al-Azhar warned that boycotting the election was equivalent to disobeying one's parents, since Egypt was the mother of all Egyptians (implying that Sisi was their father).[109] It was hardly surprising, though, since no real choice was offered: none of the major competing lists could be labelled as opposition to the new-old regime. Egypt's parliament under Hosni Mubarak had on occasion included more opponents to his regime than Sisi's new parliament. The prominent roles in this political circus were played by former members of the security and military apparatuses, wealthy businessmen with a wide resort to "political money" (i.e. vote buying), and "diehard Mubarak-era figures".[110] The first expressed concern of newly elected MPs after the first stage of the election was to revise the constitution in order to extend the duration of the presidential mandate and grant the president greater powers.[111]

Neoliberal Constancy

As for the dissatisfaction that Amnesty International's report mentioned, it was fed above all by the economic policy of the Sisi era, which accelerated markedly after the presidential election, with Mahlab in the prime-ministerial seat. The linchpin of this policy was naturally compliance with the dictates of the IMF – the common thread running through successive governments since the Mubarak era, with only a mild attempt by the Beblawi cabinet to act differently in its initial phase by resorting to stimulus spending. In this respect, the Sisi regime – the most repressive government of Egypt in the neoliberal era – went significantly further down the road than its predecessors. This much comes clearly through the balance-sheet included in the IMF's consultation report published in February 2015 (the first such report since 2010), which provides an overview of the state of Egypt's economy. The country's overall economic development from the 2011 uprising until Morsi's overthrow is summarised as follows:

The political turmoil of January 2011 triggered a sharp capital account reversal and left growth depressed, while policy accommodation widened fiscal and external imbalances. The protracted political and institutional uncertainty, a perception of rising insecurity, and sporadic unrest dented confidence. Large capital outflows ensued, along with declining investment and tourism:

- Real GDP dropped by 0.8 percent in calendar year 2011 and growth only recovered to about 2 percent annually in the following years, weighed by continued disruption of domestic production due to political turmoil, and widespread energy shortages and electricity blackouts.

- The fiscal deficit and debt rollover needs soared, pushing up domestic borrowing costs. Delayed reforms, lower revenue, and rising wage, subsidy, and interest payments led to double-digit budget deficits reaching close to 14 percent of GDP in 2012/13.

- Faced with capital outflows, weak foreign direct investment (FDI), and widening current account deficits, the Central Bank of Egypt (CBE) supplied large amounts of foreign currency to stabilise the exchange rate. While this provided an anchor to maintain confidence, it depleted international reserves from $35 billion (6.8 months of imports) at end-2010 to $14.5 billion (2.5 months) in June 2013. Exchange rate pressures were particularly strong in December 2012 and the first half of 2013, when reserves were only supported by sizable official financing from Gulf countries, rapid depreciation, and foreign exchange rationing, which compressed imports and generated a parallel market.

- Social outcomes, which were already lagging, deteriorated further post-2011. Unemployment peaked at 13.4 percent in 2013/14, with the highest levels found among youth and women. Poverty rose to 26.3 percent in 2012/13, with another

20 percent of the population estimated to be close to the poverty line.

Thus, by June 2013, Egypt's economy was in a precarious position with low growth, high unemployment, wide fiscal and external imbalances, and low reserves buffers.[112]

The IMF report then expresses a thinly veiled criticism of the Beblawi cabinet's policy:

> In 2013/14, two stimulus packages and revenue shortfalls widened the budget deficit to 13.8 percent of GDP, notwithstanding large external grants. To support domestic demand, the government raised infrastructure and social spending by 1.8 percent of GDP, increased the minimum wage for government workers by 70 percent, and raised wages of teachers and doctors. The budget sector deficit was contained only thanks to grants from Gulf countries of 3.8 percent of GDP. Budget sector debt rose to 95.5 percent of GDP, while general government debt rose to 90.5 percent of GDP (a lower level because of cross holdings of debt by social insurance funds).[113]

This is followed with clear relief and satisfaction at the course taken by the Mahlab cabinet: "The 2014/15 budget represents a *policy shift* as the authorities implemented bold energy price and tax hikes at the outset of the fiscal year to reduce the deficit."[114]

> *Egypt has chosen a path of adjustment and reform which, if followed resolutely, will lead to economic stability and growth.* The choice is epitomised by reform of fuel subsidies, which have been at the heart of Egypt's structural and fiscal problems for years. The significant increase in fuel prices and the commitment to multi-year subsidy reform was a transformative and welcome step.[115]

The irony is that this criticism of Beblawi's stimulus policy and praise of Mahlab's orthodox alignment were approved by none other than Hazem Beblawi himself, who was elected as IMF executive director (i.e. a member of the IMF Executive Board) for Middle East Arab countries in October 2014. The policy shift lauded by the IMF staff started in July 2014 with price hikes for fuel products ranging between 41 and 78 per cent, and for electricity of 20 per cent. These energy subsidy cuts (euphemistically called "subsidy reform" in IMF-speak) triggered what Heba Saleh, writing in the venerable *Financial Times*, described as "a wave of public disgruntlement", noting that "for millions of Egyptians living in poverty, the price rises – which come after years of dithering and with no accompanying mitigating measures for the poor – represent *yet more hardship imposed by an uncaring government*."[116] In a style typical of the man and his regime, Sisi called out the army to contribute to the sweetening of the pill by staging some window-dressing:

> In recognition of popular discontent with the price rises, the army – now the backbone of Sisi's regime – on Monday [7 July] announced it was selling cheap products in its network of shops and using its own fleet to lay on extra bus services in the capital to protect the people from "exploitative" drivers and traders.
>
> Unleashing a string of obscenities against Sisi and the government, Mohamed Ibrahim, a driver in Imbaba, said that a 25 per cent increase in minibus fares allowed by the authorities did nothing to offset the price rises. "We have had enough," he shouted. "Enough of this expensive life and enough of this exploitation."
>
> His colleagues complained that it was not just diesel that had gone up, but also engine oil – a twice-weekly expense crucial to keeping their decrepit vehicles on the road. "We blame the man in charge," said Ahmed al-Sayed. "Before this increase I thought he would sort out the country and bring down prices."[117]

If the subsidy cuts could be implemented without sparking riots this time – in contrast with the famous riots prompted in Egypt in 1977 by an attempt to implement similar cuts with regard to basic foodstuffs – it is to a large extent because of the climate of fear created by the ongoing bloody repression of the Muslim Brotherhood and the licence to kill granted to security forces in enforcing the ban on protests. In a national televised address on 7 July, Sisi had personally justified the cuts as an indispensable economic measure. Everybody sensed that the man who oversaw the Rabi'a massacre (in which at least ten times more people were killed than in the 1977 riots) was not going to backtrack on his decision in the face of riots, like Anwar al-Sadat in 1977, let alone scrap the "reform" on his Facebook page in the face of mere public outcry, like Mohamed Morsi had done in 2012. The people could see that every street protest was systematically attributed to Muslim Brotherhood "terrorists", and dealt with accordingly.

The overall dictatorial climate reigning over Egypt, and a sense of resignation after several years of turmoil, combined to allow the measure to go through. The result was that the final consumers at the very wide base of the social pyramid ended up bearing the brunt, despite all government assurances to the contrary and the IMF's specious attempt to present the measures as "mildly progressive".[118] The predicament is well expressed by a taxi driver who spoke to Nada Rashwan:

> The government can say what it wants, but it cannot control those who will exploit the situation to raise prices further. The private minibus drivers doubled the fares within minutes of the gas prices decree. ... Things were hard as they were, and now everybody will be affected by these price raises.
>
> I was surprised to find an additional $42 tax while renewing the taxi's license this morning. The employee looked at me and said "Sisi's president now, there's nothing you can do." I hate to admit it, but he's right. I didn't think things were going to turn out that way at all after 30 June. It seems more and more like a mistake and we will pay for it.[119]

The IMF's balance-sheet endorses the Egyptian government's adoption of the Fund's guidelines for a fiscal deficit reduction that is supposed to help achieve "inclusive growth". The budget deficit is to be drastically reduced over five years by means of

- carrying through the "subsidy reform" by continuing to raise fuel and electricity prices, as depicted above;

- "containing the wage bill" – in a way that will weigh heavily on the 27 per cent of Egypt's labour force who are public sector workers and employees, and will contribute significantly to increasing already rising unemployment: the government set a ceiling for public sector wages, subjected bonuses to income taxes and discontinued the automatic inclusion of bonuses in basic wages after five years. New hires require approval by the finance ministry, and the use of public entities' own resources for additional rewards to employees has been discontinued. This is supplemented with "an attrition scheme" limiting the number of retirees to be replaced.[120]

- cutting non-priority expenditure – needless to say, the least productive and useful expenditure of the Egyptian state, which is the massive amounts it dedicates to its armed forces, especially the amounts spent on arms purchases from abroad that significantly aggravate Egypt's current trade deficit, is nowhere mentioned, covered as it is by the general taboo imposed on discussing the military budget.

  With Sisi at the helm, the Egyptian military's frenzy to equip itself with the most expensive and unnecessary gadgetry has gone wild. One recent deal gives a clear idea of the very heavy toll taken by foreign military purchases on Egypt's economy: the $5.7 billion deal concluded with France in February 2015 by which Egypt became the first foreign buyer of the expensive Rafale fighter jet in two decades. Egypt will receive twenty-four of these jets at a time when the French armed forces themselves will receive only twenty-six of them over the next five years (down from eleven per year), due to budgetary restraint.[121]

- reforming the tax system – mainly by creating a "fully fledged" value-added tax (VAT), i.e. a *regressive* consumption tax, along with a pretence of implementing a marginal increase in taxes on high incomes (presently limited at 25 per cent in Egypt, compared to 35 per cent in Turkey and 45 per cent in China), capital gains and property.

Following IMF guidelines that have been adapted in order to minimise the risk of provoking riots – as has occurred so many times over the years since the international financial institutions started enforcing "structural adjustment programs" (SAPs) – the Egyptian "subsidy reform" is accompanied by "cash transfer schemes" that are purported to offset the effect of price hikes for the poorest, and to replace an unfair regressive system of subsidies benefiting all with a fairer one specifically targeting the poor.[122] This pretence of fairness completely disregards even moderately critical studies such as the survey of the implications of IMF subsidy reform policies in Arab countries undertaken by a group of NGO researchers, and published a full year before the IMF report on Egypt. The survey states the obvious problems that affect such devices, whose principal function is to make the cuts more palatable, and which are similar in nature to the problems that affect the IMF's "poverty reduction strategy" schemes:

> Although energy subsidies are regressive, disproportionately favoring the rich, the repeal of these subsidies is more likely to harm than help the poorest segments of society. In the near-term, the unwinding of subsidies cannot serve as the panacea for the serious budgetary and fiscal difficulties facing most Arab states. By continuing to press Arab governments to remove subsidies, the IMF has inadequately responded to the sweeping social and political changes stemming from the 2011 uprisings and subsequent period of unrest. ...
>
> Theoretically, the IMF proposes the expansion of social safety nets as a way to offset the negative impact of subsidy removal on the poor. *In practice, however, social protection schemes are underdeveloped and*

*often non-existent in Arab countries, and are thus incapable of cush-
ioning the poor against rising prices. In many instances, corruption and
the absence of transparency mechanisms further complicate the task of
distributing social welfare benefits.*[123]

The World Bank's answer to this kind of criticism, believe it or
not, is to extol the virtues of inequality: the Bank describes "pro-
poor growth accompanied by increased inequality" as a "legitimate
goal that should be pursued". This, we are told, is "in line with the
idea that, at very low levels of incomes, an increase in inequality may
signal an improvement in overall living conditions while very low
levels of inequality may simply signal widespread poverty."[124] The
rationale here is typically neoliberal: improvement is sought in the
form of a minority lifting itself slightly out of poverty, rather than
in the eradication of poverty through social programs benefiting
the poorest as a priority, and thus diminishing inequality.

Egypt's "inclusive growth" – a current catchword in the IMF's
opportunist vocabulary, like "pro-poor growth" in the World Bank's
– is predicated on the private sector's role. In conformity with the
neoliberal creed that rules the world capitalist economy under the
Fund's clerical guidance, the government's role is primarily "to foster
private sector-led growth".[125] Thus, neither Egypt's government
nor the IMF envisage an increase in public investment, as would
normally be expected for a country where investment as a whole
has remained significantly lower than its development needs since
the late 1980s, when public investment followed a steady trend of
decline. Although private – foreign and domestic – investment
was boosted for a while by the surge in oil prices that began in the
late 1990s, it did not compensate for the massive decline in public
investment.[126]

The reason for the failure of the neoliberal private-led model
in the Arab region is discussed at length in *The People Want*. In a
nutshell, the crucial factor relates to the rentier and (neo)patrimonial
nature of the state, as well as to overall political conditions that are
not conducive to long-term developmental investment, in Egypt

no more than in other Arab countries.[127] After its oil-fuelled boost, which led it to a peak in 2008, private investment in Egypt fell as a consequence of the global Great Recession. Needless to say, it continued to decline with the effects of the political turmoil unleashed in 2011. Thus, the IMF staff remains cautious in not anticipating a significant rise in private investment for the fiscal years 2014/15 to 2018/19.[128] And yet, faithful to the monetarist dogma of fiscal restraint and low debt, the Fund does not advocate the massive increase in public investment that Egypt so glaringly needs.

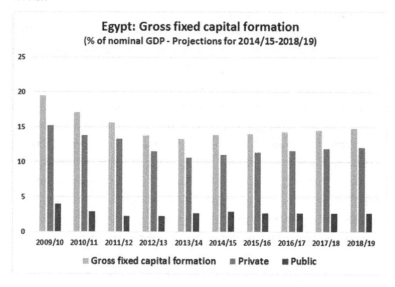

Data source: IMF

Megalomania and Megaprojects

In lieu of the socially oriented, publicly funded New Deal à la Nasser that the Egyptians had been led to expect, Abdul-Fattah al-Sisi offered them an exercise in smoke and mirrors: a pharaonic scheme, the bulk of which is conditioned by hypothetical foreign direct investment – primarily from the Gulf oil monarchies. The IMF staff listed the Sisi government's six "megaprojects" in its report, but was wise enough to incorporate only one – or more accurately only the first stage of one megaproject – in its projections for Egypt's economy: the one project that was already well advanced at the time the report was written.[129] One key reason for this circumspection was, no doubt, the fact that similar schemes, if not the very same, have been toyed with for quite some time, and had been included in the plans of successive governments, from Mubarak, or even Sadat, to Morsi.

To give them a semblance of reality, Sisi's megaprojects were at the centre of a pompous international economic conference that his government convened in Sharm el-Sheikh on 13–15 March 2015. IMF Managing Director Christine Lagarde started her speech on that occasion by quoting – partly in the Arabic original, and rather clumsily – from a verse by Egypt's most famous poet, Ahmad Shawqi, popularised by Egypt's most famous singer Umm Kulthum: "Aspirations cannot be attained through *wishful thinking*, but through toil and perseverance" (in the English translation that she read).[130] Lagarde's warning against wishful thinking was a prelude to her providing a list of conditions in need of fulfilment, summarising the guidelines of the above-quoted IMF staff report: the full neoliberal recipe, spiced with a reference to social spending.

The Sharm el-Sheikh conference was designed to be heralded to the Egyptian public as a fundraising success, with the staged signing of several investment agreements (especially energy-related deals) that had been negotiated and approved some time before – several of them under Sisi's predecessors, Morsi included – and postponed until then. Nonetheless, Sisi himself declared at the end of the conference that he needed twice as much as the $150 billion investment promises that his government boasted to have received – leaving aside their highly hypothetical character. This was also a way for him to pre-empt a highly likely failure to achieve the economic miracle that he promised by putting the blame in advance on foreign investors' stinginess.

That said, whether most of Sisi's flagship megaprojects see the light of day or not, they are quite revealing of the socio-economic logic that informs his regime. Consider the two most prominent of them – one partly achieved and the other still in the realms of fantasy: the Suez Canal project and the project of a new capital city to replace Cairo as Egypt's political and administrative hub. The Suez Canal Corridor Development Project had been under consideration since the era of Anwar al-Sadat. It involves an ambitious plan to build a new Ismailia City and develop existing Suez ports, along with new tunnels and production facilities. But its central feature is the digging of a new waterway – the New Suez Canal – complementing the existing canal, in order to increase its capacity and reduce the time it takes for ships to travel through it. It became one of the bones of contention between Sisi and Morsi when the latter planned to undertake the project in partnership with Qatar, without military participation.[131]

Sisi's government launched the New Suez Canal project in August 2014, with much fanfare. Since this was ostentatiously designed to enhance his appropriation of Gamal Abdel-Nasser's mantle, and since the latter's name is associated with the canal's nationalisation, it was not appropriate to invite foreign capital to invest in exchange for ownership rights. This would have been all the more inappropriate because this specific project was actually pursued as much for political as for economic reasons, if not more so. The idea was to give the Egyptian public the impression that they were embarking on a major new developmental journey, combined with a sense of renewed ownership of the development of their own country. Hence, foreign capital was not invited to participate: the project was financed through a call to the Egyptian public to buy investment certificates bearing an enticing interest rate of 12 per cent.

In a pattern that is typical of the new-old regime, the armed forces were heavily involved in designing and digging the new waterway, allowing for its achievement in one year instead of the three years that had been planned for.[132] This feat took a heavy toll on the workers, under conditions reminiscent of those encountered by the forced labourers who first dug the canal in the nineteenth century.[133] The New Suez Canal was inaugurated with a huge display of pomp and circumstance, including military bragging, on 6 August 2015, in the presence of a range of foreign dignitaries to whom Sisi modestly declared that they were contemplating "Egypt's gift to the world". Egypt's mosques were even instructed to invoke the Prophet Muhammad's feats on the occasion. The London *Economist* astutely commented:

> As a feat of brawn it is impressive ... As a political stunt it is big, too ... In economic terms, however, the expansion of the Suez Canal is a questionable endeavour at a time when the government is struggling to provide adequate services to its citizens. True, the channel is a significant source of revenue. Last year it pumped $5.5 billion into an economy weakened by years of turmoil. But both this sum and the number of ships transiting the canal have been flat since 2008.
>
> Egyptian officials claim that the $8.2 billion project, which expands capacity to 97 ships per day, will more than double annual revenues to some $13.5 billion by 2023. That, however, would require yearly growth of some 10%, a rosy projection given that in the entire period from 2000 to 2013 world seaborne shipping grew by just 37%, according to UNCTAD. A recent forecast from the IMF suggests that in the decade up to 2016 the annual rate of growth for global merchandise trade will have averaged 3.4%.
>
> Before its expansion the Suez Canal was operating below its capacity of 78 vessels a day. It could already handle all ships except the very biggest oil tankers. By the estimate of one Egyptian economist, the maximum growth of revenue that the new dredging

now allows from the passage of slightly bigger oil tankers amounts to just $200m a year.[134]

Whereas the New Suez Canal was Sisi's "Nasser-like" project – the most urgent one politically, all the more in that it was the most feasible – his other flagship megaproject is of truly *pharaonic* scope: the Capital, as it was called, is meant to be an entirely new capital city built in the desert between Cairo and Suez, on a gross land area of 700 square kilometres, including twenty-one residential districts with 1.1 million residential units for 5 million inhabitants (of whom only 5 per cent will have the privilege of residing in the city centre), 91 square kilometres of solar and wind energy farms, a 16-square-kilometre airport area, a 5.6-square-kilometre business district, 4.2 square kilometres of retail malls, a 4-square-kilometre theme park, 40,000 hotel rooms, and 1,250 mosques and churches.[135] The housing minister announced that the cost of the project would be $45 billion initially, and that its first phase would be executed on 105 square kilometres and involve moving the parliament, presidential palaces, government ministries and foreign embassies to the new capital over three to five years, while further development of the total area would carry on over forty years.[136]

In stark contrast with the New Suez Canal, a crucial particularity of this new capital city is that the national share in the capital of its development company will be only 24 per cent, while the rest will be foreign-owned. Egypt's contribution to the project is in fact restricted to the land provided by the government.[137] The project was to be executed by Capital City Partners, a private real estate investment fund meant for global investors and created for this specific purpose by Mohamed Alabbar, a business tycoon from the United Arab Emirates and top adviser to the emir of Dubai. Of Alabbar, Capital City Partners' website says bumptiously that, in the past two decades, he "led ambitious mega-developments of a value of over US$24 billion in over 15 countries, and helmed the creation of global icons that inspire humanity."[138]

Alabbar is founder and chairman of Emaar Properties, a gigantic real estate development company specialising in megaprojects and known especially for the development of Burj Khalifa, currently the world's tallest tower, located in Dubai. Initially intended to be called Burj Dubai, the tower was eventually named after the emir of neighbouring Abu Dhabi and president of the United Arab Emirates, Khalifa bin Zayed Al Nahyan, in exchange for his consent to bail out the project after it became mired in debt against the background of the global economic crisis, a few years before its completion in 2010. Alabbar's involvement in the Egyptian megaproject created problems in his own company.[139] Unsurprisingly, the agreement between the Egyptian government and Capital City Partners stalled in June, and was replaced in September with a new memorandum of understanding signed with the state-owned China State Construction Engineering Corporation.[140]

Irritated by this lousy start, Sisi set a two-year deadline for the completion of the project's first phase by the end of 2017.[141] Commenting on this announcement in October 2015, *Mada Masr* cogently noted that, in March 2014, when he was still minister of defence, Sisi had launched a housing megaproject of the armed forces in partnership with the UAE-based Arabtec, promising to deliver 1 million units of housing by 2020 for a cost of $40 billion: construction was to begin in late 2014, with the first homes delivered in early 2017. Work on that project had not yet started in October 2015,[142] the projected price of units having risen out of the reach for ordinary Egyptians. This is why the prospects of implementation of the new Capital City project are met with widespread scepticism, even though the New Suez Canal project had been completed in one year thanks to heavy military involvement.

But the most compelling reason for scepticism about the new Capital City project is related more to its economic, ecological and social dimensions than to its implementation. No observer could fail to note that the close to thirty new cities built in Egypt since 1977 failed to attract more than a small portion of the population

(7 million out of over 90 million inhabitants) – often the wealthiest, as is true of New Cairo, whose project was launched in 2000 and whose inhabitants are still less than one-quarter of the 6 million it was meant to host. This is at a time when more than one-quarter of all Egypt's housing units are empty – and even more than that in new cities.[143] David Sims, one of the most informed experts on Egypt's urban planning and land management, makes this very perceptive and bitter comment:

> There is still quite a bit of land around the capital both inside and on the near desert. There is public, security, and army land that could be used to make logical extensions to the city. There was land beside Manshiyat Nasir that is now part of Uptown Cairo. Why would that land have been sold at LE100 [LE = Egyptian Pound] per square meter to a businessman from Dubai? Because he had connections with the army, which was just sitting on the land. In the end, he made LE165,000,000 out of this deal and now we have Uptown Cairo. The cheapest unit there is LE4,000,000. The actual plan is to build 10,000 units. That number will, at best, even with maids, house maybe 50,000 people. Right next door you have Manshiyat Nasir with a population of 650,000 people. But did anyone say "Why don't you use some of that new land for the rotten services or for decamping some of that mess in Manshiyat Nasir?" There was not a word from human rights types, the intelligentsia, or anybody else.
>
> The new towns are largely a failure. Only New Cairo and Sixth of October have succeeded in attracting enough real estate development of the kind that Egypt needs like a hole in the head. They are used to generate false dreams, hope, fill up the front page of the newspapers, and are all [funded by] Gulf investors.
>
> These are investments. This is not just an Egyptian problem, this is happening all over now. It is because property is the most lucrative way to invest family or corporate capital. They build a villa for the son or rent it to some desperate expatriate who wants a nice place. That is what is happening in Katameya Heights. For every place that

is rented out at $5,000 a month, the hope value of all the other units increases. This is very hard to stop. If all that stuff you see along the road on the way to the American University in Cairo in New Cairo ever became inhabited there would not be any water left so it is probably just as well that it is empty.[144]

American University of Cairo professor Khaled Fahmy reacted to the new Capital City project in the same spirit, while also emphasising the lack of democracy:

> The problem with our city, like the problems of our country, is not that there is too many of us, but that our repeated governments insist on cutting us out from any decisions pertaining to our city, or our country. And the very manner in which the decision to move the capital outside Cairo has been taken is the best illustration of our government's insistence on ignoring us.
>
> No. Cairo's problems [are] not caused by too many Cairenes. Cairo's problems are caused by the complete lack of any effective, democratic institutions in which we could have a say in how our city is being run. The governor of Cairo, like the governor of Giza (its sister city), is not elected, but chosen from the ranks of the military or the police, his prime mandate being the pacification of the city and keeping it under control. Our municipal bodies, although elected, have no financial or administrative independence, and, as such, they have become a hotbed of rampant corruption. We don't even have a say in how to run our streets or our buildings.
>
> And instead of addressing the root of the problem and allowing us a say in how we shape our own lives and fulfill our dreams, the government is boasting about its ability to raise billions of dollars from friendly governments and business tycoons from all over the world, only to spend these deeply needed billions on chasing mirages in the desert.[145]

In revealing the nature of his new-old regime, Sisi's two flagship megaprojects are in full conformity with the dominant rentier character of the regional states – a feature that, along with these states' despotic nature, determines a pattern of investment in which rent-related and real estate projects are favoured. The Suez Canal is, of course, one of the Egyptian state's main sources of rent. As for the urban development megaproject, I explained in *The People Want* "why the building trade, in particular, is a flourishing sector in the region. It stands at the intersection of land speculation, encouraged by the pursuit of safe-haven investments in real estate, and a commercial and tourist-oriented service economy heavily fuelled by the regional oil rent – by both capital and consumers from the rentier states."[146]

The Military's Takeover of Egypt

In addition to this rentier feature, the military dimension of the Egyptian state permeates the two megaprojects, as it pervades the new-old regime through and through. Egypt's military-industrial complex was considerably expanded and qualitatively transformed in the 1970s under Anwar al-Sadat. Nasser's successor inherited a classical combination of a hypertrophied military apparatus and state-owned military industries, typical of a country in a protracted war condition and ruled by military dictatorship. Sadat compensated the reduction in the military's direct political role by granting them the possibility of taking advantage of the economic liberalisation (*infitah*) that he implemented in his drive to dismantle and reverse the Nasserist legacy. The armed forces were thus allowed to develop a business complex in various industries and ventures of a civilian nature. This led the military-industrial complex to become increasingly a competitor of the private sector – and here lies one main source of friction between the military and Hosni Mubarak's son Gamal, who epitomised the crony capitalism that had prospered under his father and was poised to succeed him – had the military not objected.[147] As Zeinab Abul Magd explained:

[T]he military businesses were competitors or were competing with the old business tycoon investments, because the old business tycoon[s] of the Mubarak regime were owners of heavy industries in steel, in cement, in [chemicals], and such things. And the military was also building factories of cement and steel and heavy industry. So the military was competing with them, and this created a lot of tension between the military and the old business tycoon[s] of Mubarak and Gamal Mubarak, which also helped with the military taking the side of the 2011 Revolution.[148]

The true character of the post-Morsi phase of transition towards increased military dominance was exposed from the very beginning in the circumstances surrounding the Beblawi cabinet's economic policy of mild Keynesian inspiration, as noted by *Bloomberg Businessweek*:

The army has been expanding its businesses since the 1970s. ... Now it is filling a vacuum created by the end of the Mubarak era, when Hosni and his son Gamal controlled the fates of many tycoons. The Mubaraks' influence has vanished, and companies run by their supporters, which before 2011 would have won bids, are not assured of success now.

This became clear when a government stimulus package of 30 billion Egyptian pounds ($4 billion) was announced in August 2013, financed in large part by the UAE. A close look at the distribution of funds suggests the army got half the projects, including paving roads and industrial infrastructure deals, according to Mohamed Farouk, a member of the Egyptian Council for Economic Issues. None of the contracts, he says, went to the big construction companies, a departure from the Mubarak era.[149]

The same observation was made by Samer Atallah a few months later:

The military is simply no longer content to stay out of politics in exchange for certain economic privileges. Their old "rule but not govern" formula is increasingly being rejected in favor of a greater stake in politics that will safeguard economic rents. To guarantee this economic expansion, the army has appointed military-affiliated personnel to key government posts. Two days after the military overthrow of Mohammed Morsi on July 3, 2013, for instance, Sisi's mentor Mohamed Farid el-Tohamy was selected as head of the General Intelligence Directorate. A few days before the violent dispersal of the Rabaa sit-in, the army backed the appointment of governors who were mostly retired military generals. [In October 2014], Khaled Abdel-Sallam al-Sadr, another retired general, was appointed as secretary-general of parliament, a position that runs the legislative body's daily operation and manages which laws will be debated.

Also within a short period after the July 3 military takeover, the army-backed government issued an executive decree expanding ministers' powers to sign contracts without competitive bidding. Infrastructure projects, including those covered by a $4.9 billion stimulus package mostly funded by the UAE, were thus earmarked to military-affiliated enterprises.[150]

Under Sisi's presidency, Egypt's armed forces were directly involved in the construction of the New Suez Canal, as already noted, with the financial opacity that is characteristic of their enterprises. They thereby displayed a pattern of cronyism in relation to the private sector worthy of Gamal Mubarak – as if they had removed him only to replace him in the same business. This pattern is described well by Abdel-Fattah Barayez:

> With time the military ceded some of its share of [the New Suez Canal Development] project to the private sector firms to benefit from their expertise and to ensure the timely completion of this politically significant initiative. More than seventy private sector companies were brought on board, including construction giants Orascom and Ayubco.

Interestingly, the military followed a similar approach in [a] power plants project. It brought in the privately owned Al Swidi and Orascom as partners in efforts to build turbines in Asyut and Damietta. Rather than crowding out private competition, then, the military ceded part of its share – and thus potential economic return – to the private sector. It did so in order to secure the successful advancement of national projects that are seen as essential to the legitimisation of the Sisi regime.[151]

Opaque as military business could be, commented *Bloomberg Businessweek*, "What is clear is that the canal – the latest in a long line of megaprojects – will cement the Egyptian armed forces' central role in Egypt's economy, sidelining other businesses and civilian institutions."[152] Indeed. All major economic projects under Sisi will tend inevitably to confirm this central role, as Shana Marshall concluded in a well-informed survey of the evolution of Egypt's military's economic empire over the past few years:

For most of the Egyptian Armed Forces' recent history, its role in the economy has been defined less by its dominance of megaprojects and more by its ability to leverage marginal influence across an enormous range of enterprises financed by both foreign capital and wealthy Egyptian businessmen. ... This form of military economic interference has rarely been onerous enough to deter would-be investors in sectors such as energy, petrochemicals, and real estate, which are where foreign investment in Egypt has long been concentrated. It is, however, enough to ensure that the military remains an important gatekeeper for investment in new projects.

Sisi's security measures – including a law that formalised the military's role in protecting critical infrastructure (previously the remit of police) – are likely to enhance that gatekeeping role by generating additional contacts and linkages between the generals and the businessmen that finance this infrastructure. Such conditions suggest that future foreign investment is likely to be more concentrated in ventures where the military has a stake – not less.[153]

If it takes off, the new Capital City project will be no exception to this economic gatekeeping rule. It will greatly contribute to the ongoing enhancement and expansion of the economic role of the military. In early December 2015, Sisi issued a decree authorising the armed forces to create real estate development companies alone or in partnership with private companies, including foreign companies. This was obviously a prelude to the military's heavy involvement in the new Capital City project, especially since part of the land allocated for it belongs to the armed forces.[154] Egyptian entrepreneurs and businessmen have been protesting more and more openly at the military's encroachment on their areas of activity, which they see as utterly unfair competition given that the armed forces enjoy many privileges with regard to taxation, energy prices, free use of military equipment and manpower, and priority contracting.[155]

Another, more classical, aspect of the military dimension of the new Capital City project has been overlooked by most commentators. It is related to a well-known historical pattern, namely the spatial displacement of the nerve centre of power in keeping with a strategic counter-revolutionary rationale. This could not have escaped the trained eye of a specialist in the strategic dimension of architecture like Léopold Lambert, who stressed the similarities of the Egyptian megaproject with "Georges-Eugène Haussmann's masterplan to radically transform Paris between 1853 and 1870, which is well-known to have facilitated the counter-insurrectionist military movements once implemented" – an allusion to the bloody repression (some 10,000 killed in one single Bloody Week, according to a moderate estimate) of the 1871 Paris Commune – as well as with "the appropriation of the brand new Brazilian capital by the military dictatorship in 1964":

The military understands that, despite their overwhelming domination, the control of an urban fabric is easier to implement when undertaken at the source, in the designing phase of the city. It is thus not that surprising to see a soldier-president deciding to create a new city, where military control will be fully part of the agenda (whether it is explicit as such, or not). ...

Incorporating the governmental, consular and economic entities of Cairo, this new capital is likely to increase the social fragmentation of a city, whether it is indeed incorporating a certain degree of privatization or not. Cairo is already using distance as a means of social segregation – it is not the only city in the world – and the relocation of the middle and higher social classes fifty miles further is part of such a strategy. ...

Distance is however not the only favoring condition for control. The very physicality of the new city, almost always makes it easier to implement a control of its space than in the context of an historical city. The reason for this holds in the practice of architecture design itself: a masterplan, whether designed by one or several offices, always corresponds to a vision anticipating the organization in space of the bodies living in it.[156]

This view is confirmed by Mohamed Elshahed, another architect writing in a remarkable issue of Lambert's review *The Funambulist* on militarised cities. In his contribution on Cairo's militarised landscape, of which the new Capital City project is but a natural extension, Elshahed observes that the master plan for the new Capital shows no open public spaces: "The complicity of designers in denying the Egyptian public the possibility of a large open space despite the events of 2011 [or rather because of them – GA] shows that militarization of urban space can often begin on the architect's drawing boards."[157] In that sense, the Capital is the military's response to Tahrir Square. In light of which, Lambert is absolutely right to stress that the new Capital City project "should not be judged for its success or, rather, its success [i.e. its actual implementation] is precisely what should be feared here."[158]

Whither Egypt?

The strategic lesson of all of the above is that no revolution in Egypt will succeed in dismantling the military-security state unless it manages to win the hearts and minds of the troops, instead of committing the fatal mistake of seeking the support of the brass, as was the case in both 2011 and 2013. Short of this, the top of the military-security pyramid, which is a crucial component of the top of the social pyramid, will not hesitate to bloodily crush any mass movement, whatever the cost in human lives. In that sense, the Rabi'a massacre is a harbinger of the repression to come, should Sisi – who has proved that he is much more inclined to mass-scale brutal repression than any of Egypt's previous presidents – face an uprising against him similar to the one that put an end to Mubarak's presidency.

This is not at all a remote possibility: as explained above, the social and economic conditions have steadily continued to worsen in Egypt since 2011, arousing a high level of social protest. Despite Sisi's and his fans' conviction that his iron fist would bring stability and foreign-funded prosperity to the country, the new-old regime did not even succeed in stemming the most basic expression of class struggle: workers' protests. Although, according to ECESR data, the total number of these protests in 2014 (1,655) represented a decline from the all-time peak reached in 2013 (2,239), exceeding the peak reached the year before (1,969), they were still more than their number in 2011 (1,400) – the year of the uprising. This is all the more noteworthy because the number for 2011 represented a huge leap in comparison with all preceding years, the previous all-time peak (728) having been reached in 2009.[159] The year 2015 was inaugurated yet again by a massive strike of the 24,000 textile workers of Mahalla. According to the data provided by the El-Mahrousa Center for Socioeconomic Development, the nine-month period from January to September 2015 saw significantly more workers' protests on average than the nine-month period from April to December 2014, with peaks in February–April and June.[160]

In a judgement intended to intimidate the working class –
a glaring confirmation of the *ubuesque* reputation that Egypt's
judiciary deservingly acquired in the Sisi era – the High
Administrative Court issued a ruling on 18 April 2015 banning
strikes and allowing the dismissal of strikers on the grounds that
strike action contravened the Sharia. This judgement – worthy of
the Saudi kingdom where unions, collective bargaining, strikes
and public demonstrations are all banned – was met with a general
outcry in left and liberal opposition circles, appalled to see that they
had contributed to toppling the Muslim Brotherhood only to reap
a misuse of religion that the Brothers themselves would have found
difficult to condone.[161] It came as a prelude to the implementation,
beginning in July, of a new civil service law that was enacted in
March, prior to the Sharm el-Sheikh international conference, in
further compliance with IMF dictates. Presented as fundamentally
aimed at reforming Egypt's administrative apparatus by curbing
bureaucratic inefficiencies in order to encourage investment, the
law has a negative effect on the income and conditions of work
of most of Egypt's 7 million civil servants, changing the system of
bonuses and paid leave and increasing managerial powers, including
the power to dismiss.[162]

On 10 August, thousands of Real Estate Tax Authority
employees gathered in central Cairo in the most important
industrial action of its kind since Morsi's overthrow, reminiscent
of the action that the same employees had initiated in 2007, before
founding the country's first independent union in fifty years. The
regime did not dare apply against them its very repressive Protest
Law, which provides for imprisonment of up to seven years and
fines in case of the unauthorised gathering of more than ten persons
in a public place. Nor was the ruling by the High Administrative
Court used against the strikers, needless to say. This event was
compounded a few days later by a more unusual type of strike, and
a most significant one: on 22 August, hundreds of low-ranking
police officers went on strike for two days, organising a sit-in in
front of the security directorate of the Sharqiya governorate in the

Nile Delta. Like many of Egypt's public-sector workers, they were demanding unpaid bonuses, along with access to the hospitals used by their higher-ranking counterparts. It was not the first time low-ranking policemen were protesting: in February 2014, they had undertaken similar actions in front of the security directorates of Alexandria and Kafr al-Sheikh, demanding an increase in their risk allowance, end-of-service benefits and "martyr" compensations. They also demanded modern weapons and tougher punishment for assaults on the police, as well as the dismissal of the interior minister at the time, Mohamed Ibrahim.

The government tried to repress the Sharqiya policemen's action by sending in the Central Security Forces (CSF) on the second day. In response to the tear gas that the latter fired to disperse them, the policemen fired shots into the air, prompting the CSF soldiers to withdraw from the scene. Chanting *Irhal!* ("Leave!"), a slogan much used since the beginning of the Arab uprising in 2011, the policemen demanded the dismissal of the minister of interior, Magdy Abdel-Ghaffar, who was appointed in March 2015 in replacement of Ibrahim. The Sharqiya policemen received expressions of support from their counterparts across Egypt, in a development highly worrying to the regime.[163] As a result, they were no more subjected to the repressive laws than the real estate tax employees, in spite of their unlawful use of their weapons. The interior minister had to resort to ridiculous arguments to explain its unusual leniency.[164]

Although police officers are part of the state's repressive apparatus, their lower ranks belong to poor sections of the population, and earn modest incomes that contrast sharply with the incomes and privileges of the top ranks.[165] Their action pointed to the crucial vulnerability of the military-security apparatus in Egypt, which is classically – in particular for bodies relying on conscription – the fact that it ultimately reflects the country's overall social stratification. The CSF conscripts' uprising in 1986 was one of the most outstanding eruptions of social anger in Egypt's pre-2011 history, second only to the 1977 food riots. In 1986, the

CSF conscripts – who were paid much less than those in the army – were protesting against a one-year extension of their three-year mandatory term of service. Their revolt, which involved some 25,000 of them, became violent, with hotels and nightclubs being set on fire. At that time, the Mubarak regime managed to repress them brutally by resorting to the armed forces, including air force helicopters, killing close to one hundred conscripts and dismissing most of the mutineers, with heavy punishments inflicted on many. The Sisi regime's very different attitude towards the low-ranking police officers' mutinies in 2014 and 2015 is thus the best evidence of the state's general weakening in the wake of the 2011 uprising, in spite of the new-old regime's outward bravado.

In late October 2015, tens of thousands of workers went on strike again for more than ten days on the issue of bonus payments. The movement was led once again by the Mahalla textile workers. It ended victoriously, the government – a new cabinet headed by Sherif Ismail having been sworn in on 19 September – ceding to the workers' pressure for fear of increased social anger in a period of ongoing parliamentary elections. This was a further indication, following many others, of the fact that the Egyptian revolutionary process that had begun in January 2011 was far from over.

The struggle goes on, despite frantic efforts by the new-old regime to shore up its dwindling popularity by resorting with ever-increasing intensity to consent-seeking gestures borrowed from the George W. Bush handbook of the "war on terror". As the experience of that handbook's author amply showed, the success of this political device in achieving consent hinges on the success of its self-fulfilling prophecy in increasing terrorism. Bush brilliantly succeeded in expanding terrorism globally, but the efficiency of US security apparatuses in preventing further attacks on US soil was ultimately fatal to his popularity, once the trauma of 9/11 had faded away. Unlike the former US president, Sisi can be confident that his own security apparatuses will not be so efficient in checking terrorism on Egyptian soil. However, he faces an unsolvable dilemma in the fact that the terrorist activities that can enhance consent to his regime are at the same time certain to thwart his economic ambitions and contribute to the deterioration of Egypt's socio-economic conditions in a way that can only further undermine his popularity. The expected response of a man of his background to such a dilemma, eventually, is simply to increase repression.

Unless the strategic conundrum of the Egyptian revolution with regard to the military-security state is successfully addressed – an eventuality that requires a higher degree of organisation and strategic thinking than what has existed in the past – future upsurges risk being met with a further escalation in bloody repression. This would throw more fuel on the terrorist fire, which tends increasingly to spill out from the Sinai, within which it has been mostly circumscribed up to the time of writing.[166] The barbaric manner of the ejection of the Muslim Brotherhood from Egyptian politics has already led to a radicalisation of part of its membership, especially among the youth, in a way that may well end up swelling the ranks of the barbaric al-Qaida–ISIS axis.[167] In Egypt, as in the whole Arab region, the alternatives on offer remain, more than ever, radical progressive social and political change or a deepening clash of barbarisms.

Conclusion

"Arab Winter" and Hope

Yet in every winter's heart there is a quivering spring, and behind the veil of each night there is a smiling dawn. Thence did my despair turn into a form of hope.

Gibran Khalil Gibran,
"Letter to May Ziadeh" (1920)

As mentioned in the Introduction to this book, the successful Iran-backed offensive launched by the Syrian regime in the spring of 2013, followed by the 3 July coup in Egypt and its bloody consequences, ushered in a region-wide counter-revolutionary phase involving a chain reaction in the countries that experienced the mass uprisings of 2011. Only in Bahrain had the upsurge been defeated early on, due to the repressive support of the Saudi "big brother" to the monarchy. It deterred the radicalisation of the opposition and its recourse to arms.[1] Everywhere else, the situation evolved into various shapes of one and the same essence: the clash between the two regional counter-revolutionary camps – the forces of the old regime and its Islamic fundamentalist contenders.

Libya and Yemen: Two Variations on the Same Tune

Libya was directly and naturally affected by the coup in neighbouring Egypt. The 7 July 2012 election of the General National Congress

– the first ever free election in Libya, sixty years after independence – had seen a remarkable turnout of over 60 per cent of registered voters. Assessing it shortly thereafter, I noted the poor score that the Libyan Muslim Brotherhood (its Justice and Construction Party) had achieved only a few days after their neighbouring Egyptian co-thinkers had won the presidential elections, on top of the parliamentary elections they had dominated a few months earlier.[2] This took place against the backdrop of a Libyan situation that I described as one in which "the armed forces have been dismantled and replaced by a host of militias formed in the course of the civil war; the changes have been so far-reaching and rapid that the prevailing situation is dangerously chaotic."[3]

Libya's first year after the fall of Muammar Gaddafi witnessed one of the most vibrant instances of "blooming" of the "Arab Spring", with a civil society blossoming in several hundred organisations of all kinds, from democratic to feminist, from cultural to social, filling the void created by the collapse of a totalitarian state that had suppressed modern civil society for four decades.[4] Unfortunately, this was soon overwhelmed by armed chaos. The lack of a recognised and able leadership of the uprising allowed the militias to fill the void created by the collapse of the armed apparatuses of Gaddafi's state. This was facilitated by the inept and weak decision of the National Transition Council, under pressure from the militias, to grant their members pay from public coffers, thus turning them into a privileged category compared to the remaining members of the regular armed forces. The alternative would have been to demand that they join overhauled state-controlled armed bodies. At the very least, the payroll should have been limited to those who had really taken part in the civil war. Instead, the consequence of empowering the militias without real constraints was that, in less than a year after the fall of Gaddafi, the number of their enrolled men had jumped tenfold, to 250,000.[5]

Unsurprisingly, tensions continued to be exacerbated between the two camps that had united in the fight against Gaddafi's regime: on the one hand, the Libyan Muslim Brotherhood, backed by its

Egyptian counterpart, along with a range of Islamic fundamentalist militias that sprang up in the country during the uprising and civil war, and even more so in their aftermath; on the other hand, the civilian and military remnants of Gaddafi's state, wary that the Islamic fundamentalists' claim to rule Libya could put their jobs in jeopardy, along with liberal, secularist, feminist and left-wing groups that shared their wariness for political reasons. The remnants of the state worried all the more since the Islamic camp wanted to purge state bodies of anyone who had been involved with Muammar Gaddafi's regime, in a way reminiscent of the anti-Baath purge implemented in US-occupied Iraq.[6] This second camp fell in 2014 under the military hegemony of General Khalifa Haftar, a former companion of Gaddafi who had broken with him in the late 1980s, joined the US-backed Libyan opposition in exile, and lived in the United States from 1990 until his return to Libya in 2011.

Emboldened by the anti-Morsi coup in neighbouring Egypt, Haftar led the reconstituted remnants of the Libyan armed forces in the spring of 2014 in an offensive aimed at ridding the country of the "terrorists", by which he meant the Islamic fundamentalist militias. He thus became a magnet for former Gaddafi tribal partisans, humiliated by the same militias. His move was the final and decisive episode in pitching the country into a second civil war, accompanied by the division of Libya's long coastal territory between areas dominated by competing factions – Haftar's forces in the east and far west, the Muslim brotherhood-led camp (Libya Dawn) in the Tripoli-Misrata area, with self-styled Islamic State forces (improperly called ISIS outside Iraq and Syria) managing to take control of the central region of Sirte (Gaddafi's birthplace)[7] – not to mention other locally autonomous militias.

Haftar's dictatorial approach led the Islamic fundamentalist camp to portray him as a would-be reincarnation of Gaddafi, whose legacy it purports to be the true eradicator as it claims exclusive revolutionary legitimacy for itself. The truth, however, is that Haftar's model is not, and could not be, that of Gaddafi. It was actually the military commander turned authoritarian head of state in neighbouring Egypt, Abdul-Fattah al-Sisi, whose war-on-terror vocabulary Haftar adopted. To a large extent, Libya's second civil war is an extension on Libyan soil of the confrontation between the Sisi regime and Egypt's Muslim Brotherhood, with the United Arab Emirates involved along with Cairo on Haftar's side, and Qatar and Turkey backing the Islamic fundamentalist camp.[8]

In parallel to the turn of events igniting the civil war in Libya, a similar process unfolded in Yemen. The so-called "Yemeni solution" praised by Barack Obama in 2012 as a model for Syria was based on a Saudi-sponsored agreement between former president Ali Abdallah Saleh and the opposition, concluded in November 2011. By virtue of this agreement, Saleh handed the presidency to his vice president, Abd Rabbuh Mansur Hadi (a step that was formalised through a presidential election held in February 2012, with Hadi as sole candidate), resulting in the formation of a government of national unity. I concluded my assessment in October 2012 as follows:

> Ali Saleh continues to play a direct, central role in Yemeni polit-
> ics as the leader of the majority party in parliament; his son still
> commands the Republican Guard and his nephew is still Director
> of National Security. Of all the victories of the great Arab uprising
> down to the time of writing, the Yemeni victory has, incontestably,
> been the most superficial. Not only has the change to which the
> uprising gave rise left the underlying causes of the explosion intact;
> it has not even gone far enough to usher in a period of temporary,
> relative stabilisation before the revolution pursues its course – or the
> country sinks into chaos.

The ingredients for a plunge into chaos were, to be sure, completely overwhelming. The rickety compromise of November 2011 could not last. It created a duality of power in the country, thus facilitating the spectacular growth of all sorts of armed groups, including al-Qaida, with entire regions falling out of state control into their hands.[9] For the new president to be able to rule, he needed to dismantle Saleh's grip over a major section of the state, starting with its military-security apparatuses. Hadi did indeed begin in 2012 gradually to demote Saleh's men from key positions. Then, in April 2013, he removed Ahmed Saleh, the former president's son, from his position as commander of the Republican Guard and Special Forces, and appointed him as an ambassador abroad.[10] These measures could only incense Ali Saleh, who was not willing to cede his positions of power, but intended on the contrary to restore his family and clan's rule in the Yemeni state as soon as conditions ripened for a takeover.

"There is no doubt that Mr Saleh still wields enormous power here," wrote Robert Worth in a *New York Times* report in January 2014.[11] "He remains the leader of Mr Hadi's own political party, to the president's chagrin. Many in the military are still loyal to him." The report astutely described the unfolding of what became the dominant feature of Yemen's situation in the course of that same year, 2014, against a background of increasing sectarian polarisation in the country:[12]

Recently, [Mr Saleh] has signaled an alliance of sorts with the Houthis, an insurgent group in the far north-west with which he fought a bitter, intermittent war for years. The Houthis have grown into a broad national political movement since 2011, fueled largely by a hatred of Islah, the Yemeni Islamist party that is the equivalent of the Muslim Brotherhood. Mr Saleh hates them both, but he clearly also resents Mr Hadi, who frequently disparages him.[13]

Saleh did indeed strike an alliance with the Huthi movement, an Islamic fundamentalist rebellion from within the same Zaidi sect of Shi'i Islam to which he himself belongs. This was despite the fact that the Huthi rebellion had presented a major armed challenge to Saleh's rule for many years, and had joined the uprising against him in 2011.[14] This unlikely alliance soon materialised to enable what was reductively and inaccurately described as a "Huthi offensive", sweeping the country from north to south in the course of 2014. In fact, it was to a large extent a counter-offensive involving the forces loyal to Saleh, as Helen Lackner emphasised in January 2015:

> How did the Huthis rise from being a minority regional politico-military movement to taking complete control over the formal state in less than one year? Long suspected by most Yemenis, but ignored by the international community, and denied by both concerned parties, the alliance between the Huthis and Saleh has been the main factor behind their military success. The vast majority of the Huthis' armed forces are military and security units loyal to Saleh who follow his orders. Moreover even senior Huthi leaders take orders from Saleh, as revealed by a recently leaked telephone conversation between Saleh and Abdul Wahed Abu Ras (Huthi representative at the NDC) where the former orders the latter to coordinate activities with Saleh loyalists, to ensure they control the country's borders; they even discuss the appointment of the next Prime Minister: Abu Ras meekly acquiesces. Last week, it also emerged that the military refused to obey the Minister of Defence's order to protect the Presidential Palace and other strategic locations in Sana'a: the only group who fought back were the President's personal guard, suffering heavy casualties.
>
> Last September, people wondered how the Huthis managed to take control of the capital, Sana'a, without firing a shot; the answer is clearly that the army and security forces made no move to defend the legitimate regime of President Hadi. ... It was also thanks to Saleh's military forces that the Huthis defeated the al Ahmars and the Islah party in Amran Governorate, where they burned down the houses of the leading shaykhs.[15]

Saleh had been emboldened to act by the turn of events in Egypt since the July 2013 coup. He saw the conditions for a similar comeback of his family's regime gathering in the increasing chaos into which the country had been sinking since he stepped down – a chaos he did his best to stoke, as it could only work in his favour. Indeed, a growing number of Yemenis came to "appreciate the relative stability during his rule", as a June 2014 report noted, offering the following illustration: "In an indication of the reactionary spirit, pictures of Saleh's son, Ahmed Ali Saleh, often beside Egyptian General Abdelfattah al-Sisi, have become common in the capital."[16] Saleh senior himself did not hide his enthusiastic admiration for Egypt's new "strong man", as in his symptomatic statement to *Al-Ahram Weekly* in November 2014 that "the Arab Spring is bad and that it was backed by the Zionists. But there is a bright candle now with the presence of President Abdel-Fattah Al-Sisi at the top of the pyramid of power in Egypt, and with the elimination of the Muslim Brotherhood ... "[17]

The intricacies of Yemeni society, one of the most complex of Arab societies,[18] thus produced yet another variant of the regional pattern of confrontation between two counter-revolutionary camps. There, the Zaidi–Shi'i old regime's men, in alliance with a Zaidi–Shi'i Islamic fundamentalist force, clashed with the Sunni coalition of forces that had issued from the uprising, in which the Muslim Brotherhood and other Sunni fundamentalists played a prominent role in alliance with left and nationalist groups (the Joint Meeting Parties alliance). Meanwhile the terroristic al-Qaida and Islamic State gained ground – taking advantage, as elsewhere, of civil war.[19] In short, this was a situation bearing a striking resemblance to the Syrian alignment of forces. One major difference, however, was that foreign direct involvement in the civil war in Yemen was not that of Iran and Russia on the side of the old regime, as in Syria, but that of a Saudi-led coalition on the side of the post-uprising opposition-turned-government. The Saudi bombing of Yemen has been murderous and destructive, even though it pales in comparison to Russia's bombing and Iran's involvement in Syria.

The Tunisian "Model" and Its Limits

Sisi's 2013 coup also had, most naturally and inevitably, a huge impact on the fourth Arab country along with Egypt, Libya and

Yemen, where the Muslim Brotherhood – in the Tunisian case, their local sister organisation, the Ennahda Movement – had come to power in the wake of the 2011 Arab uprising. Assessing the prospects of the Ennahda-dominated Tunisian government in October 2012, my prognosis was that the economy's performance under its stewardship would be "worse than under the dictatorship":

> This is due to a number of factors: the instability of post-dictatorial Tunisia; Ennahda's incompetence when it comes to capitalist management; Tunisian capitalism's mistrust of a populist, petty-bourgeois movement of religious inspiration that includes a hardcore fundamentalist component and has taken an accommodating stance toward the Salafists; and, above all, the movement's inability to forestall the intensification of social struggles whose protagonists have been emboldened by the uprising's victory.[20]

This, I asserted, was one reason why the Ennahda-dominated government had "adopted so accommodating a stance toward the repressive apparatus bequeathed it by the dictator".[21] Another reason – the most important one, to be sure – was plainly revealed in the words of Ennahda's founder-president himself, Rached al-Ghannouchi, when he addressed a delegation of Salafists paying him a visit in his movement's headquarters. In the video that was leaked and broadcast in October 2012, creating a scandal, Ghannouchi explains to his visitors why conditions in Tunisia were not appropriate for adding a reference to the Sharia into the new constitution, which the Constituent Assembly elected in October 2011 was then drafting.[22]

His main argument was that the key pillars of power – media, economy, administration, army and police – were in the hands of the secular elite, and that it was necessary to take this balance of forces into consideration, lest the Tunisian Islamic movement come to know a fate similar to that of its counterpart in neighbouring Algeria, where a bloody coup suppressed it just as it was about to win the parliamentary elections of January 1992. Thus, it was unwise to try to impose a reference to the Sharia, whereas there was a broad agreement on including a reference to Islam as the Tunisian state's religion – a fact that Ghannouchi regarded as a key achievement to be consolidated. For that, he exhorted his Salafist visitors to create associations and Quranic schools in order to spread their message until the balance of forces became more appropriate for further steps in Islamising the country.

Salafism started growing after the Tunisian uprising as one result of the frustration of expectations in the aftermath of Ben Ali's downfall, all the more because the workers' movement – the powerful Tunisian General Labour Union, also known by its French acronym, UGTT, which is by far the most important organised social movement in Tunisia[23] – and the Tunisian Left – which is coalesced in the Popular Front and has become hegemonic in the UGTT's leadership since 2011 – failed to harness those frustrations. Likewise, dissensions appeared within Ennahda itself between those sensitive to Salafist pressure and the moderates.[24]

The combination of increasing Salafist-perpetrated attacks and assassinations with the overall performance of Ennahda in government led in Tunisia to results similar to those brought by the Muslim Brotherhood's presidential year in Egypt: growing fear and anger in broad sectors of society that included the secular-minded and feminists, naturally, but also the workers' movement, which had been threatened with physical violence by Ennahda's militia.[25] As in Egypt, the old regime's men – the Tunisian "deep state" and the old political elite – exploited that fear and anger in order to stage a comeback. The assassination on 6 February 2013 of Chokri Belaid, one of the leading figures of the Tunisian Popular Front, led to a huge outpouring of mass anger against Ennahda, which was held responsible for creating the political conditions for the assassination, when not accused of having directly perpetrated it.

The assassination a few months later, on 25 July, of Mohamed Brahmi – another prominent figure of the Popular Front – led to the foundation on the next day of the National Salvation Front (NSF), bringing together the Popular Front's key parties as well as

Nidaa Tounes ("Tunisia's call") and a few centre-left and liberal groups. Founded in 2012 in order to fill the vacuum created by the dissolution of Ben Ali's ruling party, Nidaa Tounes is basically composed of old regime's men, with a few liberal and centre-left figures added to them in order to offer a semblance of change. The Tunisian NSF was thus the equivalent of its Egyptian namesake; it even included a Tunisian Tamarrod, though this failed to reproduce the Egyptian original's success. The NSF called for a popular anti-Ennahda rally on 6 August 2013, which turned out to be a true Tunisian equivalent of Egypt's 30 June 2013 anti-Muslim Brotherhood mobilisation. There remain two major differences between the two countries in this respect: the key role of the workers' movement in the mobilisation and the absence of direct army role, Tunisia being a country with no tradition of military rule. Other components of the "deep state" were nonetheless part of the action.

Sadri Khiari, a Tunisian observer who cannot be suspected of a priori hostility to Ennahda, neatly described the 6 August rally:

> No one can deny the extraordinary scale of the national mobilisation that expressed itself [on 6 August 2013]. Impressive logistics, mysterious funding sources, suspicious complicities, of course. But only resentment, bad faith or wilful blindness can pretend that the gathering of such a huge crowd by Tunisian standards is simply a result of manipulation. Bourgeois from La Marsa, unemployed from Menzel Bouzaïene, wage-earners from everywhere, "post-modern" artists, people coming only for fun or to be "in" – in short, an astonishing social patchwork dominated by the "middle classes" – that's probably true as well. Leftists of the worst kind, good-looking democrats, all kinds of trade-unionists, communists, Arab nationalists and *Hezbfrancists* ["France's party" people], progressives by sentiment, hard and soft secularists, people nostalgic for Bourguibism [Bourguiba was the founder of modern Tunisia, whose regime Ben Ali continued in a more corrupt form] and occasional Bourguibists, partisans of "enlightened" military

rule and others of worker-management democracy, people with no opinion and other *khobzistes* [from *khubz*, Arabic for bread, meaning *opportunists*], this messy diversity is a fact; no one can deny it, as no one can deny the demonstrators' multiple motivations, the dissonant slogans, and the fundamental contradictions that run like a thread between the diverse social interests that converged in Bardo Square.

It would be quite inept, however, or stupidly polemical, not to recognise in this paradoxical gathering the fully justified expression of a discontent or serious worry with regard to Tunisia's future, which is broadly shared in the whole country and – by virtue of different interests – by all social categories.[26]

The result in Tunisia of the events of 6 August was also similar to that of those in Egypt on 30 June, in the sense that they opened the way to what is, in essence, a comeback of old-regime men: Nidaa Tounes won a plurality in the October 2014 parliamentary election, and its leader, Beji Caid Essebsi, was elected president of Tunisia in the November 2014 presidential election, a few months after the election of his Egyptian counterpart Abdul-Fattah al-Sisi. But here again there are important differences between the two processes, the major factor in this respect being Ennahda's attitude.

Already quite impressed by the tragic repression of his Algerian co-thinkers, Ghannouchi was no doubt appalled by the tragic downfall of his Egyptian fellows only a few weeks before 6 August. In striking contrast to the Egyptian Muslim Brotherhood's foolish intransigence, he thus accepted a compromise whereby the Ennahda-dominated government would give way to a "technocratic" transitional government in January 2014, which oversaw the elections held in autumn of the same year. It may very well be that Ghannouchi was relieved that his movement came second in the parliamentary election. In any event, Ennahda – again, in stark contrast with its Egyptian co-thinkers – put forward no candidate of its own to the presidential election, contenting itself with supporting the incumbent president, the Ennahda-friendly liberal Moncef Marzouki.

Another key factor in facilitating the smooth return of the old regime was the role played by the Left, and the ability of the powerful UGTT to act as a political power broker in Tunisia. A dominant section of the Tunisian Left organised in the Popular Front leaned towards an electoral and political alliance with Nidaa Tounes. In fact, the Popular Front contributed decisively to bringing Nidaa Tounes back in from the cold, where it had been confined as a result of being reviled by both the Left and Ennahda, as representing the ousted old regime. By entering into the NSF alliance with Nidaa Tounes, the Tunisian Left contributed to the rehabilitation of the latter, as did the assassinations' impact in stoking up fear of Islamic fundamentalism and a longing for a strong state.

The UGTT thus acted as a mediator between the two class enemies of its working-class constituency: Nidaa Tounes and Ennahda. Moreover, it did so by bringing back in from the cold its direct nemesis, the employers' association, UTICA (the French acronym for Tunisian Union of Industry, Trade and Handicrafts), which was just as reviled as the old regime's political elite, since a dominant part of its membership consisted of the politically connected crony capitalists who had prospered under Ben Ali. (The World Bank noticed the existence of this crony capitalism only after the dictator's downfall, so much so that it suddenly adopted a revolutionary tone – only a tone, of course – in describing Tunisia's upheaval as an *unfinished revolution*.[27]) The UGTT's mediation allowed the process to be smooth; however, as Hèla Yousfi wrote,

> if the UGTT, first architect of the national dialogue, has more or less succeeded in appeasing the political tensions thanks to a laboriously constructed consensus, one cannot fail to observe that this consensus has been reduced to power-sharing between the old ruling elite and the new elite that emerged from the ballot box, thus widening the gap between two antagonistic visions of democracy: the vision that crystallises the democratic claim around party representativeness

and electoral competition, and the vision that considers that there is no viable democracy as long as social demands are not placed at the centre of the priorities and political alternatives on offer. The UGTT that agrees to forge a united front with the bosses, in order to be able to find a negotiated equilibrium between the various political and social forces, takes the risk of seeing its own capacity for social action weakened.[28]

One important result of the Tunisian power transition having proceeded in a much smoother and more peaceful way than the Egyptian one is that a coalition government – dominated by old-regime men and members of Nidaa Tounes, but including one minister representing Ennahda – took office in February 2015. This was the result of Nidaa Tounes not having secured enough parliamentary votes for a more restrictive cabinet, but also of its preference for a coalition with Ennahda over one with the Popular Front, part of which was willing to partner with the new-old ruling party.

This outcome greatly delighted Washington and the European Union, which had wished a similar scenario might have been possible in Egypt. After all, like the SCAF and Muslim Brotherhood in Egypt, Nidaa Tounes and Ennahda share a dedication to a neoliberal socio-economic perspective – so much so that the mood of reconciliation went so far as to allow the coalition government to draft a "reconciliation law" granting amnesty to businessmen and civil servants who had committed financial crimes or misused public funds. They would be amnestied in exchange for their admission of guilt and willingness to pay back their ill-gotten gains with 5 per cent interest – a transaction that undermined the transitional justice procedure that had been painstakingly put in place in December 2013.[29] The Norwegian Nobel Committee was so pleased that it awarded the 2015 Nobel Peace Prize to the Tunisian National Dialogue Quartet, composed of the UGTT, UTICA and two other partners of the mediation between Nidaa Tounes and Ennahda – the lawyers' guild and a human rights organisation.[30]

Accelerating the political-security dimension of this same backward process, the terrorist attacks perpetrated by Islamic State members in March and June 2015 were an occasion for the adoption of an "anti-terrorist law" denounced by human rights organisations as a threat to civil rights and liberties. The mantra of the "war on terror" has served as a justification for a return to the foreground of prominent members of Ben Ali's security apparatuses.[31] Tunisia is thus walking back with long strides into a restoration of the old regime, under the presidency of the world's third-oldest head of state after Zimbabwe's Robert Mugabe and Queen Elizabeth II of England.

The frustration of the 2011 "youth revolution" was thus complete. Under such circumstances, it was no wonder that Tunisian youth boycotted the elections en masse, like their Egyptian counterpart, with over 70 per cent of those under thirty-one abstaining in 2014.[32] Equally, it was no surprise that Tunisia, the Arab country whose youth had the strongest reasons for hope in 2011, was the country from where the largest contingent of young people relative to its population has joined the so-called Islamic State. The root causes of the social exasperation that led to the self-immolation of Mohamed Bouazizi on 17 December 2010 to act as a spark setting on an all-engulfing fire have only been aggravated by the pursuit of neoliberal policies against a backdrop of political turmoil. Anouar Boukhars aptly summarised this calamitous situation:

> The economy remains fragile, with real growth stalling at an estimated 2.8 percent in 2014. External imbalances, rising inflation (6.5–7 percent), and a 9.2 percent deficit in public finances are major sources of stress for a government under pressure to put its fiscal house in order, tackle high unemployment (15 percent), and make investments in the marginalised areas of the country's interior and border regions.
>
> The size of the informal economy, which has grown exponentially to reach 50 percent of gross domestic product, also drags on economic growth. Contraband merchandise from Algeria and Libya is traded not just in the border regions but throughout the

country. Competition from informal vendors has led several local firms to go out of business.

The severe economic crisis the country has experienced in the four years after the revolution has contributed to this rising trend of informality. But there are also structural determinants of the black economy, chiefly bureaucratic corruption, excessive regulation, high taxes, and exorbitant start-up costs. The off-the-books business will continue to thrive as long as the state is unable to provide alternatives in the formal economy and tackle corruption. ...

The disparity between Tunisia's coastal areas and its precariously marginalised periphery is a source of destabilization and a threat to democratic consolidation. The last four years have not improved the economic experience of these regions.[33]

The Arab Left and the Strategic Challenge

The frustration of the hopes created by revolutions is a classical source of the development of terrorism, as a fringe expression of that frustration. The frustration of the hopes created by the French revolutionary situation of May–June 1968 and the wave of youth revolt that swept Europe in that same year led to the emergence of a left-wing terrorism, of which the main theatres were France, Germany and Italy. Other countries witnessed a similar phenomenon.

The frustration of the hopes created by the 2011 "Arab Spring" is likewise one major source of recruits to Islamic fundamentalist terrorism, drawing young people from around the Arab region. Terroristic escapism follows the easiest available path: in the late 1960s and the 1970s, the counter-hegemonic ideology was predominantly radical-left at the global level, including in the Arab region. For reasons that I explained at length in *The People Want* and other writings, it is Islamic fundamentalism that has become the dominant counter-hegemonic ideology in the Arab region since the 1980s. It is hence naturally on the escapist outskirts of

Islamic fundamentalism that the current frustration is manifesting itself regionally.

Present-day Islamic fundamentalist terrorism is, however, incomparably more brutal and powerful than the left-wing terrorism of yesteryear, to say nothing of the fact that it stands at the opposite, far-right end of the political spectrum. It is not a terrorism that the global powers can fight with police means alone, but one that they are fighting with missiles and military planes. The spectacular development and expansion of the so-called Islamic State over the four years that have followed the 2011 "Arab Spring", while its terrorist offshoots were engaging all over the world in a macabre competition with al-Qaida, has become the most blatant expression of the degeneration of the New World Order heralded by George Bush senior on 11 September 1990 into a "new world disorder".[34]

Barack Obama faces the prospect of leaving the scene with a more catastrophic balance sheet in his running of the US empire, especially in the crucially strategic Middle East, than that of any president before him. This is no small feat for a man who succeeded George W. Bush, the president who held this record himself. Obama managed to take the disaster bequeathed to him by his predecessor to new and significantly lower depths. In the face of this fast-spreading fire, the Obama administration – with John Kerry in the role of secretary of state, about whom the *Financial Times* mordantly observed that he "has demonstrated boundless confidence in his ability to solve problems if he can only bring the concerned parties together in one room"[35] – is acting like an overwhelmed and overstretched fire brigade, along with its United Nations and European Union partners. They are engaged in trying to foster compromises and reconciliations along the lines of the Tunisian model of coalition government in all major theatres of the 2011 Arab uprising: in Syria as well as in Libya, Yemen, and even in Egypt, where the fire brigade rightly believes that Sisi is stoking up the fire in his unrealistic determination to disable the Muslim Brotherhood by repressive means.

As in the Syrian case, the best one can hope at this juncture is that such conciliatory efforts be crowned with success. Arresting the tragedies that have followed the "Arab Spring" has indeed become the priority of priorities – a matter of extremely urgent basic humanitarian necessity. At the same time, whereas reconciliation and coalition building between the two counter-revolutionary camps in the Arab region – with the exception of the terrorist lunatic fringe, of course, since one key motivation of the reconciliation efforts is precisely that the two camps together might manage to eradicate it – represent the best scenario from the point of view of the Western powers, it happens to be – quite unusually – the best scenario from a progressive point of view as well.

Had the Tunisian reconciliation between the old regime and Ennahda not been successful in bringing them into coalition, the alternative might have been the disastrous collaboration of a major section of the Tunisian Left with Nidaa Tounes. This would have further jeopardised – and in the long term – the Popular Front's chances of crystallising and channelling the steadily increasing social anger, which is doomed to be exacerbated by the same neoliberal policies that are producing similar results throughout the region, after having been instrumental in provoking the 2011 uprising. The Tunisian scene would have continued to be dominated by the confrontation between the two counter-revolutionary forces of the old regime and Ennahda. With the coalition in place, the Popular Front found itself in the best position to act as the key upholder of the 17 December 2010 Revolution, and as the major political opposition to the two counter-revolutionary camps, reconciled in their common adherence to the neoliberal framework.

Alas, the Left in the Arab region has so far proved incapable of decisively opening a regional third way – not a Tony Blair-like Third Way, which is no more than neoliberalism with a smiling face, but a third pole equally opposed to the two rival poles of the regional counter-revolution: the old regime and the Islamic fundamentalists, both of them fierce enemies of the key progressive aspirations of the 2011 Arab Spring. Instead, the regional Left has developed over recent years a tradition of allying with one of the two reactionary poles against the other.[36] A section of the Left supported the regimes in the name of confronting Islamic fundamentalism, which it mislabelled as "fascism" for the sake of legitimising this betrayal of everything progressives should stand for. This was most blatantly the case in Algeria following the 1992 coup, but also in Egypt under Mubarak and Tunisia in the early 1990s – in other words, everywhere the Islamic fundamentalist movement had grown to the point of becoming a serious contender for power.

Another part of the regional Left, led by its genuine and resolute opposition to the dictatorial regimes, sought alliances with the Muslim Brotherhood. The 2005 Damascus Declaration for National Democratic Change was one such alliance. When the 2011 uprising began, this collaboration took a new shape with the participation of the most prominent component of the Syrian Left in the now-infamous Muslim Brotherhood-dominated Syrian National Council.[37] Aziz al-Azmeh had the following comment on the initial experience:

> During the period of what was called the civil society movement in Damascus, and the Damascus Spring which preceded the Arab Spring, a short while after Bashar al-Assad's inheritance of power, I made clear my view ... that the advocacy of "historic compromises" with forces opposed to modernity, democracy and secularism, such as the Muslim Brothers, under unclear circumstances and from a standpoint of organisational weakness, and the belief that democracy is a vague unqualified slogan, a magic formula that is supposed to heal all social and political illnesses – all this is very naive. ...
>
> Many years before the major events and conflicts that have taken us by surprise in recent years, I was convinced that the Islamic discourses (people were then focusing on the Brothers more than on ISIS) about democracy are more populist than democratic ... and that such forces are no partners in any historic compromise seeking the public interest. My critics said that I was passing "judgement

on intentions". This accusation is accurate and I plead guilty: in stating my position, I made a political judgement, and a political judgement without a judgement on intentions is void. There is no room for courtesy in political judgements.[38]

Al-Azmeh is right to emphasise the fact that the Muslim Brotherhood – or any groups subscribing to religious fundamentalism, whatever its religion – cannot be trusted to be true democrats, since democracy fundamentally contradicts their vision of the world. He is also right to criticise the illusion that the Left, in entering into alliance with the Muslim Brothers on vague terms and from a position of huge organisational imbalance in the latter's favour, can keep them on the desired path. However, this leaves open the issue of more limited and tactical alliances, since political action cannot be based solely on assessing the intentions of others; clearly, it must also be based on one's own goals and intentions, and the degree to which a certain set of tactics can serve the strategic goal.

The Egyptian Left encountered such dilemmas in the present century's first decade, as Maha Abdelrahman relates:

The most divisive issue over which even short-term, tactical coalitions stumbled was the desired level of confrontation of the regime and its security apparatus. For the left, the Nasserists, and youth groups from across the political spectrum, the radicalization effect of the Second Palestinian Intifada and the ensuing revival of street politics was an opportunity to expand the boundaries of confrontation with the regime. Activists seized the chance to increase the ceiling of political demands and to take their struggle out onto the streets. The MB, on the other hand, is an organization with a track record of political horse-trading and behind-the-scenes deals as part of its conciliation with the Sadat and Mubarak regimes. Members of the group were much more reluctant to openly challenge the government by taking to the street at every opportunity. This fundamental difference in strategy raised any number of tensions between the MB and rival groups.[39]

Indeed, as in Syria, where the Muslim Brotherhood, soon after the Damascus declaration was issued, entered into a sectarian-motivated, Saudi-backed alliance with a key pillar of Hafez al-Assad's regime who had broken with his master's heir, the Egyptian mother organisation made several compromises with Mubarak up to its collaboration with the SCAF, as described in Chapter 2. Maha Abdelrahman nevertheless gives a positive account of the Egyptian experience of alliance:

> The short-term, tactical cooperation between unlikely bedfellows served a clear function during the last decade of Mubarak's rule. Where successive authoritarian regimes had for decades success-fully weakened political opposition forces through a mix of tactics including co-optation, divide and rule, repressive legal measures and the use of naked violence, the divided and weak opposition could only sustain protest movements against the regime by swelling their numbers in the form of alliances. ...
>
> These coalitions, however, were short-term, tactical formations rather than long-term strategic alliances. They did not demand any meaningful compromises over fundamental issues or require working together towards long-term strategic goals. With the downfall of Mubarak and the advent of a new political phase, mostly dominated by the military, these old coalitions became irrelevant.[40]

One may wonder, however, whether the alliances referred to remained short-term and tactical truly by the will of their left-wing participants, or rather by that of the Muslim Brotherhood, which had a very short-term, opportunistic and self-seeking relation to such alliances with groups which were like mice compared to its own elephantine dimensions. The truth is that, for the most important Egyptian left-wing group involved in that experience, the alliance with the Muslim Brotherhood did not become "irrelevant" with Mubarak's downfall. As we saw in Chapter 1, this group, Hamdeen Sabahy's Karama Party, participated in the 2011–12 parliamentary elections as part of a Muslim Brotherhood-dominated alliance, thus missing a major opportunity to start to constitute a third pole, in the way it went on to do with such success in the presidential election a few months later.

The key point that emerges from both symmetrical attitudes found on the Left towards the old regimes and their Islamic fundamentalist competitors is the past failure of the major components of the Arab Left to remain true to the values that they proclaim, or that any true Left should be proclaiming. A Left that is actively and resolutely engaged in the full range of social and democratic struggles on behalf of all the exploited and downtrodden – championing feminist values as much as national liberation values, and boldly upholding secularism along with the democratic rights of the religious (which any well-understood secularism should be the first to defend: a woman's right to wear the hijab as much as a woman's right to go bareheaded) – such a Left can only enter into short-term tactical alliances with forces standing at the opposite end of the spectrum with respect to any of its core values.

It can on occasion and for purely tactical reasons *strike together* with "unlikely bedfellows" – whether with Islamic forces against old-regime forces, or vice-versa – but it should always be *marching separately*, clearing its own fundamental path at equal distance from the two reactionary camps. Tactical short-term alliances can be concluded with the devil if need be; but the devil should never be portrayed as an angel on such occasions – such as by calling the Muslim Brotherhood "reformist" or the old regime forces "secular", thus trying to prettify their deeply reactionary nature.

The huge revolutionary potential that was released across the Arab-speaking region starting from 17 December 2010 is far from extinguished. It is still very much alive, even when smouldering under the ashes of a civil war such as the one devastating Syria. And despite the overwhelming feeling of backlash and setback to worse than prior to 2011 that the ongoing tragedies understandably inspire, the truth is that there have been quite a few positive achievements of the regional uprising other than the irruption of "the people's will" onto the scene. As paradoxical as it may sound, one of the most prominent Arab feminists, the Tunisian Ahlem Belhadj, reminds us that one of the issues on which there have been positive gains from Morocco to Tunisia, Egypt and even Yemen is the advancement of women's rights – even though such advances still fall far short of an end to gender oppression, needless to say.[41]

In 2015, its fifth year, the regional revolutionary process has seen the unexpected surge of an impressively large cross-sectarian social protest movement in Iraq and Lebanon – two countries in which sectarianism was deemed to be a most powerful deflector of class dynamics, perverting any horizontal social struggle into vertical sectarian antagonism. Nevertheless, there is no denying that, from 2013 onwards, the Arab Spring has turned into an Arab Winter, and a harsh and biting one at that. There will certainly be more seasons to come: this much is certain, and a source of hope.

The key to turning a future Arab Spring into a durable one – achieving the transition into a new era of human development and emancipation for the entire Arab-speaking region and beyond – is to build the resolutely independent progressive leaderships that have hitherto been so cruelly lacking. Without such leaderships, it will not be possible to radically overturn the socio-political order to produce one in which state resources and the national wealth are truly mobilised in the interests of the people. And, short of this, the region is doomed to remain caught in the inferno of the clash of barbarisms: there will be no "democratic" miracle to turn this part of the world into a paragon of capitalist liberalism.

Notes

Introduction

1. Samuel Huntington, *The Third Wave: Democratization in the Late Twentieth Century*, Norman, OK: University of Oklahoma Press, 1991.

2. Francis Fukuyama, "The End of History", *National Interest*, no. 16 (Summer 1989).

3. One of the potential causes of a "third reverse wave" identified by Huntington was "a general international economic collapse on the 1929–30 model" (Huntington, *Third Wave*, p. 293).

4. Freedom House, *Freedom in the World 2008*, Washington, DC: Freedom House, 2008, p. 1.

5. Freedom House, *Freedom in the World 2010*, Washington, DC: Freedom House, 2010, p. 1.

6. Freedom House, *Freedom in the World 2011*, Washington, DC: Freedom House, 2011.

7. Freedom House, *Freedom in the World 2012*, Washington, DC: Freedom House, 2012, p. 1.

8. Samuel Huntington, *The Clash of Civilizations and the Remaking of World Order*, New York: Touchstone, 1997, p. 29.

9. Huntington, *Third Wave*, p. 315.

10. Ibid., p. 307.

11. Francis Fukuyama, *The End of History and the Last Man*, New York: Avon, 1992, p. 45.

12. Ibid., p. 46.

13. Francis Fukuyama, "History Is Still Going Our Way", *Wall Street Journal*, 5 October 2001.

14. Ibid.

15. Francis Fukuyama, "Is China Next?", *Wall Street Journal*, 12 March 2011. This article confirms that Fukuyama's grasp of Chinese realities is much better than his understanding of Islam or the Middle East.

16. Rebecca D. Costa, "Acclaimed Political Scientist, Francis Fukuyama, Forecasted Arab Uprising During Clinton Years", 5 May 2011.

17. See Jannis Grimm, *Mapping Change in the Arab World: Insights from Transition Theory and Middle East Studies*, Berlin: Stiftung Wissenschaft und Politik, June 2013. A good example of theoretical disturbance in the face of a chaotic revolutionary process is the unconvincing attempt to devise an ad hoc category of "authoritarian-democratic hybrid" in Alfred Stepan and Juan Linz, "Democratization Theory and the 'Arab Spring'",

Journal of Democracy, vol. 24, no. 2 (April 2013), pp. 15–30. For a critique of democratic transition theory, see Jamie Allinson, "Class Forces, Transition and the Arab Uprisings: A Comparison of Tunisia, Egypt and Syria", *Democratization*, vol. 22, no. 2 (2015), pp. 294–314, and, in the same issue of *Democratization*, Raymond Hinnebusch, "Globalization, Democratization, and the Arab Uprising: The International Factor in MENA's Failed Democratization", pp. 335–57.

18. For a good discussion of these Cold War theses, see Bogdan Denitch, *After the Flood: World Politics and Democracy in the Wake of Communism*, London: Adamantine, 1992.

19. Barack Obama, "Remarks by the President on Egypt", Washington, DC: White House, 11 February 2011. *Silmiyya* is the Arabic word for "peaceful" in the feminine gender (as it was implicitly relating to "demonstration" which is feminine in Arabic).

20. This is discussed at length in the first two chapters of Gilbert Achcar, *The People Want: A Radical Exploration of the Arab Uprising*, trans. G. M. Goshgarian, London: Saqi, and Berkeley, CA: University of California Press, 2013.

21. As Leon Trotsky rightly predicted in 1936:

> If ... a bourgeois party were to overthrow the ruling Soviet caste, it would find no small number of ready servants among the present bureaucrats, administrators, technicians, directors, party secretaries and privileged upper circles in general. A purgation of the state apparatus would, of course, be necessary in this case too. But a bourgeois restoration would probably have to clean out fewer people than a revolutionary party. ...
>
> With energetic pressure from the popular mass, and the disintegration inevitable in such circumstances of the government apparatus, the resistance of those in power may prove much weaker than now appears.

Leon Trotsky, *The Revolution Betrayed: What Is the Soviet Union and Where Is It Going?*, trans. Max Eastman, New York: Pathfinder, 1980, pp. 253, 287.

22. An example of the lack of distinction between the levels of change and of attention to the fundamental issue of development dynamics can be found in Lucan Way's otherwise stimulating comparative assessment: "Comparing the Arab Revolts: The Lessons of 1989", *Journal of Democracy*, vol. 22, no. 4 (October 2011), pp. 17–27.

23. See Achcar, *The People Want*, pp. 77–79. I have abstained from using Weber's category of "sultanism" to describe an extreme degree of patrimonialism characterised by "discretion", as it is hardly relevant in societies with many traditional constraints in addition to being heavily tinged with Orientalism – unlike Stepan and Linz, who used it as a key category in "Democratization Theory and the 'Arab Spring'" (pp. 27–29).

24. I borrowed the concept of "triangle of power" from C. Wright Mills, *The Power Elite*, New York: Oxford University Press, 1956. See Achcar, *The People Want*, p. 179.

25. Achcar, *The People Want*, pp. 17–18.

26. See ibid, Chapter 3, for a survey of the development of Islamic fundamentalism prior to 2011.

27. On Qatar's policy as it has developed since the mid-1990s in rivalry with the Saudi kingdom, see ibid., pp. 126–41.

28. On Qatar's role, see Elizabeth Dickinson, "The Case Against Qatar", *Foreign Policy*, 30 September 2014, and David Roberts, "Is Qatar Bringing the Nusra Front in from the Cold?", *BBC News*, 6 March 2015. On Turkey's role, see Barney Guiton, "'ISIS Sees Turkey as Its Ally': Former Islamic State Member Reveals Turkish Army Cooperation", *Newsweek*, 7 November 2014, and Fehim Taştekin, "Turkish Military Says MIT Shipped Weapons to al-Qaeda", *Al-Monitor*, 15 January 2015.

29. The revolutionary pole is assessed in Achcar, *The People Want*, Chapter 4.

30. "Conditional, messianic prophecy is not the anticipation of an event foretold, be it confident or resigned, but an awakening to the possibility of its advent. A reflexive knowledge, in which what is known incessantly modifies what is possible, its temporal mode is the present, not the future. Prophecy, then, is the emblematic figure of all political and strategic discourse." Daniel Bensaïd, *Marx for Our Time: Adventures and Misadventures of a Critique*, trans. Gregory Eliott, London: Verso, 2002, pp. 55–56.

31. Achcar, *The People Want*, p. 290.

32. Huntington, *Third Wave*, p. 46.

33. The different outcomes in each of the six countries that witnessed a popular uprising in 2011 – Tunisia, Egypt, Yemen, Bahrain, Libya and Syria – are explained and assessed in Achcar, *The People Want*, Chapter 5.

Syria: The Clash of Barbarisms

1. Gilbert Achcar, *The People Want: A Radical Exploration of the Arab Uprising*, trans. G. M. Goshgarian, London: Saqi, and Berkeley, CA: University of California Press, 2013, pp. 225–27.

2. "The barrel bomb is essentially a large, home-made incendiary device. An oil barrel or similar cylindrical container filled with petrol, nails or other crude shrapnel, along with explosives. With an appropriate fuse, they are simply rolled out of a helicopter. The first recorded use of such weapons goes back to late August 2012." (Jonathan Marcus, "Syria Conflict: Barrel Bombs Show Brutality of War", *BBC News*, 20 December 2013). See the poignant article by the executive director of Human Rights Watch, Kenneth Roth, "Barrel Bombs, Not ISIS, Are the Greatest Threat to Syrians", *New York Times*, 5 August 2015.

3. See "FIM-92 Stinger-RMP", at Deagel.com, 31 March 2015.
4. Roketsan, an affiliated company of the Turkish Armed Forces Foundation, produces Stinger missiles. See <http://www.roketsan.com.tr/en/kurumsal/>.
5. Nour Malas, "Syrian Rebels Get Missiles", *Wall Street Journal*, 17 October 2012.
6. Matt Schroeder, *Fire and Forget: The Proliferation of Man-Portable Air Defence Systems in Syria*, Small Arms Survey, Issue Brief, no. 9 (August 2014).
7. Martian2, "Syria: Chinese FN-6 MANPADS Shoots Down Two Russian Mi-8/17 Helicopters", *Pakistan Defence*, 1 April 2013.
8. C. J. Chivers and Eric Schmitt, "Arms Shipments Seen from Sudan to Syria Rebels", *New York Times*, 12 August 2013.
9. Ibid.
10. Adam Entous and Julian E. Barnes, "Rebels Plead for Weapons in Face of Syrian Onslaught", *Wall Street Journal*, 12 June 2013.
11. Ibid. There were other high-ranking supporters of this same option:

> Testifying before the Senate Armed Services Committee, Defense Secretary Leon E. Panetta acknowledged that he and the chairman of the Joint Chiefs of Staff, Gen. Martin E. Dempsey, had supported a plan [in 2012] to arm carefully vetted Syrian rebels. But it was ultimately vetoed by the White House, Mr Panetta said, although it was developed by David H. Petraeus, the CIA director at the time, and backed by Hillary Rodham Clinton, then the secretary of state. ...
> Neither Mr Panetta nor General Dempsey explained why President Obama did not heed their recommendation. But senior American officials have said that the White House was worried about the risks of becoming more deeply involved in the Syria crisis, including the possibility that weapons could fall into the wrong hands.

Michael Gordon and Mark Landler, "Senate Hearing Draws Out a Rift in US Policy on Syria", *New York Times*, 7 February 2013.
12. Muhammad Idrees Ahmad, "Obama's Legacy Is Tarnished as Putin Fills the Vacuum in Syria", *The National* (UAE), 10 October 2015.
13. "Remarks by the President on the Situation in Iraq", Washington, DC: White House, Office of the Press Secretary, 19 June 2014. This was the second time Barack Obama had resorted to the same argument: a few days earlier, he had told National Public Radio: "When you talk about the moderate opposition, many of these people were farmers, or dentists or maybe some radio reporters who didn't have a lot of experience fighting." Greg Myre, "More Diplomacy, Fewer Military Missions: 5 Obama Statements Explained", NPR, 29 May 2014. As former Syria adviser in the Obama administration, Frederic Hof, rightly commented:

Leave aside the historical precedent of American rabble – farmers, smithies, shopkeepers and the like – being elevated to decent degrees of military proficiency by arms and trainers from abroad. ... The question that arises, however, is why President Obama fails to mention the tens of thousands of Syrian Army officers and soldiers who abandoned the Assad regime rather than participate in that regime's campaign of mass homicide. Why is the totality of what the president calls 'the moderate opposition' characterised by him as entirely civilian, and therefore inadequate, in nature? And why does he *not* assume that a healthy percentage of the farmers, teachers, pharmacists, dentists, and radio reporters to whom he refers have had significant prior military training as conscripts in Syria? Does he think that Syria has had an all-volunteer military force for the past fifty years?

Frederic Hof, "Syria: Farmers, Teachers, Pharmacists, and Dentists", *MENASource*, Atlantic Council, 20 June 2014.

14. "Vice President Biden Speaks to the John F. Kennedy Jr. Forum" (audio recording), Washington: *The White House*, 2 October 2014, <https://www.youtube.com/watch?v=UrXkm4FImvc>.
15. Gen. Martin Dempsey, "Letter to The Honorable Eliot L. Engel", 19 Aug. 2013, available at <http://www.loufisher.org/docs/syria/dempsey.pdf> (emphasis added).
16. Maria Abi-Habib and Stacy Meichtry, "Saudis Agree to Provide Syrian Rebels with Mobile Antiaircraft Missiles", *Wall Street Journal*, 14 Feb. 2014.
17. Michael Crowley, "White House Debates 'Game Changer' Weapon for Syria", *Time*, 21 April 2014.
18. Anthony Cordesman, "US Options in Syria: Obama's Delays and the Dempsey Warnings", CSIS, 23 August 2013.
19. Ellen Knickmeyer, Maria Abi-Habib and Adam Entous, "Advanced US Weapons Flow to Syrian Rebels", *Wall Street Journal*, 18 April 2014.
20. Bureau of Political-Military Affairs, "MANPADS: Combating the Threat to Global Aviation from Man-Portable Air Defense Systems", Washington, DC: US Department of State, 27 July 2011.
21. Ibid.
22. Obama's reply to the *New Republic* on the moral issue, that one of the questions he has to ponder on this issue was "How do I weigh tens of thousands who've been killed in Syria versus the tens of thousands who are currently being killed in the Congo?" (Franklin Foer and Chris Hughes, "Barack Obama Is Not Pleased: The President on His Enemies, the Media, and the Future of Football", *New Republic*, 27 January 2013), is the worst possible argument: trying to excuse one's failure to rescue in one place by pointing to one's failure to rescue in another. It is actually aggravating the scope of the moral crime (see my comment on ethics, the Congo and so on in Gilbert

Achcar, *The Clash of Barbarisms: The Making of the New World Disorder*, trans. Peter Drucker, 2nd edn., London: Saqi, and Boulder, CO: Paradigm, 2006 [1st edn, New York: Monthly Review Press, 2002], Chapter 1, on "narcissistic compassion") while playing the trick of not comparing what could actually be done in both cases. On this, see Natalie Nougayrède's powerful article, "If Barack Obama Ever Had a Strategy for Syria, It's Been Turned on Its Head", *Guardian*, 10 August 2015. Nougayrède rightly concludes that "Obama's apparent indifference to the plight of Syrian civilians – not just the fact that he failed to work out a solution – will be part of his legacy."

23. "Remarks by the President to the White House Press Corps", Washington, DC: White House, Office of the Press Secretary, 20 August 2012 (emphases added). Shortly after, in September 2012, Frederic Hof resigned from his State Department post as adviser on Syrian political transition to Secretary of State Hillary Clinton: "I knew that Syria was plunging into an uncharted abyss – a humanitarian abomination of the first order. And I knew that the White House had little appetite for protecting civilians (beyond writing checks for refugee relief) and little interest in even devising a strategy to implement President Barack Obama's stated desire that Syrian President Bashar Assad step aside." Frederic Hof, "I Got Syria So Wrong", *Politico*, 14 October 2015.

24. See in particular Achcar, *The People Want*, Chapter 6, "Co-opting the Uprising", pp. 237–50. In his above-mentioned *New York Times* article, "Barrel Bombs, Not ISIS, Are the Greatest Threat to Syrians", Human Rights Watch's executive director, Kenneth Roth, put his finger on this central reason for US reluctance to stop the Assad regime's war crimes: "One reason for soft-pedaling is a fear that ending the barrel-bomb attacks might undermine Mr Assad's ability to cling to power, and thus facilitate an Islamic State takeover."

25. Hillary Rodham Clinton, *Hard Choices*, New York: Simon & Schuster, 2015, p. 386 (emphasis added).

26. Ibid., p. 392 (emphasis added).

27. Ibid., p. 394.

28. The Arabic name is Al-Dawla al-Islamiyya fil-'Iraq wal-Sham. In addition to Syria, Al-Sham (Bilad al-Sham) encompasses Lebanon, British Mandate Palestine, Jordan and adjacent parts of Turkey and Sinai. The organisation is widely designated by the English acronyms ISIS, or ISIL where L stands for Levant (a French Orientalist term that used to designate the countries of the Eastern Mediterranean), or as Daesh or Daish (a simplified transliteration of the commonly used Arabic acronym Da'ish, equivalent to ISIS).

29. White House, "Press Conference by the President", Washington, DC: White House, 2 October 2015, <https://www.whitehouse.gov/the-press-office/2015/10/02/press-conference-president>.

30. Ahmad, "Obama's Legacy Is Tarnished".

31. On R2P, see Médecins Sans Frontières, *Responsibility to Protect*, *Dialogue 8*, April 2009, <http://www.msf.org.uk/sites/uk/files/MSF_Dialogue_No8__

R2P_200904012144.pdf>, and Noam Chomsky, "The Responsibility to Protect", lecture given at the UN General Assembly, New York, 23 July 2009, <http://www.chomsky.info/talks/20090723.htm>. On the discussion of R2P with regard to Syria, see Robert Murray and Alasdair McKay, eds, *Into the Eleventh Hour: R2P, Syria and Humanitarianism in Crisis*, Bristol, UK: E-International Relations, 2014.

32. PBS, "Former US Ambassador Says He Could 'No Longer Defend' Obama Administration's Syria Policy", *PBS Newshour*, 3 June 2014.

33. Cordesman, "US Options in Syria".

34. Jeffrey Goldberg, "Hillary Clinton: 'Failure' to Help Syrian Rebels Led to the Rise of ISIS", *Atlantic*, 10 August 2014 (emphases added).

35. "Vice President Biden Speaks to the John F. Kennedy Jr Forum".

36. On the role of the Iranian regime and its proxies, see the reports by Naame Shaam, *Iran in Syria: From an Ally of the Regime to an Occupying Force*, September 2014, and *Silent Sectarian Cleansing: Iranian Role in Mass Demolitions and Population Transfers in Syria*, May 2015, both available online. See also Eskandar Sadeghi-Boroujerdi, *Salvaging the "Axis of Resistance," Preserving Strategic Depth*, Dirasat, no. 1, Riyadh: King Faisal Center for Research and Islamic Studies (November 2014), and Phillip Smyth, *The Shiite Jihad in Syria and Its Regional Effects*, Washington, DC: Washington Institute for Near East Policy, 2015.

37. For a sophisticated analysis of the urban sociology of the Syrian uprising in its early phase, see Salwa Ismail, "Urban Subalterns in the Arab Revolutions: Cairo and Damascus in Comparative Perspective", *Comparative Studies in Society and History*, vol. 55, no. 4 (2013), pp. 865–94.

38. Ibrahim al-Amin, "Al-Shara' Yakhruj 'an Samtihi: al-Hall al-'Askari Wahm, wal-Hall bi-Taswiya Tarikhiyya", *Al-Akhbar*, 17 December 2012.

39. Ibid.

40. See François Burgat, "Testimony of General Ahmed Tlass on the Syrian Regime and the Repression", *Noria*, April 2014.

41. "Takfiri" designates the brand of Islamic fundamentalism that declares whole branches of Islam or individual Muslims infidels or apostates. This term has come in recent years to be exclusively used for Sunni fundamentalist tendencies, especially those inspired by Wahhabism. See Aaron Zelin and Phillip Smyth, "The Vocabulary of Sectarianism", *Foreign Policy*, 29 January 2014.

42. On the sectarianisation of the Syrian uprising and its general dynamics, see François Burgat and Bruno Paoli, eds, *Pas de printemps pour la Syrie. Les clés pour comprendre les acteurs et les défis de la crise (2011–2013)*, Paris: La Découverte, 2013.

43. Haytham Manna – former spokesperson abroad for the National Coordination Committee of Democratic Change Forces (the coalition of left-wing and nationalist groups and individuals that rejected the Syrian National Council when it was formed in 2011 and advocated a negotiated solution to the crisis) – related to me in November 2013 how dissidents in

the city of Deraa (from where he originates) found AK-47 rifles wrapped in blankets laid at their doors in the early stage of the uprising. This was later confirmed by a key Alawite member of the Syrian military security, talking to the Abu Dhabi-based English-language daily *The National*:

> Weapons were made available to radical elements of the opposition in key hotspots, including Deraa and Idlib, the former military intelligence officer said. "This is not something I heard rumours about, I actually heard the orders, I have seen it happening," the officer said. "These orders came down from [Military Intelligence] headquarters Damascus." The officer remains angry about the strategy of stoking radicalism, saying it was a key reason why he left his post.

Phil Sands, Justin Vela and Suha Maayeh, "Assad Regime Set Free Extremists from Prison to Fire up Trouble during Peaceful Uprising", *The National*, 21 January 2014.

44.

> In May 2011, after the first protests broke out in Syria, the Syrian government released from the Saydnaya military prison some of its most high-value detainees imprisoned for terrorism, the first in a series of general amnesties. At least nine went on to lead extremist groups in Syria, and four currently serve the Islamic State, statements from the extremist groups and interviews with other rebels show.
>
> Mr Ali, the Syrian ambassador to Lebanon, said Damascus had released only common criminals in the amnesties, who were then offered money by extremist groups to fight against the government. "When Syria released these people, they hadn't committed terrorist crimes," he said. "They were just criminals. In 2011, there were calls for freedom and accusations that Damascus was imprisoning people, so we hosted several amnesties [to demonstrate] our goodwill."
>
> Bassam Barabandi, a diplomat in Syria's foreign ministry at the time who has since defected, offered a different explanation. "The fear of a continued, peaceful revolution is why these Islamists were released," he said. "The reasoning behind the jihadists, for Assad and the regime, is that they are the alternative to the peaceful revolution. They are organised with the doctrine of jihad and the West is afraid of them."

Maria Abi-Habib, "ISIS Gained Momentum Because Al-Assad Decided to Go Easy on It", *Wall Street Journal*, 22 August 2014.

45. Martin Chulov, "Why ISIS Fights", *Guardian*, 17 September 2015.

46.

The Syrian government facilitated the predecessor to the Islamic State – al Qaeda in Iraq – when that group's primary target was US troops then in the country.

In 2007, US military forces raided an al Qaeda training camp in Sinjar, northern Iraq. They uncovered a trove of documents outlining Damascus's support to the extremists, according to the US Military Academy at West Point, which publicly released the records. The Sinjar records detailed the flow of extremists from across the Middle East to the Damascus airport.

Syrian intelligence agents detained the fighters as they landed in the capital, holding them at the [Saydnaya] military prison on the city's outskirts. If deemed a threat to the country, they would remain imprisoned, the records indicate. But if their intentions were solely to fight US troops in Iraq, Syrian intelligence would facilitate their flow across the border, the records show. Making that journey were many Saudis and Libyans – the same nationalities that today bolster the ranks of the Islamic State.

Mr Maliki's former spokesman, Ali Aldabbagh, said in an interview that he attended heated meetings in Damascus during which Baghdad asked Mr Assad to stop the flow of al Qaeda militants across the border. He said Syria brushed off the requests.

Abi-Habib, "ISIS Gained Momentum".

47. Wikileaks, Cable from the US Embassy in Damascus, Canonical ID: 10DAMASCUS158_a, "When Chickens Come Home to Roost: Syria's Proxy War in Iraq at Heart of 2008–09 Seidnaya Prison Riots", 24 February 2010. Catherine al-Talli's name has been corrected from "Tali" (see <http://carnegie-mec.org/publications/?fa=48713>).

48. Patrick Seale, *Asad: The Struggle for the Middle East*, London: I.B. Tauris, 1990.

49. David Lesch, *The New Lion of Damascus: Bashar al-Asad and Modern Syria*, New Haven, CT: Yale University Press, 2005, p. 187.

50. Wikileaks, "When Chickens Come Home to Roost".

51. I described how the G. W. Bush administration tried in Iraq to circumvent its own claims of "democracy promotion" in Achcar, *The Clash of Barbarisms*, Chapter 4, as well as in Noam Chomsky and Gilbert Achcar, *Perilous Power: The Middle East and US Foreign Policy*, ed. Stephen Shalom, 2nd edn, Boulder, CO: Paradigm, 2008.

52. See the statements by Iraqi and US officials quoted in Tony Badran, "The 'Lebanonization' of Iraq", *NOW*, 22 December 2009, <https://now.mmedia.me/lb/en/commentary/the_lebanonization_of_iraq>. On Iraqi Baathists' role in al-Qaida and ISIS, see Liz Sly, "The Hidden Hand Behind the Islamic State Militants? Saddam Hussein's", *Washington Post*, 4 April

2015, and Isabel Coles and Ned Parker, "The Baathists: How Saddam's Men Help Islamic State Rule", *Reuters*, 11 December 2015.

53. Wikileaks, Cable from the US Embassy in Damascus, Canonical ID: 10DAMASCUS159_a, "Syrian Intelligence Chief Attends CT Dialogue with S/CT Benjamin", 24 February 2010.

54. Peter Neumann, "Suspects into Collaborators", *London Review of Books*, vol. 36, no. 7 (3 April 2014). See also Hani Nasira, "Min Aghasi ila al-Nusra: Khibrat al-Asad fi Ikhtiraq al-Jihadiyyin", *Ma'had Al-'Arabiyya lil-Dirasat*, 16 June 2013, and Muhammad Habash, "Abu al-Qa'qa' ... Dhikrayat ... al-Tariq ila Da'ish", *All4Syria*, 7 October 2014. The best-informed books on ISIS, its rise and the Assad regime's role in that process, are Michael Weiss and Hassan Hassan, *Isis: Inside the Army of Terror*, New York: Regan Arts, 2015; Jean-Pierre Filiu, *From Deep State to Islamic State: The Arab Counter-Revolution and its Jihadi Legacy*, London: Hurst, 2015; and, on ISIS as well as the whole galaxy of Syrian jihadism, Charles Lister, *The Syrian Jihad: Al-Qaeda, the Islamic State and the Evolution of an Insurgency*, London: Hurst, 2015.

55. Rita Faraj, "Riyad al-As'ad lil-Ra'y: 'Anasir al-Qa'ida' iza Dakhalat Suriyya fa bil-Ta'awun ma' al-Mukhabarat al-Jawwiyya", *Al-Ra'y* (Amman), 13 May 2012. In their excellent book, Michael Weiss and Hassan Hassan quote Laith Alkhouri, an internet security expert specialised in al-Qaida, who told them that he had seen a Syrian Air Force Intelligence document stating that they have "about 250 informants in the ranks of ISIS" (*Isis: Inside the Army of Terror*, p. 199).

56. Chulov, "Why Isis Fights".

57. On Jabhat al-Nusra, see in particular Lister, *The Syrian Jihad*.

58. On the evolution of Turkey's role and its relations with al-Nusra/ISIS, see Asli Ilgit and Rochelle Davis, "The Many Roles of Turkey in the Syrian Crisis", *Middle East Report Online*, 28 January 2013; Semih Idiz, "ISIS emerges as threat to Turkey", *Al-Monitor*, 25 March 2014; Aaron Stein, "Turkey's Evolving Syria Strategy", *Foreign Affairs*, Snapshot, 9 February 2015; Martin Chulov, "Is Vladimir Putin Right to Label Turkey 'Accomplices of Terrorists'?", *Guardian*, 24 November 2015.

59. Haswani was a central target of EU sanctions imposed in March 2015:

> A Syrian businessman responsible for orchestrating millions of dollars' worth of secret oil and gas trades between the Assad government and its supposed sworn enemy, the Islamic State of Iraq and the Levant, or ISIS, is among 13 individuals and organisations hit with sweeping new economic sanctions by the EU. George Haswani, a Syrian-Greek businessman with "direct access" to Syrian president Bashar al-Assad, is responsible for broking contracts between ISIS and the Syrian regime, according to a diplomat familiar with the new EU sanctions. Mr Haswani's company, HESCO – one of Syria's largest engineering firms – also operates a natural gas production facility in Tabqa that is jointly run

by ISIS and the Syrian regime, the diplomat added. The sanctions against Mr Haswani are one of the first official acknowledgments from Western governments that ISIS and Damascus are working closely together in key areas in a clandestine relationship that sustains the jihadis with significant income.

Sam Jones, "New EU Syria Sanctions Reveal Regime Collusion with Isis", *Financial Times*, 7 March 2015.

On HESCO's revealing range of clients (ISIS not included, naturally), see the company's website: <http://www.hescoco.com/>.

60. Erika Solomon, "The ISIS Economy: Meet the New Boss", *Financial Times*, 5 January 2015. For an overview of ISIS's finances, see Frank Gunter, "ISIL Revenues: Grow or Die", *Foreign Policy Research Institute*, June 2015. See also Rim Turkmani, *ISIL, JAN and the War Economy in Syria*, London: LSE, 30 July 2015, and the excellent *Financial Times* series: Erika Solomon, Guy Chazan and Sam Jones, "ISIS INC: How Oil Fuels the Jihadi Terrorists"; Erika Solomon, Robin Kwong and Steven Bernard, "Inside ISIS INC: The Journey of a Barrel of Oil", 14 October 2015; Erika Solomon and Ahmed Mhidi, "ISIS INC: Syria's 'Mafia-Style' Gas Deals with Jihadis", 15 October 2015; Erika Solomon and Ahmed Mhidi, "ISIS: The Munitions Trail", 30 November 2015; and Erika Solomon and Sam Jones, "ISIS INC: Loot and Taxes Keep Jihadi Economy Churning", 14 December 2015.

61. On Ahrar al-Sham, one of the key components of the Islamic fundamentalist armed opposition, see Erika Solomon, "Syrian Islamist Rebel Group Looks to the West", *Financial Times*, 14 August 2015; Mariam Karouny, "Resilient insurgent group Ahrar al-Sham to play bigger role in Syria", *Reuters*, 22 September 2015; Sam Heller, "Ahrar al-Sham's Revisionist Jihadism", *War on the Rocks*, 30 September 2015; and the interview with Hassan Hassan by Dylan Collins, "A Growing Jihadist Presence in Syria's Opposition", *Syria Deeply*, 30 November 2015.

62. Yvonne Ridley, "EXCLUSIVE: Shaikh Hassan Abboud's Final Interview", *MEMO Middle East Monitor*, 22 September 2014.

63. See Anne Barnard, "Assad's Forces May Be Aiding New ISIS Surge", *New York Times*, 2 June 2015.

64. Jeffrey White, "Russia in Syria (Part 2): Military Implications", Washington Institute, 15 September, 2015. See also Christoph Reuter, "The West's Dilemma: Why Assad Is Uninterested in Defeating Islamic State", *Spiegel Online International*, 8 December 2015.

65. On the role of the Syrian Muslim Brotherhood, see Raphaël Lefèvre, "Islamism Within a Civil War: The Syrian Muslim Brotherhood's Struggle for Survival", Washington, DC: Brookings Institution, August 2015.

66. The Islamic Front was preceded by the Syrian Islamic Front. On the latter, see Aron Lund, *Syria's Salafi Insurgents: The Rise of the Syrian Islamic Front*, Stockholm: Swedish Institute of International Affairs, March 2013.

67. Weiss and Hassan, *Isis: Inside the Army of Terror*, p. 181 (emphasis in original).

68. Hamit Bozarslan called this policy "destroying one's society to ensure its durability", in *Révolution et état de violence. Moyen-Orient 2011–2015*, Paris: CNRS, 2015, pp. 134–50. On the Assad regime's sectarianism, see Achcar, *The People Want*, pp. 209–16, and Yassin al-Haj Saleh, "al-Sultan al-Hadith: Al-Manabiʿ al-Siyasiyya wa al-Ijtimaʿiyya lil-Taʾifiyya fi Suriya", *Al-Jumhuriyya*, 26 and 30 January and 4 February 2015.

69. Weiss and Hassan, *Isis: Inside the Army of Terror*, pp. 167–68.

70. Syrian Network for Human Rights, *The Society's Holocaust: Most Notable Sectarian and Ethnic Cleansing Massacre* [*sic*], London: SNHR, 16 June 2015.

71. Achcar, *Clash of Barbarisms*.

72. Gilbert Achcar, "Letter to a Slightly Depressed Antiwar Activist" (14 April 2003), reprinted in Achcar, *Eastern Cauldron: Islam, Afghanistan, Palestine and Iraq in a Marxist Mirror*, trans. Peter Drucker, New York/London: Monthly Review/Pluto, 2004, pp. 262–63 – originally posted on ZNet at <http://zcomm.org/znetarticle/letter-to-a-slightly-depressed-antiwar-activist-by-gilbert-achcar/>.

73. Carl von Clausewitz, *On War*, ed. and trans. Michael Howard and Peter Paret, Princeton, NJ: Princeton University Press, 1989, p. 89.

74. For a panorama of the Syrian Left, see Akram al-Bunni, "An Analysis of the Realities of the Syrian Left", in Jamil Hilal and Katja Hermann, eds, *Mapping of the Arab Left: Contemporary Leftist Politics in the Arab East*, Ramallah: Rosa Luxemburg Stiftung Regional Office Palestine, 2014, pp. 104–26. For a discussion of the role of the Syrian Left in the Syrian revolution, see Salameh Kaileh, "Hawla Dawr al-Yasar al-Suri fil-Thawra", in Mohamed Elagati *et al.*, *Al-Yasar wal-Thawrat al-ʿArabiyya*, Cairo: Muntada al-Badaʾil al-ʿArabi lil-Dirasat/Rosa Luxemburg Stiftung, 2013, pp. 47–63.

75. Quoted in Achcar, *Eastern Cauldron*, p. 168, where I analysed the corruptive process that affected the PLO (esp. pp. 129–74).

76.

> The al-Bab [quarter in Aleppo] of Ramadan 2012 had offered one of the most encouraging signs of the anti-Assad revolution. The FSA presence guarding the town was mostly financed by local merchants, not foreign donors, and perhaps because it was salaried by the community it protected, it exhibited none of the taints of corruption or venality that would come to characterise the larger rebel camp later.

Weiss and Hassan, *Isis: Inside the Army of Terror*, pp. 214–15.

77. Sardar Saadi, "David Harvey: Reclaiming the City from Kobane to Baltimore" (interview), *Roarmag*, 26 May 2015. Strikingly, romantic notions about the PYD are not the preserve of anarchist circles and publications seduced by

references from PKK leader Abdullah Öcalan to Murray Bookchin. Even the *Financial Times* gave it a prominent place by publishing a long article of similar inspiration: Carne Ross, "Power to the People: A Syrian Experiment in Democracy", *Financial Times*, 23 October 2015.

78. See the reports by Human Rights Watch, *Under Kurdish Rule: Abuses in PYD-run Enclaves of Syria*, New York: HRW, June 2014, and Amnesty International, *"We Had Nowhere Else to Go": Forced Displacement and Demolitions in Northern Syria*, London: Amnesty International, October 2015.

79. Here is a statement by Salih Muslim, the key leadership figure within the PYD:

> I would like to stress that the air strikes of the coalition have saved many civilian lives, and they have contributed to the resistance of the YPG. I therefore express my hope that these strikes continue as they have great impact on strengthening the bonds of friendship between our people and the forces defending peace and democracy in the world. On behalf of my party and the people of Kobani, I would like to thank the US led international coalition and the people around the world for their support of our people in its plight.

"PYD Leader Thanks US Led Coalition against ISIS", 10 October 2014, <http://civiroglu.net/2014/10/10/pyd-leader-thanks-us-led-coalition-against-isis/>. See also Sharmila Devi, "Kobane Official Calls for More Outside Help to Defeat ISIS", *Rûdaw*, 5 November 2014, and the reportage by Patrick Cockburn, remarkably uncritical of US airstrikes and an arms and ammunition airdrop in defence of Kobani: "War against ISIS: PKK Commander Tasked with the Defence of Syrian Kurds Claims 'We Will Save Kobani'", *Independent*, 11 November 2014. Cockburn's work has been a major reference for the knee-jerk "anti-imperialist left" in their denunciation of any form of US support for the Syrian uprising since its early stage.

80. See my discussion of the ethics of democracy and anti-imperialism in Achcar, *The People Want*, pp. 238–39.

81. See Hassan Hassan and Bassam Barabandi, "Kurds Can't Be Syria's Saviors", *Foreign Policy*, 18 November 2015, and Aron Lund, "Syria's Kurds at the Center of America's Anti-Jihadi Strategy", Carnegie Endowment for International Peace, 2 December 2015.

82. See the useful study by Fabrice Balanche, "Syria's Kurds Are Contemplating an Aleppo Alliance with Assad and Russia", *PolicyWatch 2499*, Washington Institute for Near East Policy, 7 October 2015. See also Sarkawt Shamsulddin, "The US, Russia Competition to Win YPG", *NRT*, 13 October 2015; Tim Arango and Anne Barnard, "Turkey Expresses Concern to US and Russia Over Help for Syrian Kurds", *New York Times*, 14 October 2015;

and Jonathan Steele, "The Syrian Kurds Are Winning!", *New York Review of Books*, 3 December 2015.

83. Quoted in Maher Samaan and Anne Barnard, "For Those Who Remain in Syria, Daily Life Is a Nightmare", *New York Times*, 15 September 2015.

84. See Kheder Khaddour, *The Assad Regime's Hold on the Syrian State*, Beirut: Carnegie Middle East Center, July 2015. On the Syrian armed forces, see, by the same author, "Assad's Officer Ghetto: Why the Syrian Army Remains Loyal", Beirut: Carnegie Middle East Center, November 2015, and Dorothy Ohl, Holger Albrecht and Kevin Koehler, "For Money or Liberty? The Political Economy of Military Desertion and Rebel Recruitment in the Syrian Civil War", Beirut: Carnegie Middle East Center, 24 November 2015.

85. Anthony Cordesman, "Beyond Partisan Bickering: Key Questions About US Strategy in Syria", CSIS, 17 September 2015.

86. Ibid.

87. In his address to the UN General Assembly on 28 September 2015, Ban Ki-moon affirmed: "Five countries in particular hold the key [of a solution for Syria]: the Russian Federation, the United States, Saudi Arabia, Iran and Turkey." ("Address to the General Assembly", UN News Centre, 28 September 2015). Qatar, however, has been playing a key role in the Syrian events since 2011.

88. See for example Mark Mazzetti, Eric Schmitt and David Kirkpatrick, "Saudi Oil Is Seen as Lever to Pry Russian Support from Syria's Assad", *New York Times*, 3 February 2015. For a strategic assessment of the "oil war" from an Iranian regime perspective, see Kaveh Afrasiabi, "The Oil War II and How Iran Can Strike Back", *Iran Review*, 2 December 2014.

89. Pamela Falk, "US Doesn't Really Want Assad to Fall, Russian Ambassador Claims", *CBS News*, 15 September 2015.

90. "Iranian President in US after Nuclear Deal; Russia Launches Airstrikes in Syria", *CNN's Amanpour*, 2 October 2015 (emphasis added).

91. Mark Urban, "What is Putin's End Game in Syria?", *BBC News*, 23 September 2015.

92. Ian Black and Saeed Dehghan, "Iran Ramps Up Troop Deployment in Syria in Run-Up to 'Anti-Rebel Offensive'", *Guardian*, 14 October 2015.

93. Bashar al-Assad, "Al-Ra'is al-Asad: al-Ma'raka Ma'rakat Mihwar Mutakamil Yumaththil Manhajan min al-Istiqlaliyya wal-Karama", *SANA*, 26 July 2015. On the Assad regime's territorial strategy, see Fabrice Balanche, "Insurrection et contre-insurrection en Syrie", *Geostrategic Maritime Review*, no. 2 (Spring/Summer 2014), pp. 36–57, and Aron Lund, "The Political Geography of Syria's War: An Interview with Fabrice Balanche", Carnegie Endowment for International Peace, 30 January 2015. On the Syrian war economy, see Samer Abboud, "Capital Flight and the Consequences of the War Economy", *Jadaliyya*, 18 March 2013; Jihad Yazigi, "Syria's War Economy", European Council on Foreign Relations, April 2014; Syrian Centre for Policy Research, *Syria War on Development:*

Socioeconomic Monitoring Report of Syria, October 2013, *Syria Squandering Humanity: Socioeconomic Monitoring Report on Syria*, May 2014, and *Syria Alienation and Violence: Impact of Syria Crisis Report 2014*, March 2015, Damascus: SCPR with UNRWA and UNDP; David Butter, *Syria's Economy: Picking up the Pieces*, London: Chatham House, June 2015; and Hamoud al-Mahmoud, "The War Economy in the Syrian Conflict: The Government's Hands-Off Tactics", Carnegie Endowment for International Peace, 15 December 2015.

94. The phrase "useful Syria" is a reference to French colonial vocabulary. It was Maréchal Hubert Lyautey, resident-general of the French protectorate of Morocco until 1925, who distinguished between "geographical Morocco" and "useful Morocco".

95. Sammy Ketz, "Syria Regime 'to Accept De Facto Partition' of Country", *AFP*, 24 May 2015.

96. For an analysis of Putin's goal, see Alexei Malashenko, "Putin's Syrian Bet", *Le Monde Diplomatique*, November 2015.

97. Jim Heintz, "Russia Says Islamic State Group Not the Only Target in Syria" and "Russia Defends Its Military Action in Syria", *Associated Press*, 1 October 2015. Putin's spokesman, Dmitry Peskov, made the news in the summer of 2015 for wearing a $620,000 watch at his wedding – see Leonid Bershidsky, "Where Did Putin's Spokesman Get a $620,000 Watch?", *Bloomberg View*, 3 August 2015.

98. Ian Black, "Wake-Up Call on Syrian Army Weakness Prompted Russian Intervention", *Guardian*, 1 October 2015.

99. John Kerry, "Remarks at a Meeting on International Peace and Security and Countering Terrorism", US Department of State, 30 September 2015.

100. John McCain, "Statement by Senator John McCain on Obama Administration's 'Deconfliction' Talks with Russia on Syria Airstrikes", Senator John McCain's website (<http://www.mccain.senate.gov>), 1 Oct. 2015.

101. This has actually been the case since 2012 with regard to Moscow. See Helene Cooper and Mark Landler, "US Hopes Assad Can Be Eased Out with Russia's Aid", *New York Times*, 26 May 2012.

102. John Kerry, "Interview with Nicolle Wallace, Mike Barnicle, Mark Halperin, Richard Haass, and Katty Kay of MSNBC's *Morning Joe*", US Department of State, 29 September 2015.

103. White House, "Press Conference by the President".

104. Neil Quilliam, "Five Reasons Why the Inclusion of Assad in a Political Transition in Syria Is Destined to Fail", *Newsweek*, 29 September 2015.

105. "Al-Khatib: Al-Taqa'us al-Dawli wara' Istiqalati", *Al-Jazeera*, 25 March 2013.

106. See Salam Al-Saadi, "Changes in Syria's Armed Opposition", *Sada* (CEIP), 11 December 2015. On the Riyadh meeting, see also Ibrahim Hamidi, "Mu'tamar al-Riyadh Yad'am al-Hall al-Siyasi, wa Hay'a li-Tashkil Wafd al-Mufawadat", *Al-Hayat*, 11 December 2015, and Aron Lund, "Syria's

Opposition Conferences: Results and Expectations", Carnegie Endowment for International Peace, 11 December 2015.

107. Amin, "Al-Shara' Yakhruj 'an Samtihi". In June 2015, Farouk al-Sharaa was reported to have been severely beaten by the Assad regime's militiamen: Bahiyya Mardini, "Anba' 'an Muhawalat Tasfiyat Faruq al-Shara'", *Elaph*, 28 June 2015.

108. Frederic Hof, "The Self-Government Revolution that's Happening under the Radar in Syria", *Washington Post*, 26 July 2015.

109. Ibid.

Egypt: The "23 July" of Abdul-Fattah al-Sisi

1.   Marx actually paraphrased this famous passage from a letter sent to him by Friedrich Engels on 3 December 1851. Karl Marx and Friedrich Engels, *Collected Works*, vol. 38, London: Lawrence & Wishart, 1982, pp. 503–6.

2.   The French Revolutionary (or Republican) Calendar was used in France from 1793 to 1805, and for a short period by the 1871 Paris Commune.

3.   See Sarah Brun, "La Farce à l'épreuve du tragique au XXe siècle", in Milagros Torres and Ariane Ferry, eds, *Tragique et comique liés, dans le théâtre, de l'Antiquité à nos Jours (du texte à la mise en scène)*, Rouen: CEREdi, 2012.

4.   See the typology of coups in Gilbert Achcar, *The People Want: A Radical Exploration of the Arab Uprising*, trans. G. M. Goshgarian, London: Saqi, and Berkeley, CA: University of California Press, 2013, pp. 177–78. See also the comparison between 1952 and 2011 (p. 15).

5.   Ibid., p. 274 (emphasis added).

6.   Ibid., p. 282.

7.   Ibid., p. 293.

8.   This is explained at length in ibid.

9.   See Gehad El-Haddad's testimony in Edmund Blair, Paul Taylor and Tom Perry, "Special Report: How the Muslim Brotherhood Lost Egypt", *Reuters*, 26 July 2013.

10. Among the critics were senior figures of the Egyptian Brotherhood based in Europe such as Youssef Nada, the Brotherhood's financial manager, who described the Consultative Council's decision to field a presidential candidate as a "catastrophe". Youssef Nada with Douglas Thompson, *Inside the Muslim Brotherhood*, London: Metro, 2012, p. 266. Kamal al-Hilbawi, founder of the Muslim Association of Britain (MAB) and formerly the Brotherhood's spokesman in the West, resigned in protest against the same decision.

11. Matthew Kaminski, "Khairat Al Shater: The Brother Who Would Run Egypt", *Wall Street Journal*, 22 June 2012.

12. Ibid. (emphasis added).

13. Achcar, *The People Want*, p. 189.

14. For this episode, as well as the whole period from January 2011 until the spring of 2013 (when it was first published), a useful source is the account by Mustafa Bakri of the relations between the SCAF and the Brotherhood from the SCAF's perspective, in Mustafa Bakri, *Al-Jaysh wal-Ikhwan: Asrar Khalf al-Sitar*, Cairo: Al-Dar al-Misriyya al-Lubnaniyya, 2013. Bakri confirms that Sisi had been Tantawi's and the whole SCAF's choice to succeed the old field marshal, and that Tantawi and Anan wanted to retire. At the same time, Bakri echoes Sisi's quite unconvincing excuse for lending himself to Morsi's particular staging of that changing of the guard. The latter fact may explain Sami Anan's later opposition to Sisi, who seems also to have frustrated his plan of running for president. See "Fi Zull al-Sira'at dakhil al-Mu'assassa al-'Askariyya: Tahdidat lil-Fariq Sami 'Anan bi-Waqf Muzakkaratihi aw Kashf 'Ilaqatihi bi-Mawqi'at al-Jamal", *Shabakat al-Marsad al-Ikhbariyya*, 10 October 2013.

15. Translated here from the Arabic original at <http://gate.ahram.org.eg/News/262873.aspx>.

16. Michael Birnbaum, "Egypt's Morsi Emerges as Key Player", *Washington Post*, 21 November 2012.

17. Bradley Klapper and Julie Pace, "Why Obama is Standing with Egypt's President Morsi", *Associated Press*, 28 November 2012.

18. "English Text of Morsi's Constitutional Declaration", *Ahram Online*, 22 November 2012.

19. The student membership of Sabahy's Popular Current and El-Baradei's Constitution Party protested against the presence of remnants of the Mubarak regime (*fulul*) in the NSF. See "Youth of anti-Morsi Parties Reject Coalition with 'Mubarak Remnants'", *Ahram Online*, 28 November 2012.

20. Cairo Institute for Human Rights Studies (CIHRS), *Al-Ittihadiyya "Presidential Palace" Clashes in Cairo 5 and 6 December 2012*, Cairo: CIHRS, December 2012.

21. Paul Taylor, "Exclusive: Egypt's 'Road Not Taken' Could Have Saved Mursi", *Reuters*, 17 July 2013.

22. On Morsi's economic policy up to October 2012, see Achcar, *The People Want*, pp. 279–82. For a balance-sheet of his year of economic policy, see also Muhammad Muslim, *Tabdid al-Asatir: Al-Azma al-Iqtisadiyya fi Misr*, Cairo: Al-Mubadara al-Misriyya lil-Huquq al-Shakhsiyya, May 2013.

23. On the FJP's u-turn, see Wael Gamal, "La lil-Iqtirad 'ala Mabadi' al-Sunduq wal-Ganzouri wa Man Tabi'ahuma", *Al-Shuruq*, 20 August 2012.

24. Dina Ezzat, "President Morsi Could Face a Summer of Discontent", *Ahram Online*, 27 December 2012.

25. "'Ishrin Alf 'Amil bi-Ghazl al-Mahalla Yudribun 'an al-'Amal wa Yutalibun bi-Tanahhi Morsi 'an al-Hukm", *Al-Shuruq*, 15 July 2012.

26. On the dynamics of this wave as it unfolded after 2011, see Joel Beinin, *The Rise of Egypt's Workers*, Washington, DC: Carnegie Endowment for International Peace, June 2012; Mostafa Ali, "Wave of Strikes: Egypt Labour

Fights Back, Capital Draws a Line", *Ahram Online*, 31 July 2012; Nadine Abdalla, "Egypt's Workers – From Protest Movement to Organized Labor", Berlin: Stiftung Wissenschaft und Politik, October 2012; Anne Alexander and Mostafa Bassiouny, *Bread, Freedom, and Social Justice: Workers and the Egyptian Revolution*, London: Zed Books, 2014; Joel Beinin and Marie Duboc, "Mouvement ouvrier, luttes syndicales et processus révolutionnaire en Égypte, 2006-2013", in Michel Camau and Frédéric Vairel, eds, *Soulèvements et recompositions politiques dans le monde arabe*, Montreal: Presses de l'Université de Montréal, 2014, pp. 121–42; Marie Duboc, "Reluctant Revolutionaries? The Dynamics of Labour Protests in Egypt, 2006–13", in Reem Abou-El-Fadl, ed., *Revolutionary Egypt: Connecting Domestic and International Struggles*, Abingdon, UK: Routledge, 2015, pp. 27–41 (this multi-authored volume is a useful contribution to the study of various aspects of the Egyptian upheaval, including topics that are rarely addressed); and Joel Beinin, *Workers and Thieves: Labor Movements and Popular Uprisings in Tunisia and Egypt*, Stanford, CA: Stanford University Press, 2015.

27. The figure for the twelve months of Morsi's presidency is calculated on the basis of the data provided in ECESR, *Al-Ihtijajat al-'Ummaliyya fi Misr 2012*, Cairo: Al-Markaz al-Misri lil-Huquq al-Iqtisadiyya wal-Ijtima'iyya, 2013, and *Taqrir Al-Ihtijajat al-Sanawi 2013*, Cairo: ECESR, 2014.

28. *Taqrir Al-Ihtijajat al-Sanawi 2013*. The report for the year 2012 does not give a monthly breakdown of workers' protests, making it impossible to calculate the total for the twelve months of Morsi's presidency.

29. Dar al-Khadamat al-Niqabiyya wal-'Ummaliyya, *Hal al-'Ummal fi Hukm al-Ikhwan: 'Am min Intihakat al-Hurriyyat al-Niqabiyya fi Fatrat Hukm Mursi*, Cairo: CTUWS, June 2013.

30. Bakri, *Al-Jaysh wal-Ikhwan*, pp. 411–46.

31. Asma Alsharif and Yasmine Saleh, "Special Report: The Real Force behind Egypt's 'Revolution of the State'", *Reuters*, 10 October 2013.

32. Dina Ezzat, "Egypt: The President, the Army and the Police", *Ahram Online*, 27 December 2012.

33. Muhammad Tantawi, "Mudir al-Kulliyya al-Harbiyya Yakshuf: al-Daf'a 109 Harbiyya biha Abna' lil-'Ikhwan'", *Al-Yawm al-Sabi'*, 18 March 2013; "Khawf min Akhwanat al-Jaysh bi-Misr ba'da Qubul Dafa'at Muttasila bil-Jama'a", *Al-Arabiyya.net*, 19 March 2013; Bakri, *Al-Jaysh wal-Ikhwan*, p. 434.

34. Bakri, ibid.

35. Ibid., p. 447.

36. Ibid., p. 446.

37. Ibid., p. 447.

38. Ibid., p. 451.

39. Muhammad Salah, "Hamdin Sabahi lil-Hayat: Khuruj 'Adil lil-'Askar wa Tantawi Yastahiq al-Takrim iza Hakama Qatalat al-Shuhada'", *Al-Hayat*, 19 January 2012.

40. "Hamdin Sabbahi khilal Liqa'ihi ma' Wafd Markaz Carter", Hamdeen Sabahy's *Facebook* page, 18 June 2012.

41. Ekram Ibrahim, "Why Did Sabbahi – 'One of Us' – Do So well?", *Ahram Online*, 25 May 2012.

42. Al-Ishtirakiyyun al-Thawriyyun, "'Ala Tariq Istikmal al-Thawra: Al-Ishtirakiyyun al-Thawriyyun fi Hamlat Tamarrud", Revolutionary Socialists' website, 19 May 2013, <http://revsoc.me/-14836>.

43. Heba El-Shazli, "Where Were the Egyptian Workers in the June 2013 People's Coup Revolution?", *Jadaliyya*, 23 July 2013.

44. On the distinction between market bourgeoisie and state bourgeoisie, see Achcar, *The People Want*, p. 76.

45. Benjamin Barthe, "Egypte: les apprentis sorciers de Tamarrod", *Le Monde*, 17 July 2013.

46. Alsharif and Saleh, "Special Report".

47. Yasmine Saleh and Paul Taylor, "The Egyptian Rebel Who 'Owns' Tahrir Square", *Reuters*, 8 July 2013. On the role of the interior ministry in the summer of 2013, see also Alsharif and Saleh, "Special Report".

48. Barthe, "Egypte: les apprentis sorciers".

49. Dalia Othman, "'Al-Jaysh' lil-Sha'b': Lan Nazall Samitin ... wa sa-Nahmi Iradatakum", *Al-Masry al-Youm*, 24 June 2013.

50. Dalia Othman and Muhammad al-Bahrawi, "Al-Jaysh 'bayn al-Nas' ... wa Mursi Yuhaddid wa Yatahakkam ... wa-'al-Tahrir': Irhal", *Al-Masry al-Youm*, 27 June 2013.

51. Ibid.

52. Yusri al-Badri and 'Isam Abu-Sdayra, "Masirat Dubbat al-Shurta lil-'Tahrir' Tutalib bi-Rahil Mursi", *Al-Masry al-Youm*, 1 July 2013.

53. Yusri al-Badri et al., "'Azl Mursi bi-Amr al-Sha'b", *Al-Masry al-Youm*, 4 July 2013; this was later confirmed by Morsi's prime minister Hisham Qandil: "Qandil: Mursi Wafaqa 'ala Ijra' Istifta' 'ala Istimrarihi Lakin Ba'd al-Intikhabat al-Barlimaniyya", *Al-Watan*, 25 July 2013.

54. Saleh and Taylor, "Egyptian Rebel". Mahmoud Badr told the same story to *Le Monde*'s Barthe: see Barthe, "Egypte: les apprentis sorciers".

55. Charles Levinson and Matt Bradley, "In Egypt, the 'Deep State' Rises Again", *Wall Street Journal*, 12 July 2013.

56. Salah, "Hamdin Sabahi lil-Hayat".

57. Thousands of demonstrators gathered spontaneously in Tahrir Square chanting that slogan in protest against the results of the presidential election's first round as soon as they were announced on the evening of 27 May 2012. Yasmin al-Gayushi and Peter Magdi, "Alaf fil-Tahrir Yarfudun Natijat al-Intikhabat wa Yahtufun 'La Fulul wa la Ikhwan, Lissah al-Thawra fil-Maydan'", *Al-Dustur al-Asli*, 28 May 2012.

58. "Awwal Bayanat 'al-Tayyar al-Sha'bi': al-Hukuma al-Jadida Tu'akkid annahu la Khilaf Haqiqi bayn al-Ikhwan wa 'al-'Askari'", *Al-Watan*, 3 August 2012.

59. Ghassan Charbel, "Ajaza Mursi 'an al-Ijaba wa Qala 'Uriduka ma'i Na'iban

lil-Ra'is' ... Shi'ar 'Yasqut Yasqut Hukm al-'Askar' Adarra al-Thawra wa Qarraba bayn al-Jaysh wal-Ikhwan", *Al-Hayat*, 26 June 2013.

60. Ibid.

61. Ghassan Charbel, "Sabbahi: Mursi lam Ya'ud Yumaththil al-Thawra wa '30 Yunyu' li Waqf al-Istibdad 'al-Ikhwani'", *Al-Hayat*, 27 June 2013.

62. Ghassan Charbel, "Sabbahi: Al-Jaysh Quwwa Wataniyya Asila wa ayy Tadakhkhul lahu sa-Yakun li-Marhala Intiqaliyya", *Al-Hayat*, 28 June 2013.

63. Ibid.

64. "Mona Makram-Ebeid on Egypt's Political Future" (video), Washington: Middle East Institute, 11 July 2013 (online; statement at minute 6).

65. Max Weber, *Economy and Society*, Berkeley, CA: University of California Press, 1978, vol. 1, pp. 293–95.

66. Karl Marx, *The Civil War in France*, in Marx and Engels, *Collected Works*, vol. 22, 1986, p. 333.

67. Ibid., p. 332-33.

68. Weber, *Economy and Society*, vol. 1, p. 295 (emphasis added).

69. Ibid., p. 289.

70. Definition of "Referendum" at <http://legal-dictionary.thefreedictionary. com/referendum>.

71. John Locke, *Second Treatise of Civil Government*, 1689, Chapter XIV, sec. 168.

72. "When the government violates the rights of the people, insurrection is for the people and for each portion of the people the most sacred of rights and the most indispensable of duties." Art. 35 of the French "Declaration of the Rights of Man and Citizen" of 1793.

73. The "monopoly of the legitimate use of physical force" is taken from Max Weber's classic definition of the modern state, in his famous 1919 lecture "Politics as Vocation", available at <http://anthropos-lab.net/wp/wp-content/uploads/2011/12/Weber-Politics-as-a-Vocation.pdf>.

74. "Nanshur al-Nass al-Kamil li-Kalimat al-Ra'is Muhammad Mursi min Maydan al-Tahrir", *Akhbarak*, 30 June 2012, <http://goo.gl/NDV56i>.

75. It all looked very much like the Algerian military's appointment of the progressive Mohamed Boudiaf as president (chairman of the High Council of State) in January 1992, in order to lure the liberals and the left into supporting their coup against the Islamic Salvation Front. Boudiaf tried to live up to his principles; he was assassinated after only six months.

76. On the building of the independent workers' movement in Egypt, see in particular Alexander and Bassiouny, *Bread, Freedom, and Social Justice*.

77. On Kamal Abu Aita's role as minister of the labour force, see Jano Charbel, "Labor Activist Wades into the Deep State", *Mada Masr*, 30 September 2013; Safa' Srur, "Kamal Abu-'Aita ... al-Wazir Yumazziq Dafatir al-Munadil al-'Ummali", *Al-Masry al-Youm*, 6 February 2014. For an assessment of the general state of Egypt's independent workers' unions in the Sisi era, see Jano Charbel, "Whatever Happened to Egypt's Independent Unions?", *Mada*

Masr, 1 May 2015; Brecht De Smet and Seppe Malfait, "Trade Unions and Dictatorship in Egypt", *Jadaliyya*, 31 August 2015.

78. Al-Markaz al-Misri, *Taqrir Al-Ihtijajat al-Sanawi 2013*.

79. Ibid.

80. One of the very first articles posted on the Muslim Brotherhood's website after the coup was titled (after the name of the Coptic Pope, Tawadros II) "Tawadros's Military Republic". It affirmed: "It is possible to say that Tawadros leads now his military republic, which has overthrown the legitimate regime and legitimate Muslim president – a republic that does not respect the rights of Muslims." Hilmi al-Qa'ud, "Jumhuriyyat Tawadrus al-'Askariyya", originally posted on *Ikhwan online* on 5 July 2013 and still available at <http://arabic.alshahid.net/columnists/94958?fb_source=pubv1>.

81. David Kirkpatrick, Peter Baker and Michael Gordon, "How American Hopes for a Deal in Egypt Were Undercut", *New York Times*, 17 August 2013.

82. See Alsharif and Saleh, "Special Report". This disproves Hazem Kandil's unconvincing attempt to interpret the Egyptian events through the lens of a struggle between two poles within a "triangle of power", with the army standing on one side, and the security and political apparatuses on the other. (Hazem Kandil, *Soldiers, Spies, and Statesmen: Egypt's Road to Revolt*, London: Verso, 2012). That the military and security apparatuses have distinct interests and views that can translate episodically into different attitudes is beyond dispute. But to regard these differences as more important that the common interests that tie both sections of the state's hard core to the point of constituting the basis of major historical developments is quite far-fetched (see note 147, below).

83. Kirkpatrick, Baker and Gordon, "How American Hopes of a Deal in Egypt Were Undercut".

84. Human Rights Watch, *All According to Plan: The Rab'a Massacre and Mass Killings of Protesters in Egypt*, New York: Human Rights Watch, August 2014, p. 6.

85. Ibid., p. 5 (emphasis added).

86. "The Protest Law, passed in November 2013, has become a fast-track to prison. The law effectively makes protests subject to official authorisation by the Interior Ministry, while handing security forces the power to use excessive force to disperse unsanctioned demonstrations and arrest their participants." Amnesty International, *Generation Jail: Egypt's Youth Go from Protest to Prison*, London: Amnesty International, June 2015, pp. 2, 7. On the Protest Law, see also the report on human rights violations released by fourteen NGOs on 4 January 2014, *Azru' al-Zulm: Taqrir Mushtarak bayn Munazzamat wa Harakat Huquqiyya hawl Intihakat Huquq al-Insan*, available at <http://www.eipr.org/report/2014/01/05/1921>.

87. The sentencing to fifteen years in prison of the police officer convicted for the killing of Socialist Popular Alliance Party member Shaima' al-Sabbagh on 24

January 2015 is indeed an exception forced on the government by the outcry this murder provoked *even among the government's own supporters.* As Human Rights Watch's Sarah Leah Whitson rightly commented: "The sentence against al-Sabbagh's killer would serve justice but past convictions of police have been reversed on appeal, meaning there has been zero accountability for killing protesters ... Nor has there been any accountability for those in charge of Egypt's security forces, who are ultimately responsible for the widespread and systematic killings of protesters in Egypt over the past two years." Human Rights Watch, "Egypt: Officer Convicted in Protester's Killing", 11 June 2015.

88. Dina al-Khawaga, "30 Yunyu ... Min Thawra ila Inqilab", *Mada Masr*, 13 November 2013.

89. "Open Call: Egyptian Human Rights Organizations Oppressed: A Return to What Is Worse than the Pre-January 25th Era", ECESR website, 19 December 2013 <http://ecesr.org/en/urgent-open-call-egyptian-human-rights-organizations-oppressed-a-return-to-what-is-worse-than-the-pre-january-25th-era/> (emphasis added). See also the above-mentioned report by fourteen NGOs on human rights violations, *Azru' al-Zulm.*

90. For an interesting discussion of the fascistic *features* displayed by the Muslim Brotherhood, see Amr Adly, "Bayna Fashiyya Mujahada wa Ukhra Muhtamala", *Bidayat*, no. 6 (Summer 2013), pp. 86–93 (also on *Jadaliyya*).

91. Karim Ennarah, "The Politics of Mobilization and Demobilization (Part 2)", *Mada Masr*, 25 February 2014 (emphasis added).

92. The soccer metaphor was used by Sameh Naguib, a leading member of the Revolutionary Socialists, at a public meeting in London a few days after the 3 July coup, where he proudly announced that, in the revolutionary contest between Tunisia and Egypt, the score was now: Tunisia 1, Egypt 2.

93. Karl Marx, *The Eighteenth Brumaire of Louis Bonaparte*, in Marx and Engels, *Collected Works*, vol. 11, 1979, p. 176. The translation used "conspiration", which is obsolete English for "conspiracy", for an obvious stylistic reason.

94. 'Ali al-Raggal, "Al-Dhabh 'ala Mihrab al-Dawla al-Muqaddas", *Mada Masr*, 16 July 2015.

95. Juan Linz, *Totalitarian and Authoritarian Regimes*, Boulder, CO: Lynne Rienner, 2000, p. 159. Linz is actually quoting the definition he gave in "An Authoritarian Regime: The Case of Spain", his contribution to a multi-authored volume published in 1964 (Erik Allardt and Yrjö Littunen, eds, *Cleavages, Ideologies and Party Systems*, Helsinki: Transactions of the Westermarck Society, 1964, pp. 291-342).

96. On the use of Nasser's image in pro-Sisi propaganda, see Tarek El-Ariss, "Future Fiction: In the Shadow of Nasser", *Ibraaz*, June 2014.

97. For a systematic comparison of the text of the two constitutions, see Maysara 'Abdul-Haq and Lina 'Atallah, "Muqarana bayn Dustur 2012 wa Mashru' Dustur 2013", *Mada Masr*, 13 January 2014.

98. Associated Press, "Putin Backs Egypt Army Chief's Run for President", 13 February 2014.

99. ECESR, "Taqrir Al-Ihtijajat al-'Ummaliyya 2014", Cairo: Al-Markaz al-Misri lil-Huquq al-Iqtisadiyya wal-Ijtima'iyya, 1 May 2015.

100. Dina Ezzat, "El-Sisi's Silence Provokes Questions about Expected Presidential Run", *Ahram Online*, 1 March 2014. Another delaying factor, according to Ezzat, was the preference expressed by Sisi's funders among the Gulf oil monarchies that he remain in charge of the SCAF rather than assuming the role of president – a preference reflecting Washington's unhappiness at the prospect of a blatant confirmation of the military character of Egypt's new rule.

101. "Yasir Rizq: Ra'aytu al-Sisi Yabki fa Qala li Huwa Ana A'azz min al-Rasul wa Abu Bakr", *AlAssema TV*, 22 October 2015, <https://www.youtube.com/watch?v=FjGUo5mcWGQ>.

102. Jano Charbel, "Sisi Posters and the Politics of Patronage", *Mada Masr*, 25 May 2014.

103. Economist, "Egypt's Election: A Coronation Flop", *Economist*, 31 May 2014.

104. A survey conducted by the Pew Research Center one month before the election indicated that 54 per cent of Egyptians had a favourable opinion of Sisi, versus 45 per cent unfavourable, while 35 per cent had a favourable opinion of Sabahy, versus 62 per cent unfavourable. Pew Research Center, *One Year After Morsi's Ouster, Divides Persist on El-Sisi, Muslim Brotherhood*, 22 May 2014, p. 13.

105. The term *ubuesque* is explained at the beginning of this chapter.

106. Human Rights Watch, "Egypt: Year of Abuses Under al-Sisi", *Human Rights Watch*, 8 June 2015.

107. Ibid.

108. Amnesty International, *Generation Jail*, p. 24.

109. Sa'id 'Abd al-Rahim, "Shaykh al-Azhar Da'iyan lil-Taswit: Al-Muqati'un lil-Intikhbata fi Manzilat al-'Aqin", *Al-'Arabi al-Jadid*, 22 November 2015.

110. Gamal Essam El-Din, "Diehard Mubarak-Era Figures Gain Ground in 2nd Stage of Egypt's Parliamentary Polls", *Ahram Online*, 28 November 2015.

111. Gamal Essam El-Din, "Egypt's Newly Elected MPs Vow to Amend Constitution", *Ahram Online*, 3 November 2015.

112. International Monetary Fund, *Arab Republic of Egypt 2014 Article IV Consultation, IMF Country Report No. 15/33*, Washington, DC: IMF, February 2015, p. 6 (Article IV consultation reports are related to IMF surveillance of economic and financial policies).

113. Ibid., p. 11.

114. Ibid. (emphasis added).

115. Ibid., p. 23.

116. Heba Saleh, "Egyptians Rail against Government as Fuel Costs Soar", *Financial Times*, 8 July 2014 (emphasis added).

117. Ibid.

118. "The benefits of the untargeted energy price subsidies accrue mostly to high-income households in Egypt, as they tend to consume a higher quantity of energy products. Based on staff estimates, the direct effect of the July

price increases for gasoline and diesel is mildly progressive, also reflecting low car ownership among low and middle-income households." International Monetary Fund, *Arab Republic of Egypt 2014*, p. 19.

119. Nada Rashwan, "Voices from Egypt: How Will Increased Energy Prices Affect You?", *Middle East Eye*, 6 July 2014.

120. International Monetary Fund, *Arab Republic of Egypt 2014*, p. 18.

121. Julien Ponthus and John Irish, "France's Hollande Says Egypt to Buy Rafale Fighters, Frigate", *Reuters*, 12 February 2015; Noah Rayman, "The Real Reason Egypt Is Buying Fighter Jets from France", *Time*, 14 February 2015; Dominique Gallois, "Comment la vente de Rafale à l'Egypte a-t-elle été organisée?", *Le Monde.fr*, 16 February 2015.

122. On the issue of subsidies as well as economic policy more generally, see Hannah Bargawi, "Economic Policies, Structural Change and the Roots of the 'Arab Spring' in Egypt", *Review of Middle East Economics and Finance*, vol. 10, no. 3, pp. 219–46.

123. Abdulla Zaid, Hassan Sherry, Mahinour El-Badrawi and Joshua Haber, *Arab Uprisings and Social Justice: Implications of IMF Subsidy Reform Policies*, Washington, DC: New America Foundation (with ECESR and ANND), February 2014, p. 2 (emphasis added). Egypt has the highest incidence of fraud among the countries surveyed by the audit firm Ernst & Young in 2014: over 80 per cent of business executives surveyed in Egypt stated that corruption was widespread, and 44 per cent of them reported having experienced a significant fraud during the previous two years. Ernst & Young, *Overcoming Compliance Fatigue: Reinforcing the Commitment to Ethical Growth, 13th Global Fraud Survey*, London: Ernst & Young, 2015.

124. Paolo Verme et al., *Inside Inequality in the Arab Republic of Egypt: Facts and Perceptions across People, Time, and Space*, Washington, DC: World Bank, 2014, pp. 10–11. For a discussion of inequality in Egypt and the Middle East, see Facundo Alvaredo and Thomas Piketty, *Measuring Top Incomes and Inequality in the Middle East: Data Limitations and Illustration with the Case of Egypt*, Giza: Economic Research Forum, 2014.

125. For a good critical survey of neoliberal economic policies in the Arab region, see Adam Hanieh, *Lineages of Revolt: Issues of Contemporary Capitalism in the Middle East*, Chicago: Haymarket, 2013.

126. See Achcar, *The People Want*, pp. 63–64.

127. Ibid., Chapter 2, esp. pp. 55–67.

128. Figure based on data provided in International Monetary Fund, *Arab Republic of Egypt 2014*, p. 34.

129. Ibid., p. 36.

130. Christine Lagarde, "Moment of Opportunity – Delivering on Egypt's Aspirations", speech delivered on 13 March 2015 at Sharm el-Sheikh, IMF (emphasis added). The Arabic verse is: *wa ma naylu al-matalibi bil-tammani wa lakin tu'khaz al-dunya ghilaba.*

131. See Abigail Hauslohner, "Egypt's Military Expands Its Control of the Country's Economy", *Wall Street Journal*, 16 March 2014. On the strains that developed between the Egyptian armed forces and Morsi with regard to economic projects, the most comprehensive source is Shana Marshall, *The Egyptian Armed Forces and the Remaking of an Economic Empire*, Beirut: Carnegie Middle East Center, April 2015.

132. On the armed forces' role in the New Suez Canal project, see Muhammad al-Bahrawi, "Al-Liwa' Kamil al-Wazir, Ra'is Arkan al-Hay'a al-Handasiyya lil-Quwwat al-Musallaha li 'al-Masri al-Yawm': al-Sisi Hasama Mashru' 'al-Qanat al-Jadida' qabla Tawallihi al-Ri'asa", *Al-Masry al-Youm*, 1 March 2015.

133. See Jano Charbel, "What Sisi Didn't Say About Labor Conditions in Constructing the New Suez Canal", *Mada Masr*, 7 August 2015.

134. Economist, "A Bigger, Better Suez Canal – But Is It Necessary?", *Economist*, 8 August 2015.

135. All figures for the Capital–Cairo are gathered from the project's website <http://thecapitalcairo.com/index.html>.

136. Ahram Online, "Egypt Government to Have 24% Share in New Capital City: Minister", *Ahram Online*, 23 March 2015.

137. Ibid.

138. Capital City, <http://www.capitalcity-partners.com/city-partners.html>.

139. See Hadeel Al Sayegh, "Dubai Property King's Outside Deals Stir Investor Unrest", *Reuters*, 2 April 2015.

140. Mada Masr, "Talks Between Egypt and Alabbar for New Administrative Capital Hit a Snag", *Mada Masr*, 24 June 2015, and Reuters, "Egypt Signs Deal with China Construction to Build, Finance, Part of New Capital", *Reuters*, 7 September 2015.

141. Al-Hay'a al-'Amma lil-Isti'lamat, "Al-Ra'is 'Abdul-Fattah al-Sisi Yajtami' ma' Mustashar Siyadatihi lil-Mashru'at al-Qawmiyya wa Wazir al-Iskan wa Qiyadat al-Hay'at al-Handasiyya", Cairo: Al-Hay'a al-'Amma lil-Isti'lamat, 12 October 2015.

142. Mada Masr, "Sisi Sets Two-Year Deadline for Phase 1 of New Capital", *Mada Masr*, 13 October 2015. On the 2014 housing project, see Reuters, "UAE's Arabtec Agrees $40 Billion Housing Project with Egypt Army", *Reuters*, 9 March 2014.

143. New Urban Communities Authority Portal, "New Cairo", <http://www.newcities.gov.eg/english/New_Communities/Cairo/default.aspx>. On Egypt's new cities, see David Sims, *Egypt's Desert Dreams: Development or Disaster?*, Cairo: American University in Cairo Press, 2015. See also Thanassis Cambanis, "To Catch Cairo Overflow, 2 Megacities Rise in Sand", *New York Times*, 24 August 2010. On the new cities and the new capital project, see Patrick Kingsley, "A New New Cairo: Egypt Plans £30bn Purpose-Built Capital in Desert", *Guardian*, 16 March 2015, and Heba Saleh, "Egypt's New Desert Capital: Metropolis or Mirage?", *Financial Times*, 5 June 2015.

144. David Sims, "David Sims Takes a Hard Look at Egypt's Struggling Desert Development", *AUC Press e-newsletter*, February 2015.

145. Khaled Fahmy, "Chasing Mirages in the Desert", *Cairobserver*, 14 March 2015.

146. Achcar, *The People Want*, p. 86.

147. On this, as well as on the relation between the military and security apparatuses, see ibid., pp. 183–85. The socio-economic tensions between the military-industrial complex and the Mubaraks' crony capitalist coterie were much more determinant than the episodic tensions between the military and security apparatuses (see note 82, above). The latter tensions actually derived from the former.

148. Zeinab Abul Magd (interviewed by Jessica Desvarieux), "New Egypt PM & Army Set to Keep Egypt on Neo-Liberal Track", *Real News Network*, 14 July 2013. See also Stephan Roll, *Egypt's Business Elite after Mubarak: A Powerful Player between Generals and Brotherhood*, Berlin: Stiftung Wissenschaft und Politik, September 2013.

149. Sarah Topol, "In Egypt, the Military Means (Big) Business", *Bloomberg Businessweek*, 13 March 2014. A similar assessment is expressed in Amr Adly, "The Military Economy and the Future of the Private Sector in Egypt", Carnegie Middle East Center, 6 September 2014 (Arabic original in same date's *Al-Shuruq*).

150. Samer Atallah, "Seeking Wealth, Taking Power", *Sada* (CEIP), 18 November 2014.

151. Abdel-Fattah Barayez, "More than Money on Their Minds: The Generals and the Economy in Egypt Revisited", *Jadaliyya*, 2 July 2015. The list of private companies involved in the New Suez Canal project is given in 'Abir 'Abd al-Majid, "Al-Qa'ima al-Kamila li-Sharikat Hafr Qanat al-Suways al-Jadida", *Al-Yawm al-Sabi'*, 5 February 2015. On the army's economic empire in Egypt, see also Abdel-Fattah Barayez, "'An al-Jaysh wa Imbaraturiyyatihi al-Iqtisadiyya fi Misr", *Jadaliyya*, 24 October 2013.

152. Jared Malsin, "Egypt's Generals Want a New Canal", *Bloomberg Businessweek*, 21 August 2014.

153. Marshall, *Egyptian Armed Forces*, p. 20.

154. Al-'Araby al-Jadid, "Misr: Al-Sisi Yadman Wala' al-Jaysh bi-Imtiyazat Iqtisadiyya ghayr Masbuqa", *Al-'Arabi al-Jadid*, 7 December 2015.

155. Muhammad Tawfiq, "Al-Qita' al-Khas al-Misri Yatakhawwaf min Tamaddud al-Jaysh Iqtisadiyyan", *Al-'Arabi al-Jadid*, 11 December 2015. See also Naguib Sawiris's protest against military involvement in economic activities in Stephen Kalin and Michael Georgy, "Interview: Egypt's Sawiris to Diversify Orascom, Invest $500 Mln in Egypt", Reuters, 15 March 2015.

156. Léopold Lambert, "New Egyptian Capital: Architects' Intrinsic Aspiration to Work with the Military", Funambulist (website), 24 April 2015. For a most interesting perspective on the nexus between urbanism, neoliberalism, security and sexuality in Cairo (and Rio de Janeiro), see Paul Amar, *The*

Security Archipelago: Human-Security States, Sexuality Politics, and the End of Neoliberalism, Durham, NC: Duke University Press, 2013.

157. Mohamed Elshahed, "Cairo: Militarized Landscape", *Funambulist* (journal), no. 1, September 2015, p. 24.

158. Lambert, "New Egyptian Capital".

159. ECESR, "Taqrir Al-Ihtijajat al-'Ummaliyya 2014".

160. Nashwa Muhammad, *Taqrir al-Ihtijajat al-Sanawi: al-Hirak al-'Ummali fi Misr li-'Am 2014* and *Taqrir al-Hala al-'Ummaliya fi Misr: al-Rub' al-Thalith li-'Am 2015*, both Cairo: Markaz al-Mahrousa lil-Tanmiya al-Iqtisadiyya wal-Ijtima'iyya, 2015. At the time of writing, the ECESR had not published data on workers' protests in 2015.

161. See the comment of former deputy prime minister in the Beblawi cabinet, Ziad Bahaa-Eldin (who resigned in January 2014): "Egypt: Labor Day Thoughts", *Ahram Online*, 6 May 2015 (Arabic original in previous day's *Al-Shuruq*).

162. See Islam Rida, "Akhtar 6 Bunud fi 'Qanun al-Khidma al-Madaniyya'", *Al-Misriyyun*, 10 August 2015, and Waad Ahmed and Randa Ali, "Doubts Hover Over Egypt's Civil Service Law", *Ahram Online*, 19 August 2015.

163. Mada Masr, "Policemen's Associations Express Solidarity with Sharqiya Protest", *Mada Masr*, 24 August 2015.

164. Ahram Online, "Egypt's Interior Ministry Says Sharqiya Police Action Was a 'Protest Rally' Not a 'Protest'", *Ahram Online*, 25 August 2015.

165. For a discussion of this issue, see Menna Alaa El-Din, "Egypt's Lower-Ranking Officers: A Struggle for Fairness or an Abuse of Power?", *Ahram Online*, 28 August 2015.

166. See Mokhtar Awad and Mostafa Hashem, *Egypt's Escalating Islamist Insurgency*, Beirut: Carnegie Middle East Center, October 2015.

167. On the polarisation within Egypt's Muslim Brotherhood, see Nathan Brown and Michele Dunne, *Unprecedented Pressures: Uncharted Course for Egypt's Muslim Brotherhood*, Washington, DC: Carnegie Endowment for International Peace, July 2015; Steven Brooke, "The Muslim Brotherhood's social outreach after the Egyptian coup", Washington, DC: Brookings Institution, August 2015; Omar Said, "After State Crackdown and Rumors of Rifts, Brotherhood Faces Identity Crisis", *Mada Masr*, 14 August 2015 (Arabic original: "Maza Yahduth Dakhil al-Ikhwan al-Muslimin: Muqarrabun wa A'da' Yujibun", *Mada Masr*, 8 June 2015); Georges Fahmi, "The Struggle for the Leadership of Egypt's Muslim Brotherhood", Carnegie Middle East Center, 14 July 2015; Vinciane Jacquet, "Les Frères musulmans égyptiens dépassés par leur base ?", *Orient XXI* (15 September 2015); Dina Samak, "What Does the Brotherhood Really Want?", *Ahram Online*, 9 October 2015; Mohamed Hamama, "The Hidden World of Militant 'Special Committees'", *Mada Masr*, 22 December 2015 (Arabic original posted on 22 November); and Muhammad al-'Atar, "Azmat al-Ikhwan al-Muslimin fi Misr: Inshiqaq Taqlidi am Inhiyar Murtaqab?", *Sasa Post*, 21 December 2015.

Conclusion

1.

    The main obstacle in the path of the Bahraini revolution – one potentially shared by protest movements in other Gulf monarchies, such as the predominantly working-class and social movement in Oman or the predominantly political movement in Kuwait – resides in the fact that it not only faces the local monarchy, but must square off with the GCC's mammoth, the Saudi kingdom, which will intervene to save its fellow monarchies whenever they are threatened by subversion – until the day when it is itself overwhelmed by a general uprising.

    Gilbert Achcar, *The People Want: A Radical Exploration of the Arab Uprising*, trans. G. M. Goshgarian, London: Saqi Books, and Berkeley, CA: University of California Press, 2013, pp. 198–99. The struggle has carried on in Bahrain, albeit muted in comparison with the 2011 uprising. See Ala'a Shehabi and Marc Owen Jones, eds, *Bahrain's Uprising*, London: Zed, 2015.

2. Achcar, *The People Want*, pp. 260–61.

3. Ibid., p. 208.

4. See Francoise Clément and Ahmed Salah, "Post-Uprising Libyan Associations and Democracy Building in Urban Libya", *Built Environment*, vol. 40, no. 1, 2013, pp. 118–27. See also Fadil Aliriza, "Libya's Unarmed Revolutionaries", *Foreign Policy* (online), 16 August 2013.

5. See International Crisis Group, *Divided We Stand: Libya's Enduring Conflicts*, Middle East/North Africa Report, No. 130, Tripoli/Brussels: ICG, 14 September 2012.

6. See Roman David and Houda Mzioudet, *Personnel Change or Personal Change? Rethinking Libya's Political Isolation Law*, Brookings Doha Center/Stanford University Project on Arab Transitions, Paper No. 4, March 2014.

7. See Ali Bensaâd, "Comment Daech progresse en Libye", *Libération*, 12 December 2015. According to the author, the members of Gaddafi's tribe were more attracted by Haftar than by the IS.

8. On post-uprising Libya, see Peter Cole and Brian McQuinn, eds, *The Libyan Revolution and Its Aftermath*, New York: Oxford University Press, 2015. See also Frederic Wehrey, *Ending Libya's Civil War: Reconciling Politics, Rebuilding Security*, Washington, DC: Carnegie Endowment for International Peace, September 2014; Patrick Haimzadeh, "Libya's Second Civil War", *Le Monde diplomatique*, April 2015; and Mattia Toaldo, "Libya's Transition and the Weight of the Past", in Anna Bozzo and Pierre-Jean Luizard, eds, *Polarisations politiques et confessionnelles. La place de l'islam dans les "transitions" arabes*, Rome: Roma TrE-Press, 2015, pp. 77–97.

9. See Laurent Bonnefoy, "Les Trois gagnants de la révolution yéménite", *Orient XXI*, 18 July 2014.

10. See ʿAdil al-Shurbaji, *Iʿadat Haykalat al-Jaysh al-Yamani*, Doha: Al-Markaz al-ʿArabi lil-Abhath wa Dirasat al-Siyasat, May 2013, and Marwan Noman and David Sorenson, *Reforming the Yemen Security Sector*, CDDRL Working Papers No. 137, Stanford, CA: Stanford University, June 2013.

11. Robert Worth, "Even Out of Office, a Wielder of Great Power in Yemen", *New York Times*, 31 January 2014.

12. See Laurent Bonnefoy, "La Revanche inattendue du confessionnalisme au Yémen", *Orient XXI*, 18 September 2014.

13. Worth, "Even Out of Office".

14. See International Crisis Group, *The Huthis: From Saada to Sanaa*, Middle East Report No. 154, Brussels: ICG, 10 June 2014.

15. Helen Lackner, "An Introduction to Yemen's Emergency", *Open Democracy*, 25 January 2015.

16. International Crisis Group, *The Huthis*, p. 16.

17. Ahmed Eleiba, "Saleh Speaks his Mind", *Al-Ahram Weekly*, 27 November 2014.

18. For background on Yemen's post-2011 evolution, see Helen Lackner, ed., *Why Yemen Matters: A Society in Transition*, London: Saqi, 2014.

19. On the role and peculiarity of Yemen's Muslim Brotherhood, see Laurent Bonnefoy, "Au Yémen, des Frères musulmans pas comme les autres", *Orient XXI*, 8 April 2014, and Stacey Philbrick Yadav, "Yemen's Muslim Brotherhood and the Perils of Powersharing", Washington, DC: Brookings Institution, August 2015.

20. Achcar, *The People Want*, p. 268. On the situation under Ennhada's rule, see Francis Ghilès, "Still a Long Way to Go for Tunisian Democracy", *Notes Internacional* CIDOB, no. 73 (May 2013).

21. Achcar, *The People Want*, p. 269.

22. The video was shown on television. It is available online at ProLaiques Tunisie, *Video al-Ghannushi maʿ al-Salafiyyin al-Musarrab*, 9 October 2012, <https://www.youtube.com/watch?v=m5vqhT8TxRw>. One can easily tell that it has been edited in order to reduce it to the most sensational statements. However, Ghannushi confirmed on television soon after the video's release that it is authentic, albeit edited, and that his only intention was to incite the Salafists to respect the state and abide by the law. Minbar Tunisi Hurr, *Radd al-Shaykh Rashid al-Ghannushi ʿala al-Video al-Musarrab*, 11 October 2012, <https://www.youtube.com/watch?v=_ZqFW-KEljM>. On Ennahda's attitude on constitutional issues, see Monica Marks, "Convince, Coerce, or Compromise? Ennahda's Approach to Tunisia's Constitution", Brookings Doha Center Analysis Paper No. 10, February 2014.

23. On the UGTT's role in the Tunisian uprising, the most comprehensive source is Hèla Yousfi's excellent book, *L'UGTT: Une passion tunisienne*, Sfax: Med Ali Edition, 2015. For a more concise survey, see Joel Beinin, *Workers and Thieves: Labor Movements and Popular Uprisings in Tunisia and Egypt*, Stanford, CA: Stanford University Press, 2015.

24. See Fabio Merone and Francesco Cavatorta, "Ennahda: A Party in Transition", *Jadaliyya*, 25 March 2013. On the Tunisian Salafist movement, see, by the same authors, "Salafist Movement and Sheikh-ism in the Tunisian Democratic Transition", *Middle East Law and Governance*, no. 5, 2013, pp. 308–30; Fabio Merone, "Enduring Class Struggle in Tunisia: The Fight for Identity beyond Political Islam", *British Journal of Middle Eastern Studies*, vol. 42, no. 1 (2015), pp. 74–87; Monica Marks, *Tunisia's Ennahda: Rethinking Islamism in the Context of ISIS and the Egyptian Coup*, Washington, DC: Brookings Institution, August 2015. On the jihadist phenomenon, see Haim Malka, "Tunisia: Confronting Extremism", in Jon Alterman, ed., *Religious Radicalism after the Arab Uprisings*, Lanham, MD: Rowman & Littlefield, 2015, pp. 92–121, and Georges Fahmi and Hamza Meddeb, *Market for Jihad: Radicalization in Tunisia*, Beirut: Carnegie Middle East Center, October 2015.

25. For a good survey of the Tunisian experience under Ennahda, see Mohammed Hachemaoui, *La Tunisie à la croisée des chemins: quelles règles pour quelle transition?* Berlin: Stiftung Wissenschaft und Politik, August 2013.

26. Sadri Khiari, "Quand l'Histoire recule par le bon côté", *Nawaat*, 7 August 2013.

27. The World Bank first commissioned a study of the 220 firms owned by the Ben Ali family that were confiscated in the aftermath of the Jasmin revolution, and which appropriated 21 per cent of all net private-sector profits. Bob Rijkers, Caroline Freund and Antonio Nucifora, *All in the Family: State Capture in Tunisia*, Policy Research Working Paper 6810, Washington, DC: World Bank, March 2014. This was followed by special attention being devoted to cronyism, corruption, predation and rent-extraction in the Bank's general report on Tunisia, *The Unfinished Revolution: Bringing Opportunity, Good Jobs and Greater Wealth to All Tunisians*, Development Policy Review, Washington, DC: World Bank, May 2014. Needless to say, "finishing the revolution" in the understanding of the World Bank means nothing other than achieving neoliberal "good governance". On Tunisian crony capitalism under Ben Ali, see also Bob Rijkers, Leila Baghdadi and Gael Raballand, *Political Connections and Tariff Evasion: Evidence from Tunisia*, Policy Research Working Paper 7336, Washington, DC: World Bank, June 2015.

28. Yousfi, *L'UGTT*, p. 237.

29. See Tasia Wagner, "Testing Tunisia's Transition: The Law on Economic and Financial Reconciliation", Institute for Strategic Islamic Affairs, October 2015.

30. See Hèla Yousfi and Choukri Hmed, "What Is Tunisia's Nobel Prize Rewarding?", *Open Democracy*, 25 October 2015.

31. See Yezid Sayigh, *Missed Opportunity: The Politics of Police Reform in Egypt and Tunisia*, Beirut: Carnegie Middle East Center, March 2015.

32. See Amel Boubekeur, "Islamists, Secularists and Old Regime Elites in Tunisia: Bargained Competition", *Mediterranean Politics* (online), 2015.

On spaces of youth struggle, see Charles Tripp, *Battlefields of the Republic: The Struggle for Public Space in Tunisia*, LSE Middle East Centre Paper Series No. 13, December 2015. For an excellent survey of young people in popular suburbs of Tunis, see Olfa Lamloum and Mohamed Ali Ben Zina, eds, *Les Jeunes de Douar Hicher et d'Ettadhamen. Une enquête sociologique*, Tunis: Arabesques/International Alert, 2015.

33. Anouar Boukhars, *The Reckoning: Tunisia's Perilous Path to Democratic Stability*, Washington, DC: Carnegie Endowment for International Peace, April 2015, pp. 19–20.

34. See my *The Clash of Barbarisms: The Making of the New World Disorder*, 2nd edn, London: Saqi, and Boulder, CO: Paradigm, 2006 [2002]. By a cruel irony of history, it was indeed on "September 11" 1990 that George H. W. Bush delivered his New World Order speech to Congress in a prelude to the first US war on Iraq.

35. Geoff Dyer and Demetri Sevastopulo, "Kerry Walks High Wire in Talks with Putin", *Financial Times*, 18 December 2015.

36. For a panorama of the Arab Left, see Mohamed Elagati et al., *Al-Yasar wal-Thawrat al-'Arabiyya*, Cairo: Muntada al-Bada'il al-'Arabi lil-Dirasat/ Rosa Luxemburg Stiftung, 2013, and Jamil Hilal and Katja Hermann, eds, *Mapping of the Arab Left: Contemporary Leftist Politics in the Arab East*, Ramallah: Rosa Luxemburg Stiftung Regional Office Palestine, 2014.

37. See Chapter 1, above.

38. Aziz al-Azmeh, *Suriyya wa al-Su'ud al-Usuli: 'An al-Usuliyya wa al-Ta'ifiyya wa al-Thaqafa*, Beirut: Riad El-Rayyes, 2015, pp. 76–77.

39. Maha Abdelrahman, *Egypt's Long Revolution: Protest Movements and Uprisings*, Abingdon, UK: Routledge, 2015, p. 107.

40. Ibid., pp. 110–11.

41. Ahlem Belhadj, "Women's Rights and the Arab Uprisings" (online video), conference delivered at SOAS, University of London, 7 December 2015.

References and Sources

The list below includes all books, pamphlets and journal articles cited in the text, along with selected press articles. Most of these documents were available online at the time of writing, and are easy to find with a search engine. A URL is provided only for online documents that are not easy to locate.

Abi-Habib, Maria, "ISIS Gained Momentum Because Al-Assad Decided to Go Easy on It", *Wall Street Journal*, 22 August 2014.

Abboud, Samer, "Capital Flight and the Consequences of the War Economy", *Jadaliyya*, 18 March 2013.

Abdalla, Nadine, "Egypt's Workers – From Protest Movement to Organized Labor", Berlin: Stiftung Wissenschaft und Politik, October 2012.

Abdelrahman, Maha, *Egypt's Long Revolution: Protest Movements and Uprisings*, Abingdon, UK: Routledge, 2015.

'Abdul-Haq, Maysara and Lina 'Atallah, "Muqarana bayn Dustur 2012 wa Mashru' Dustur 2013", *Mada Masr*, 13 January 2014.

Abou-El-Fadl, Reem, ed., *Revolutionary Egypt: Connecting Domestic and International Struggles*, Abingdon, UK: Routledge, 2015.

Abul Magd, Zeinab, "New Egypt PM & Army Set to Keep Egypt on Neo-Liberal Track" (interviewed by Jessica Desvarieux), *The Real News Network*, 14 July 2013.

Achcar, Gilbert, *Eastern Cauldron: Islam, Afghanistan, Palestine and Iraq in a Marxist Mirror*, trans. Peter Drucker, New York: Monthly Review Press, and London: Pluto, 2004.

——, *The Clash of Barbarisms: The Making of the New World Disorder*, trans. Peter Drucker, 2nd edn, London: Saqi, and Boulder, CO: Paradigm Publishers, 2006 [2002].

——, *The People Want: A Radical Exploration of the Arab Uprising*, trans. G. M. Goshgarian, London: Saqi, and Berkeley, CA: University of California Press, 2013 (page references in this book are to the UK edition).

Adly, Amr "Bayna Fashiyya Mujhada wa Ukhra Muhtamala", *Bidayat*, no. 6, Summer 2013, pp. 86–93.

——, "The Military Economy and the Future of the Private Sector in Egypt", Carnegie Middle East Center, 6 September 2014.

Afrasiabi, Kaveh, "The Oil War II and How Iran Can Strike Back", *Iran Review*, 2 December 2014.

Ahmad, Muhammad Idrees, "Obama's Legacy Is Tarnished as Putin Fills the Vacuum in Syria", *The National* (UAE), 10 October 2015.

Ahmed, Waad and Randa Ali, "Doubts Hover Over Egypt's Civil Service Law", *Ahram Online*, 19 August 2015.

Alaa El-Din, Menna, "Egypt's Lower-Ranking Officers: A Struggle for Fairness or an Abuse of Power?", *Ahram Online*, 28 August 2015.

Alexander, Anne and Mostafa Bassiouny, *Bread, Freedom, and Social Justice: Workers & the Egyptian Revolution*, London: Zed, 2014.

Ali, Mostafa, "Wave of Strikes: Egypt Labour Fights Back, Capital Draws a Line", *Ahram Online*, 31 July 2012.

Aliriza, Fadil, "Libya's Unarmed Revolutionaries", *Foreign Policy*, 16 August 2013.

Allinson, Jamie, "Class Forces, Transition and the Arab Uprisings: A Comparison of Tunisia, Egypt and Syria", *Democratization*, vol. 22, no. 2 (2015), pp. 294–314.

Alsharif, Asma and Yasmine Saleh, "Special Report: The Real Force behind Egypt's 'Revolution of the State'", *Reuters*, 10 October 2013.

Alterman, Jon, ed., *Religious Radicalism after the Arab Uprisings*, Lanham, MD: Rowman & Littlefield, 2015.

Alvaredo, Facundo and Thomas Piketty, *Measuring Top Incomes and Inequality in the Middle East: Data Limitations and Illustration with the Case of Egypt*, Giza: Economic Research Forum, 2014.

Amar, Paul, *The Security Archipelago: Human-Security States, Sexuality Politics, and the End of Neoliberalism*, Durham, NC: Duke University Press, 2013.

Amin (al-), Ibrahim, "Al-Shara' Yakhruj 'an Samtihi: al-Hall al-'Askari Wahm, wal-Hall bi-Taswiya Tarikhiyya", *Al-Akhbar*, 17 December 2012.

Amnesty International, *Generation Jail: Egypt's Youth Go from Protest to Prison*, London: Amnesty International, June 2015.

——, *"We Had Nowhere Else to Go": Forced Displacement and Demolitions in Northern Syria*, London: Amnesty International, October 2015.

'Araby al-Jadid (Al-), "Misr: Al-Sisi Yadman Wala' al-Jaysh bi-Imtiyazat Iqtisadiyya ghayr Masbuqa", *Al-'Arabi al-Jadid*, 7 December 2015.

Ariss (El-), Tarek, "Future Fiction: In the Shadow of Nasser", *Ibraaz*, June 2014.

Assad (al-), Bashar "Al-Ra'is al-Asad: al-Ma'raka Ma'rakat Mihwar Mutakamil Yumaththil Manhajan min al-Istiqlaliyya wal-Karama", *SANA*, 26 July 2015.

Atallah, Samer, "Seeking Wealth, Taking Power", *Sada* (CEIP), 18 November 2014.

'Atar (al-), Muhammad, "Azmat al-Ikhwan al-Muslimin fi Misr: Inshiqaq Taqlidi am Inhiyar Murtaqab?", *Sasa Post*, 21 December 2015.

Awad, Mokhtar and Mostafa Hashem, *Egypt's Escalating Islamist Insurgency*,

Beirut: Carnegie Middle East Center, October 2015.

Azmeh (al-), Aziz, *Suriyya wa al-Su'ud al-Usuli: 'An al-Usuliyya wa al-Ta'ifiyya wa al-Thaqafa*, Beirut: Riad El-Rayyes, 2015.

Bahaa-Eldin, Ziad, "Egypt: Labor Day Thoughts", *Ahram Online*, 6 May 2015.

Bakri, Mustafa, *Al-Jaysh wal-Ikhwan: Asrar Khalf al-Sitar*, Cairo: Al-Dar al-Misriyya al-Lubnaniyya, 2013.

Balanche, Fabrice, "Insurrection et contre-insurrection en Syrie", *Geostrategic Maritime Review*, no. 2, Spring/Summer 2014, pp. 36–57.

———, "Syria's Kurds Are Contemplating an Aleppo Alliance with Assad and Russia", *PolicyWatch 2499*, Washington Institute for Near East Policy, 7 October 2015.

Barayez, Abdel-Fattah, "'An al-Jaysh wa Imbaraturiyyatihi al-Iqtisadiyya fi Misr", *Jadaliyya*, 24 October 2013.

———, "More than Money on Their Minds: The Generals and the Economy in Egypt Revisited", *Jadaliyya*, 2 July 2015.

Bargawi, Hannah, "Economic Policies, Structural Change and the Roots of the 'Arab Spring' in Egypt", *Review of Middle East Economics and Finance*, Vol. 10, no. 3, pp. 219–46.

Barthe, Benjamin, "Egypte: les apprentis sorciers de Tamarrod", *Le Monde*, 17 July 2013.

Beinin, Joel, *The Rise of Egypt Workers*, . Washington, DC: Carnegie Endowment for International Peace, June 2012.

———, *Workers and Thieves: Labor Movements and Popular Uprisings in Tunisia and Egypt*, Stanford, CA: Stanford University Press, 2015.

Beinin, Joel, and Marie Duboc, "Mouvement ouvrier, luttes syndicales et processus révolutionnaire en Égypte, 2006–2013", in Camau and Frédéric Vairel, eds, 2014, pp. 121–42.

Belhadj, Ahlem, "Women's Rights and the Arab Uprisings" (online video), conference delivered at SOAS, University of London, 7 December 2015.

Bensaâd, Ali, "Comment Daech Progresse en Libye", *Libération*, 12 December 2015.

Bensaïd, Daniel, *Marx for Our Time: Adventures and Misadventures of a Critique*, trans. Gregory Elliott, London: Verso, 2002.

Black, Ian, "Wake-Up Call on Syrian Army Weakness Prompted Russian Intervention", *Guardian*, 1 October 2015.

Black, Ian, and Saeed Dehghan, "Iran Ramps Up Troop Deployment in Syria in Run-Up to 'Anti-Rebel Offensive'", *Guardian*, 14 October 2015.

Blair, Edmund, Paul Taylor and Tom Perry, "Special Report: How the Muslim Brotherhood lost Egypt", *Reuters*, 26 July 2013.

Bonnefoy, Laurent, "Au Yémen, des Frères musulmans pas comme les autres", *Orient XXI*, 8 April 2014.

———, "Les Trois gagnants de la révolution yéménite", *Orient XXI*, 18 July 2014.

———, "La Revanche inattendue du confessionnalisme au Yémen", *Orient XXI*, 18 September 2014.

Boubekeur, Amel, "Islamists, Secularists and Old Regime Elites in Tunisia: Bargained Competition", *Mediterranean Politics* (online), 2015.

Boukhars, Anouar, *The Reckoning: Tunisia's Perilous Path to Democratic Stability*, Washington, DC: Carnegie Endowment for International Peace, April 2015.

Bozarslan, Hamit, *Révolution et état de violence. Moyen-Orient 2011–2015*, Paris: CNRS, 2015.

Bozzo, Anna and Pierre-Jean Luizard, eds, *Polarisations politiques et confessionnelles. La place de l'islam dans les "transitions" arabes*, Rome: Roma TrE-Press, 2015.

Brown, Nathan and Michele Dunne, *Unprecedented Pressures, Uncharted Course for Egypt's Muslim Brotherhood*, Washington, DC: Carnegie Endowment for International Peace, July 2015.

Brun, Sarah, "La Farce à l'épreuve du tragique au XXe siècle", in Torres and Ferry, eds, 2012.

Bunni (al-), Akram, "An Analysis of the Realities of the Syrian Left", in Hilal and Hermann, eds, *Mapping of the Arab Left*, pp. 104–26.

Bureau of Political-Military Affairs, "MANPADS: Combating the Threat to Global Aviation from Man-Portable Air Defense Systems", Washington, DC: US Department of State, 27 July 2011.

Burgat, François, "Testimony of General Ahmed Tlass on the Syrian Regime and the Repression", *Noria*, April 2014.

Burgat, François and Bruno Paoli, eds, *Pas de printemps pour la Syrie. Les clés pour comprendre les acteurs et les défis de la crise (2011–2013)*, Paris: La Découverte, 2013.

Butter, David, *Syria's Economy: Picking up the Pieces*, London: Chatham House, June 2015.

Cairo Institute for Human Rights Studies (CIHRS), *Al-Ittihadiyya "Presidential Palace" Clashes in Cairo 5 and 6 December 2012*, Cairo: CIHRS, December 2012.

Cambanis, Thanassis, "To Catch Cairo Overflow, 2 Megacities Rise in Sand", *New York Times*, 24 August 2010.

Camau, Michel and Frédéric Vairel, eds, *Soulèvements et recompositions politiques dans le monde arabe*, Montreal: Presses de l'Université de Montréal, 2014.

Charbel, Ghassan, "'Ajaza Mursi 'an al-Ijaba wa Qala 'Uriduka ma'i Na'iban lil-Ra'is' … Shi'ar 'Yasqut Yasqut Hukm al-'Askar' Adarra al-Thawra wa Qarraba bayn al-Jaysh wal-Ikhwan", *Al-Hayat*, 26 June 2013.

———, "Sabbahi: Mursi lam Ya'ud Yumaththil al-Thawra wa '30 Yunyu' li

Waqf al-Istibdad 'al-Ikhwani'", *Al-Hayat*, 27 June 2013.

——, "Sabbahi: Al-Jaysh Quwwa Wataniyya Asila wa ayy Tadakhkhul lahu sa-Yakun li-Marhala Intiqaliyya", *Al-Hayat*, 28 June 2013.

Charbel, Jano, "Labor Activist Wades into the Deep State", *Mada Masr*, 30 September 2013.

——, "Sisi Posters and the Politics of Patronage", *Mada Masr*, 25 May 2014.

——, "Whatever happened to Egypt's independent unions?", *Mada Masr*, 1 May 2015.

——, "What Sisi Didn't Say About Labor Conditions in Constructing the New Suez Canal", *Mada Masr*, 7 August 2015.

Chomsky, Noam, "The Responsibility to Protect", lecture given at the UN General Assembly, New York, July 23, 2009, <http://www.chomsky.info/talks/20090723.htm>.

Chomsky, Noam and Gilbert Achcar, *Perilous Power: The Middle East and US Foreign Policy*, ed. by Stephen Shalom, 2nd edn, Boulder, CO: Paradigm, 2008.

Chulov, Martin, "Why Isis Fights", *Guardian*, 17 September 2015.

——, "Is Vladimir Putin Right to Label Turkey 'Accomplices of Terrorists'?", *Guardian*, 24 November 2015.

Clausewitz (von), Carl, *On War*, ed. and trans. Michael Howard and Peter Paret, Princeton, NJ: Princeton University Press, 1989.

Clément, Francoise, and Ahmed Salah, "Post-Uprising Libyan Associations and Democracy Building in Urban Libya", *Built Environment*, vol. 40, no. 1, 2013, pp. 118–27.

Clinton, Hillary Rodham, *Hard Choices*, New York: Simon & Schuster, 2015.

——, see the entry for Goldberg.

Cole, Peter, and Brian McQuinn, eds, *The Libyan Revolution and Its Aftermath*, New York: Oxford University Press, 2015.

Coles, Isabel, and Ned Parker, "The Baathists: How Saddam's Men Help Islamic State Rule", *Reuters*, 11 December 2015.

Collins, Dylan, "A Growing Jihadist Presence in Syria's Opposition" (interview with Hassan Hassan), *Syria Deeply*, 30 November 2015.

Cooper, Helene and Mark Landler, "US Hopes Assad Can Be Eased Out with Russia's Aid", *New York Times*, 26 May 2012.

Cordesman, Anthony, "US Options in Syria: Obama's Delays and the Dempsey Warnings", CSIS, 23 August 2013.

——, "Beyond Partisan Bickering: Key Questions About US Strategy in Syria", CSIS, 17 September 2015.

CTUWS, *Hal al-'Ummal fi Hukm al-Ikhwan: 'Am min Intihakat al-Hurriyyat al-Niqabiyya fi Fatrat Hukm Mursi*, Cairo: Dar al-Khadamat al-Niqabiyya wal-'Ummaliyya, June 2013.

David, Roman, and Houda Mzioudet, *Personnel Change or Personal Change?*
    Rethinking Libya's Political Isolation Law, Brookings Doha Center –
    Stanford University Project on Arab Transitions, Paper no. 4, March 2014.

Denitch, Bogdan, *After the Flood: World Politics and Democracy in the Wake
    of Communism*, London: Adamantine, 1992.

De Smet, Brecht, and Seppe Malfait, "Trade Unions and Dictatorship in
    Egypt", *Jadaliyya*, 31 August 2015.

Dickinson, Elizabeth, "The Case Against Qatar", *Foreign Policy*, 30 September
    2014.

Duboc, Marie "Reluctant Revolutionaries? The Dynamics of Labour Protests
    in Egypt, 2006–13", in Abou-El-Fadl, ed., 2015, pp. 27–41.

Economist (The), "Egypt's Election: A Coronation Flop", *Economist*, 31 May
    2014.

———, "A Bigger, Better Suez Canal – But Is It Necessary?", *Economist*, 8
    August 2015.

Egyptian Center for Economic and Social Rights (ECESR), *Al-Ihtijajat
    al-'Ummaliyya fi Misr 2012*, Cairo: Al-Markaz al-Misri lil-Huquq al-
    Iqtisadiyya wal-Ijtima'iyya, 2013.

———, *Taqrir Al-Ihtijajat al-Sanawi 2013*, Cairo: ECESR, 2014.

———, "Taqrir Al-Ihtijajat al-'Ummaliyya 2014", Cairo: Al-Markaz al-Misri
    lil-Huquq al-Iqtisadiyya wal-Ijtima'iyya, 1 May 2015.

ECESR et al., "Open Call: Egyptian Human Rights Organizations Oppressed:
    A Return to what is Worse than the Pre-January 25th Era", ECESR website,
    19 December 2013, <http://ecesr.org/en/urgent-open-call-egyptian-
    human-rights-organizations-oppressed-a-return-to-what-is-worse-than-
    the-pre-january-25th-era/>.

Egyptian Initiative for Personal Rights et al., *Azru' al-Zulm: Taqrir
    Mushtarak bayn Munazzamat wa Harakat Huquqiyya hawl Intihakat
    Huquq al-Insan*, 4 January 2014, available at <http://www.eipr.org/
    report/2014/01/05/1921>.

Elagati, Mohamed *et al.*, *Al-Yasar wal-Thawrat al-'Arabiyya*, Cairo: Muntada
    al-Bada'il al-'Arabi lil-Dirasat/Rosa Luxemburg Stiftung, 2013.

Eleiba, Ahmed, "Saleh Speaks his Mind", *Al-Ahram Weekly*, 27 November
    2014.

Elshahed, Mohamed, "Cairo: Militarized Landscape", *The Funambulist*, no. 1,
    September 2015, pp. 20–25.

Ennarah, Karim, "The Politics of Mobilization and Demobilization (Part 2)",
    Mada Masr, 25 February 2014.

Ezzat, Dina, "Egypt: The President, the Army and the Police", *Ahram Online*,
    27 December 2012.

———, "President Morsi Could Face a Summer of Discontent", *Ahram
    Online*, 27 December 2012.

———, "El-Sisi's Silence Provokes Questions about Expected Presidential Run", *Ahram Online*, 1 March 2014.

Fahmi, Georges, "The Struggle for the Leadership of Egypt's Muslim Brotherhood", Carnegie Middle East Center, 14 July 2015.

Fahmi, Georges and Hamza Meddeb, *Market for Jihad: Radicalization in Tunisia*, Beirut: Carnegie Middle East Center, October 2015.

Fahmy, Khaled, "Chasing Mirages in the Desert", *Cairobserver*, 14 March 2015.

Falk, Pamela, "US Doesn't Really Want Assad to Fall, Russian Ambassador Claims", *CBS News*, 15 September 2015.

Filiu, Jean-Pierre, *From Deep State to Islamic State: The Arab Counter-Revolution and its Jihadi Legacy*, London: Hurst, 2015.

Foer, Franklin, and Chris Hughes, "Barack Obama Is Not Pleased: The President on His Enemies, the Media, and the Future of Football", *New Republic*, 27 January 2013.

Freedom House, *Freedom in the World 2008*, Washington, DC: Freedom House, 2008.

———, *Freedom in the World 2010*, Washington, DC: Freedom House, 2010.

———, *Freedom in the World 2011*, Washington, DC: Freedom House, 2011.

———, *Freedom in the World 2012*, Washington, DC: Freedom House, 2012.

Fukuyama, Francis, "The End of History", *The National Interest*, no. 16, Summer 1989.

———, *The End of History and the Last Man*, New York: Avon, 1992.

———, "Is China Next?", *Wall Street Journal*, 12 March 2011.

Gallois, Dominique, " Comment la vente de Rafale à l'Egypte a-t-elle été organisée?", *Le Monde.fr*, 16 February 2015.

Gamal, Wael, "La lil-Iqtirad 'ala Mabadi' al-Sunduq wal-Ganzouri wa Man Tabi'ahuma", *Al-Shuruq*, 20 August 2012.

Ghilès, Francis, "Still a Long Way to Go for Tunisian Democracy", *Notes Internacional CIDOB*, no. 73, May 2013.

Goldberg, Jeffrey, "Hillary Clinton: 'Failure' to Help Syrian Rebels Led to the Rise of ISIS", *Atlantic*, 10 August 2014.

Gordon, Michael and Mark Landler, "Senate Hearing Draws Out a Rift in US Policy on Syria", *New York Times*, 7 February 2013.

Grimm, Jannis, *Mapping Change in the Arab World: Insights from Transition Theory and Middle East Studies*, Berlin: Stiftung Wissenschaft und Politik, June 2013.

Guiton, Barney, "'ISIS Sees Turkey as Its Ally': Former Islamic State Member Reveals Turkish Army Cooperation", *Newsweek*, 7 November 2014.

Gunter, Frank, "ISIL Revenues: Grow or Die", *Foreign Policy Research Institute*, June 2015.

Habash, Muhammad, "Abu al-Qaʿqaʿ... Dhikrayat ... al-Tariq ila Daʿish", *All4Syria*, 7 October 2014.

Hachemaoui, Mohammed, *La Tunisie à la croisée des chemins: quelles règles pour quelle transition?*, Berlin: Stiftung Wissenschaft und Politik, August 2013.

Haimzadeh, Patrick, "Libya's Second Civil War", *Le Monde diplomatique*, April 2015.

Haj Saleh (al-), Yassin, "al-Sultan al-Hadith: Al-Manabiʿ al-Siyasiyya wa al-Ijtimaʿiyya lil-Taʾifiyya fi Suriya", *Al-Jumhuriyya*, 26 and 30 January, and 4 February 2015.

Hamama, Mohamed, "The Hidden World of Militant 'Special Committees'", *Mada Masr*, 22 December 2015.

Hamidi, Ibrahim, "Muʾtamar al-Riyadh Yadʿam al-Hall al-Siyasi, wa Hayʾa li-Tashkil Wafd al-Mufawadat", *Al-Hayat*, 11 December 2015.

Hanieh, Adam, *Lineages of Revolt: Issues of Contemporary capitalism in the Middle East*, Chicago: Haymarket, 2013.

Hassan, Hassan and Bassam Barabandi, "Kurds Can't Be Syria's Saviors", *Foreign Policy*, 18 November 2015.

Hauslohner, Abigail, "Egypt's Military Expands Its Control of the Country's Economy", *Wall Street Journal*, 16 March 2014.

Heller, Sam, "Ahrar al-Sham's Revisionist Jihadism", *War on the Rocks*, 30 September 2015.

Hilal, Jamil and Katja Hermann, eds, *Mapping of the Arab Left: Contemporary Leftist Politics in the Arab East*, Ramallah: Rosa Luxemburg Stiftung Regional Office Palestine, 2014

Hinnebusch, Raymond, "Globalization, Democratization, and the Arab Uprising: The International Factor in MENA's Failed Democratization", *Democratization*, vol. 22, no. 2, 2015, pp. 335-57.

Hof, Frederic, "The Self-Government Revolution That's Happening under the Radar in Syria", *Washington Post*, 26 July 2015.

———, "I Got Syria So Wrong", *Politico*, 14 October 2015.

Human Rights Watch, *Under Kurdish Rule: Abuses in PYD-run Enclaves of Syria*, New York: HRW, June 2014.

———, *All According to Plan: The Rabʾa Massacre and Mass Killings of Protesters in Egypt*, New York: HRW, August 2014.

———, "Egypt: Year of Abuses Under al-Sisi", HRW, 8 June 2015.

Huntington, Samuel, *The Third Wave: Democratization in the Late Twentieth Century*, Norman, OK: University of Oklahoma Press, 1991.

———, *The Clash of Civilizations and the Remaking of World Order*, New York: Touchstone, 1997.

Ibrahim, Ekram, "Why Did Sabbahi – 'One of Us' – Do So well?", *Ahram Online*, 25 May 2012.

Idiz, Semih, "ISIS Emerges as Threat to Turkey", *Al-Monitor*, 25 March 2014.

Ilgit, Asli and Rochelle Davis, "The Many Roles of Turkey in the Syrian Crisis", *Middle East Report Online*, 28 January 2013.

International Crisis Group, *Divided We Stand: Libya's Enduring Conflicts*, *Middle East/North Africa Report* no. 130, 14 September 2012.

———, *The Huthis: From Saada to Sanaa, Middle East Report* no. 154, Brussels: ICG, 10 June 2014.

International Monetary Fund, *Arab Republic of Egypt 2014 Article IV Consultation*, IMF *Country Report No. 15/33*, Washington, DC: IMF, February 2015.

Ismail, Salwa, "Urban Subalterns in the Arab Revolutions: Cairo and Damascus in Comparative Perspective", *Comparative Studies in Society and History*, vol. 55, no. 4, 2013, pp. 865–94.

Jacquet, Vinciane, "Les Frères musulmans égyptiens dépassés par leur base ?", *Orient XXI*, 15 September 2015.

Jones, Sam "New EU Syria Sanctions Reveal Regime Collusion with Isis", *Financial Times*, 7 March 2015.

Kaileh, Salameh, "Hawla Dawr al-Yasar al-Suri fil-Thawra", in Mohamed Elagati *et al.*, pp. 47-63.

Kaminski, Matthew, "Khairat Al Shater: The Brother Who Would Run Egypt", *Wall Street Journal*, 22 June 2012.

Kandil, Hazem, *Soldiers, Spies, and Statesmen: Egypt's Road to Revolt*, London: Verso, 2012.

Karouny, Mariam, "Resilient insurgent group Ahrar al-Sham to play bigger role in Syria", *Reuters*, 22 September 2015.

Kerry, John, John Kerry, "Interview with Nicolle Wallace, Mike Barnicle, Mark Halperin, Richard Haass, and Katty Kay of MSNBC's Morning Joe", US Department of State, 29 September 2015.

———, "Remarks at a Meeting on International Peace and Security and Countering Terrorism", US Department of State, 30 September 2015.

Khaddour, Kheder, *The Assad Regime's Hold on the Syrian State*, Beirut: Carnegie Middle East Center, July 2015.

———, "Assad's Officer Ghetto: Why The Syrian Army Remains Loyal", Beirut: Carnegie Middle East Center, November 2015.

Khiari, Sadri, "Quand l'Histoire recule par le bon côté", *Nawaat*, 7 August 2013.

Kingsley, Patrick, "A New New Cairo: Egypt Plans £30bn Purpose-Built Capital in Desert", *Guardian*, 16 March 2015.

Kirkpatrick, David, Peter Baker and Michael Gordon, "How American Hopes for a Deal in Egypt Were Undercut", *New York Times*, 17 August 2013.

Klapper, Bradley and Julie Pace, "Why Obama is Standing with Egypt's President Morsi", *Associated Press*, 28 November 2012.

Lackner, Helen, ed., *Why Yemen Matters: A Society in Transition*, London: Saqi, 2014.

———, "An Introduction to Yemen's Emergency", *Open Democracy*, 25 January 2015.

Lambert, Léopold, "New Egyptian Capital: Architects' Intrinsic Aspiration to Work with the Military", *The Funambulist* (website), 24 April 2015.

Lamloum, Olfa and Mohamed Ali Ben Zina, eds, *Les Jeunes de Douar Hicher et d'Ettadhamen. Une enquête sociologique*, Tunis: Arabesques/International Alert, 2015.

Lefèvre, Raphaël, "Islamism Within a Civil War: The Syrian Muslim Brotherhood's Struggle for Survival", Washington, DC: Brookings Institution, August 2015.

Lesch, David, *The New Lion of Damascus: Bashar al-Asad and Modern Syria*, New Haven, CT: Yale University Press, 2005.

Levinson, Charles and Matt Bradley, "In Egypt, the 'Deep State' Rises Again", *Wall Street Journal*, 12 July 2013.

Linz, Juan, *Totalitarian and Authoritarian Regimes*, Boulder, CO: Lynne Rienner, 2000.

Lister, Charles, *The Syrian Jihad: Al-Qaeda, the Islamic State and the Evolution of an Insurgency*, London: Hurst, 2015.

Locke, John, *Second Treatise of Civil Government*, 1689.

Lund, Aron, *Syria's Salafi Insurgents: The rise of the Syrian Islamic Front*, Stockholm: Swedish Institute of International Affairs, March 2013.

———, "Syria's Kurds at the Center of America's Anti-Jihadi Strategy", Carnegie Endowment for International Peace, 2 December 2015.

———, "Syria's Opposition Conferences: Results and Expectations", Carnegie Endowment for International Peace, 11 December 2015.

Mahmoud (al-), Hamoud, "The War Economy in the Syrian Conflict: The Government's Hands-Off Tactics", Carnegie Endowment for International Peace, 15 December 2015.

Makram-Ebeid, Mona, "Mona Makram-Ebeid on Egypt's Political Future" (video), Washington: Middle East Institute, 11 July 2013.

Malashenko, Alexei, "Putin's Syrian Bet", *Le Monde Diplomatique*, November 2015.

Malka, Haim, "Tunisia: Confronting Extremism", in Alterman, ed., 2015, pp. 92–121.

Marks, Monica, "Convince, Coerce, or Compromise? Ennahda's Approach to Tunisia's Constitution", Brookings Doha Center Analysis Paper no. 10, February 2014.

————, *Tunisia's Ennahda: Rethinking Islamism in the Context of ISIS and the Egyptian Coup*, Washington, DC: Brookings Institution, August 2015.

Marshall, Shana, *The Egyptian Armed Forces and the Remaking of an Economic Empire*, Beirut: Carnegie Middle East Center, April 2015.

Karl Marx, *The Eighteenth Brumaire of Louis Bonaparte*, in Marx and Engels, *Collected Works*, vol. 11, London: Lawrence & Wishart, 1979, pp. 99–197.

————, *The Civil War in France*, in Marx and Engels, *Collected Works*, vol. 22, London: Lawrence & Wishart, 1986, pp. 307–59.

Mazzetti, Mark, Eric Schmitt and David Kirkpatrick, "Saudi Oil Is Seen as Lever to Pry Russian Support from Syria's Assad", *New York Times*, 3 February 2015.

McCain, John, "Statement by Senator John McCain on Obama Administration's 'Deconfliction' Talks with Russia on Syria Airstrikes", Senator John McCain's website, 1 October 2015.

Médecins Sans Frontières (MSF), *Responsibility to Protect, Dialogue 8*, April 2009, <http://www.msf.org.uk/sites/uk/files/MSF_Dialogue_No8__R2P_200904012144.pdf>.

Merone, Fabio, "Enduring Class Struggle in Tunisia: The Fight for Identity beyond Political Islam", *British Journal of Middle Eastern Studies*, vol. 42, no. 1, 2015, pp. 74–87.

Merone, Fabio and Francesco Cavatorta, "Ennahda: A Party in Transition", *Jadaliyya*, 25 March 2013.

————, "Salafist Movement and Sheikh-Ism in the Tunisian Democratic Transition", *Middle East Law and Governance*, no. 5, 2013, pp. 308–30.

Mills, C. Wright, *The Power Elite*, New York: Oxford University Press, 1956.

Morsi, Mohamed, "Nanshur al-Nass al-Kamil li-Kalimat al-Ra'is Muhammad Mursi min Maydan al-Tahrir", *Akhbarak*, 30 June 2012, <http://goo.gl/NDV56i>.

Muhammad, Nashwa, *Taqrir al-Ihtijajat al-Sanawi: al-Hirak al-'Ummali fi Misr li-'Am 2014*, Cairo: Markaz al-Mahrousa lil-Tanmiya al-Iqtisadiyya wal-Ijtima'iyya, 2015.

————, *Taqrir al-Hala al-'Ummaliya fi Misr: al-Rub' al-Thalith li-'Am 2015*, Cairo: Markaz al-Mahrousa lil-Tanmiya al-Iqtisadiyya wal-Ijtima'iyya, 2015.

Murray, Robert and Alasdair McKay, eds, *Into the Eleventh Hour: R2P, Syria and Humanitarianism in Crisis*, Bristol, UK: E-International Relations, 2014.

Muslim, Muhammad, *Tabdid al-Asatir: Al-Azma al-Iqtisadiyya fi Misr*, Cairo: Al-Mubadara al_Misriyya lil-Huquq al-Shakhsiyya, May 2013.

Naame Shaam, *Iran in Syria: From an Ally of the Regime to an Occupying Force*, September 2014.

————, *Silent Sectarian Cleansing: Iranian Role in Mass Demolitions and Population Transfers in Syria*, May 2015.

Nada, Youssef with Douglas Thompson, *Inside the Muslim Brotherhood*, London: Metro, 2012.

Nasira, Hani, "Min Aghasi ila al-Nusra: Khibrat al-Asad fi Ikhtiraq al-Jihadiyyin", *Ma'had Al-'Arabiyya lil-Dirasat*, 16 June 2013.

Neumann, Peter, "Suspects into Collaborators", *London Review of Books*, vol. 36, no. 7 (3 April 2014), pp. 19–21.

Noman, Marwan and David Sorenson, *Reforming the Yemen Security Sector*, CDDRL Working Papers no. 137, Stanford, CA: Stanford University, June 2013.

Obama, Barack, "Remarks by the President on Egypt", Washington, DC: The White House, 11 February 2011.

————, "Remarks by the President to the White House Press Corps", Washington: White House, Office of the Press Secretary, 20 August 2012.

————, "Remarks by the President on the Situation in Iraq", Washington, DC: White House, Office of the Press Secretary, 19 June 2014.

————, "Press Conference by the President", Washington, DC: White House, 2 October 2015, <https://www.whitehouse.gov/the-press-office/2015/10/02/press-conference-president>.

————, see the entry for Foer and Hugues.

Ohl, Dorothy, Holger Albrecht and Kevin Koehler, "For Money or Liberty? The Political Economy of Military Desertion and Rebel Recruitment in the Syrian Civil War", Beirut: Carnegie Middle East Center, 24 November 2015.

PBS, "Former US Ambassador Says He Could 'No Longer Defend' Obama Administration's Syria Policy", *PBS Newshour*, 3 June 2014.

Pew Research Center, *One Year After Morsi's Ouster, Divides Persist on El-Sisi, Muslim Brotherhood*, 22 May 2014.

Qandil, Hisham, "Qandil: Mursi Wafaqa 'ala Ijra' Istifta' 'ala Istimrarihi Lakin Ba'd al-Intikhabat al-Barlimaniyya", *Al-Watan*, 25 July 2013.

Quilliam, Neil, "Five Reasons Why the Inclusion of Assad in a Political Transition in Syria Is Destined to Fail", *Newsweek*, 29 September 2015.

Raggal (al-), 'Ali, "Al-Dhabh 'ala Mihrab al-Dawla al-Muqaddas", *Mada Masr*, 16 July 2015.

Rashwan, Nada, "Voices from Egypt: How Will Increased Energy Prices Affect You?", *Middle East Eye*, 6 July 2014.

Reuter, Christoph, "The West's Dilemma: Why Assad Is Uninterested in Defeating Islamic State", *Spiegel Online International*, 8 December 2015.

Revolutionary Socialists (Al-Ishtirakiyyun al-Thawriyyun), "'Ala Tariq Istikmal al-Thawra: Al-Ishtirakiyyun al-Thawriyyun fi Hamlat Tamarrud", Revolutionary Socialists' website, 19 May 2013, <http://revsoc.me/-14836>.

Rida, Islam, "Akhtar 6 Bunud fi 'Qanun al-Khidma al-Madaniyya'", *Al-Misriyyun*, 10 August 2015.

Ridley, Yvonne, "EXCLUSIVE: Shaikh Hassan Abboud's final interview", *MEMO Middle East Monitor*, 22 September 2014.

Rijkers, Bob, Leila Baghdadi and Gael Raballand, *Political Connections and Tariff Evasion: Evidence from Tunisia*, Policy Research Working Paper 7336, Washington, DC: World Bank, June 2015.

Rijkers, Bob, Caroline Freund and Antonio Nucifora, *All in the Family: State Capture in Tunisia*, Policy Research Working Paper 6810, Washington, DC: World Bank, March 2014.

Roberts, David, "Is Qatar Bringing the Nusra Front in from the Cold?", *BBC News*, 6 March 2015.

Roll, Stephan, *Egypt's Business Elite after Mubarak: A Powerful Player between Generals and Brotherhood*, Berlin: Stiftung Wissenschaft und Politik, September 2013.

Ross, Carne, "Power to the People: A Syrian Experiment in Democracy", *Financial Times*, 23 October 2015.

Roth, Kenneth, "Barrel Bombs, Not ISIS, Are the Greatest Threat to Syrians", *New York Times*, 5 August 2015.

Saadi (al-), Salam, "Changes in Syria's Armed Opposition", *Sada* (CEIP), 11 December 2015.

Saadi, Sardar, "David Harvey: Reclaiming the City from Kobane to Baltimore" (interview), *Roarmag.org*, 26 May 2015.

Sabahy, Hamdeen, "Hamdin Sabbahi khilal Liqa'ihi ma' Wafd Markaz Carter", Hamdeen Sabahy's *Facebook* page,18 June 2012.

———, see the entry for Charbel, Ghassan.

Sadeghi-Boroujerdi, Eskandar, *Salvaging the "Axis of Resistance," Preserving Strategic Depth*, Dirasat, no. 1, November 2014, Riyadh: King Faisal Center for Research and Islamic Studies, 2014.

Said, Omar, "After State Crackdown and Rumors of Rifts, Brotherhood Faces Identity Crisis", *Mada Masr*, 14 August 2015.

Salah, Muhammad, "Hamdin Sabbahi lil-Hayat: Khuruj 'Adil lil-'Askar wa Tantawi Yastahiq al-Takrim iza Hakama Qatalat al-Shuhada'", *Al-Hayat*, 19 January 2012.

Saleh, Heba, "Egyptians Rail against Government as Fuel Costs Soar", *Financial Times*, 8 July 2014.

———, "Egypt's New Desert Capital: Metropolis or Mirage?", *Financial Times*, 5 June 2015.

Saleh, Yasmine and Paul Taylor, "The Egyptian Rebel Who 'Owns' Tahrir Square", *Reuters*, 8 July 2013.

Samak, Dina, "What Does the Brotherhood Really Want?", *Ahram Online*, 9 October 2015.

Sands, Phil, Justin Vela and Suha Maayeh, "Assad Regime Set Free Extremists from Prison to Fire up Trouble during Peaceful Uprising", *The National* (UAE), 21 January 2014.

Sayigh, Yezid, *Missed Opportunity: The Politics of Police Reform in Egypt and Tunisia*, Beirut: Carnegie Middle East Center, March 2015.

Schroeder, Matt, *Fire and Forget: The Proliferation of Man-portable Air Defence Systems in Syria*, Small Arms Survey, Issue Brief, no. 9, August 2014.

Seale, Patrick, *Asad: The Struggle for the Middle East*, London: I.B. Tauris, 1990.

Shazli (El-), Heba, "Where Were the Egyptian Workers in the June 2013 People's Coup Revolution?", *Jadaliyya*, 23 July 2013.

Shehabi, Ala'a and Marc Owen Jones, eds, *Bahrain's Uprising*, London: Zed Books, 2015.

Shurbaji (al-), 'Adil, *I'adat Haykalat al-Jaysh al-Yamani*, Doha: Al-Markaz al-'Arabi lil-Abhath wa Dirasat al-Siyasat, May 2013.

Sims, David, *Egypt's Desert Dreams: Development or Disaster?*, Cairo: American University in Cairo Press, 2015.

———, "David Sims Takes a Hard Look at Egypt's Struggling Desert Development", *AUC Press e-newsletter*, February 2015.

Sly, Liz, "The Hidden Hand Behind the Islamic State Militants? Saddam Hussein's", *Washington Post*, 4 April 2015.

Solomon, Erika, "The Isis Economy: Meet the New Boss", *Financial Times*, 5 January 2015.

———, "Syrian Islamist Rebel Group Looks to the West", *Financial Times*, 14 August 2015.

Solomon, Erika, Guy Chazan and Sam Jones, "Isis Inc: How Oil Fuels the Jihadi Terrorists", *Financial Times*, 14 October 2015.

Solomon, Erika, Robin Kwong and Steven Bernard, "Inside Isis Inc: The Journey of a Barrel of Oil", *Financial Times*, 14 October 2015.

Solomon, Erika and Ahmed Mhidi, "Isis Inc: Syria's 'Mafia-Style' Gas Deals with Jihadis", *Financial Times*, 15 October 2015.

———, "Isis: The Munitions Trail", *Financial Times*, 30 November 2015.

Solomon, Erika and Sam Jones, "Isis Inc: Loot and Taxes Keep Jihadi Economy Churning", *Financial Times*, 14 December 2015.

Smyth, Phillip, *The Shiite Jihad in Syria and Its Regional Effects*, Washington: Washington Institute for Near East Policy, 2015.

Srur, Safa', "Kamal Abu-'Aita ... al-Wazir Yumazziq Dafatir al-Munadil al-'Ummali", *Al-Masry al-Youm*, 6 February 2014.

Steele, Jonathan, "The Syrian Kurds Are Winning!", *New York Review of Books*, 3 December 2015.

Stein, Aaron, "Turkey's Evolving Syria Strategy", *Foreign Affairs*, Snapshot, 9 February 2015.

Stepan, Alfred and Juan Linz, "Democratization theory and the 'Arab Spring'", *Journal of Democracy*, vol. 24, no. 2, April 2013, pp. 15–30.

Syrian Centre for Policy Research, *Syria War on Development: Socioeconomic Monitoring Report of Syria*, Damascus: SCPR with UNRWA and UNDP, October 2013.

———, *Syria Squandering Humanity: Socioeconomic Monitoring Report on Syria*, Damascus: SCPR with UNRWA and UNDP, May 2014.

———, *Syria Alienation and Violence: Impact of Syria Crisis Report 2014*, Damascus: SCPR with UNRWA and UNDP, March 2015.

Syrian Network for Human Rights, *The Society's Holocaust: Most Notable Sectarian and Ethnic Cleansing Massacre*, London: SNHR, 16 June 2015.

Taylor, Paul, "Exclusive: Egypt's 'Road Not Taken' Could Have Saved Mursi", *Reuters*, 17 July 2013.

Taştekin, Fehim, "Turkish Military Says MIT Shipped Weapons to al-Qaeda", *Al-Monitor*, 15 January 2015.

Tawfiq, Muhammad, "Al-Qita' al-Khas al-Misri Yatakhawwaf min Tamaddud al-Jaysh Iqtisadiyyan", *Al-'Arabi al-Jadid*, 11 December 2015.

Toaldo, Mattia, "Libya's Transition and The Weight of the Past", in Bozzo and Luizard, eds, 2015, pp. 77–97.

Topol, Sarah, "In Egypt, the Military Means (Big) Business", *Bloomberg Businessweek*, 13 March 2014.

Torres, Milagros and Ariane Ferry, eds, *Tragique et comique liés, dans le théâtre, de l'Antiquité à nos jours (du texte à la mise en scène)*, Rouen: CEREdi, 2012.

Tripp, Charles, *Battlefields of the Republic: The Struggle for Public Space in Tunisia*, LSE Middle East Centre Paper Series no. 13, December 2015.

Trotsky, Leon, *The Revolution Betrayed: What Is the Soviet Union and Where Is It Going?*, trans. Max Eastman, New York: Pathfinder, 1980.

Turkmani, Rim, *ISIL, JAN and the War Economy in Syria*, London: LSE, 30 July 2015.

Urban, Mark, "What is Putin's end game in Syria?", *BBC News*, 23 September 2015.

Verme, Paolo, et al., *Inside Inequality in the Arab Republic of Egypt: Facts and Perceptions across People, Time, and Space*, Washington, DC: The World Bank, 2014.

Wagner, Tasia, "Testing Tunisia's Transition: The Law on Economic and Financial Reconciliation", Institute for Strategic Islamic Affairs, October 2015.

Way, Lucan, "Comparing the Arab Revolts: The Lessons of 1989", *Journal of Democracy*, vol. 22, no. 4, October 2011, pp. 17–27.

Weber, Max, "Politics as Vocation" (1919), available at <http://anthropos-lab.net/wp/wp-content/uploads/2011/12/Weber-Politics-as-a-Vocation.pdf>.

———, *Economy and Society*, vol. 1, Berkeley: University of California Press, 1978.

Wehrey, Frederic, *Ending Libya's Civil War: Reconciling Politics, Rebuilding Security*, Washington, DC: Carnegie Endowment for International Peace, September 2014.

Weiss, Michael and Hassan Hassan, *Isis: Inside the Army of Terror*, New York: Regan Arts, 2015.

White, Jeffrey, "Russia in Syria (Part 2): Military Implications", *The Washington Institute*, 15 September 2015.

Wikileaks, Cable from the US Embassy in Damascus, Canonical ID: 10DAMASCUS158_a, "When Chickens Come Home to Roost: Syria's Proxy War in Iraq at Heart of 2008-09 Seidnaya Prison Riots", 24 February 2010.

——, Cable from the US Embassy in Damascus, Canonical ID: 10DAMASCUS159_a, "Syrian Intelligence Chief Attends CT Dialogue with S/CT Benjamin", 24 February 2010.

World Bank, *The Unfinished Revolution: Bringing Opportunity, Good Jobs and Greater Wealth to All Tunisians*, Development Policy Review, Washington, DC: World Bank, May 2014.

Worth, Robert, "Even Out of Office, a Wielder of Great Power in Yemen", *New York Times*, 31 January 2014.

Yadav, Stacey Philbrick, "Yemen's Muslim Brotherhood and the Perils of Powersharing", Washington, DC: Brookings Institution, August 2015.

Yazigi, Jihad, "Syria's War Economy", European Council on Foreign Relations, April 2014.

Yousfi, Hèla, *L'UGTT: Une passion tunisienne*, Sfax: Med Ali Edition, 2015.

Yousfi, Hèla and Choukri Hmed, "What Is Tunisia's Nobel Prize Rewarding?", *Open Democracy*, 25 October 2015.

Zaid, Abdulla, Hassan Sherry, Mahinour El-Badrawi, and Joshua Haber, *Arab Uprisings & Social Justice: Implications of IMF Subsidy Reform Policies*, Washington, DC: New America Foundation (with ECESR and ANND), February 2014.

Zelin, Aaron and Phillip Smyth, "The Vocabulary of Sectarianism", *Foreign Policy*, 29 January 2014

Index

Stanford Studies In Middle Eastern and Islamic Societies and Cultures

Joel Beinin, editor

Jacob Mundy, *Imaginative Geographies of Algerian Violence: Conflict Science, Conflict Management, Antipolitics*
2015

Ilana Feldman, *Police Encounters: Security and Surveillance in Gaza under Egyptian Rule*
2015

Tamir Sorek, *Palestinian Commemoration in Israel: Calendars, Monuments, and Martyrs*
2015

Adi Kuntsman and Rebecca L. Stein, *Digital Militarism: Israel's Occupation in the Social Media Age*
2015

Laurie A. Brand, *Official Stories: Politics and National Narratives in Egypt and Algeria*
2014

Kabir Tambar, *The Reckonings of Pluralism: Citizenship and the Demands of History in Turkey*
2014

Diana Allan, *Refugees of the Revolution: Experiences of Palestinian Exile*
2013

Shira Robinson, *Citizen Strangers: Palestinians and the Birth of Israel's Liberal Settler State*
2013

Joel Beinin and Frédéric Vairel, editors, *Social Movements, Mobilization, and Contestation in the Middle East and North Africa*
2013 (Second Edition), 2011

Ariella Azoulay and Adi Ophir, *The One-State Condition: Occupation and Democracy in Israel/Palestine*
2012

Steven Heydemann and Reinoud Leenders, editors, *Middle East Authoritarianisms: Governance, Contestation, and Regime Resilience in Syria and Iran*
2012

Jonathan Marshall, *The Lebanese Connection: Corruption, Civil War, and the International Drug Traffic*
2012

Joshua Stacher, *Adaptable Autocrats: Regime Power in Egypt and Syria*
2012

Bassam Haddad, *Business Networks in Syria: The Political Economy of Authoritarian Resilience*
2011

Noah Coburn, *Bazaar Politics: Power and Pottery in an Afghan Market Town*
2011

Laura Bier, *Revolutionary Womanhood: Feminisms, Modernity, and the State in Nasser's Egypt*
2011

Samer Soliman, *The Autumn of Dictatorship: Fiscal Crisis and Political Change in Egypt under Mubarak*
2011

Rochelle A. Davis, *Palestinian Village Histories: Geographies of the Displaced*
2010

Haggai Ram, *Iranophobia: The Logic of an Israeli Obsession*
2009

John Chalcraft, *The Invisible Cage: Syrian Migrant Workers in Lebanon*
2008

Rhoda Kanaaneh, *Surrounded: Palestinian Soldiers in the Israeli Military*
2008

Asef Bayat, *Making Islam Democratic: Social Movements and the Post-Islamist Turn*
2007

Robert Vitalis, *America's Kingdom: Mythmaking on the Saudi Oil Frontier*
2006

Jessica Winegar, *Creative Reckonings: The Politics of Art and Culture in Contemporary Egypt*
2006

Joel Beinin and Rebecca L. Stein, editors, *The Struggle for Sovereignty: Palestine and Israel, 1993–2005*
2006